ANNALS

OF

THE FRENCH STAGE.

VOL. II.

RACINE.

ANNALS

OF

THE FRENCH STAGE

FROM ITS ORIGIN TO THE DEATH OF RACINE.

BY

FREDERICK HAWKINS.

IN TWO VOLUMES.

VOL. II.
1668—1699.

HASKELL HOUSE PUBLISHERS Ltd.
Publishers of Scarce Scholarly Books
NEW YORK, N. Y. 10012
1970

First Published 1884

HASKELL HOUSE PUBLISHERS LTD.
Publishers of Scarce Scholarly Books
280 LAFAYETTE STREET
NEW YORK, N. Y. 10012

Library of Congress Catalog Card Number: 68-24949

Standard Book Number 8383-0161-4

Printed in the United States of America

THE FRENCH STAGE.

CHAPTER I.

1668—1670.

IN a free version by himself of the Roman *Amphit-ruo*, brought out early in January, Molière obtained a counterpoise to the exceptional popularity of *Andromaque*. In more than one respect was the new piece to his honour. He wrote it with a delicacy to which the nature of the subject was hardly favourable. Schlegel, predisposed as he is to decry Molière in every way, is constrained to confess that the coarseness of the old legend is refined as much as it possibly could be without injury to its spirit and boldness. In both incident and character, too, the French *Amphitryon* is superior to the Latin original. While Jupiter (Lathorillière) is appearing to Alcmène (Mdlle. Molière) in the form of her husband, Amphitryon (Lagrange), Mercure (Ducroisy) pays court to

Cléanthis (Mdlle. Beauval), the wife of Amphitryon's serving-man Sosie (Molière). Between Alcmène and Cléanthis a most dramatic contrast is displayed, the former being a pattern of tenderness, and the latter so inveterate a scold, "though all in affection," that Mercure is induced to keep out of her way as much as he can. If Armande looked and spoke like Alcmène it must have been a remarkable triumph of art over nature. Sosie, with his fine humour and quaint philosophy, is one of the best of Molière's characters, and was doubtless represented to perfection. His rehearsal of the intended speech to Alcmène, here represented by a lantern on the ground, is irresistible. It should be observed that the oft-quoted though ungrammatical lines

> Le véritable Amphitryon
> Est l'Amphitryon où l'on dîne,

are simply a variation of one which Rotrou had inserted in *Les Sosies*, and which had become proverbial,—

> Point, point d'Amphitryon où l'on ne dîne point.

Mdlle. Lefévre, afterwards Madame Dacier, one of the most learned of her sex, refused to allow that Plautus had been eclipsed. In support of this view she wrote an elaborate dissertation, but a fear that Molière might bring her on the stage led her to carefully suppress the manuscript. Boileau, with characteristic candour, declared that he liked the ancient *Amphitryon* better than the other—an opinion which a close comparison of the two plays is not likely to bear out. One interesting point in connexion with Molière's new piece has yet to be noticed. Modified as the indecency of the story had been, it was still conspicuous enough to lend some faint colour to the assertion, so common since the production of *Tartuffe*, that he was degrading the stage. But his enemies were not so much alive to the well-being of the stage as they had alleged. In *Amphitryon*—which, by the way, was dedicated to the Prince de Condé—they saw no room for reproach.

The actress who played the sharp-tongued Cleanthis proved a decided acquisition to the company. Jeanne Olivier Bourguignon was born in Holland about 1645, and, having been deserted in infancy by her parents, was cared for by a tender-hearted old washerwoman. In her tenth year she became maid-of-all-work to the chief of a troupe of itinerant players, the great Filandre, who taught her to read and write, gave her small parts to play, and generally treated her as a daughter. The company, after a long tour in Holland and Flanders, repaired to Lyons, one of the most play-loving of French cities. Mdlle. Bourguignon here consented to transfer her services to Paphetin's troupe, the more readily as the manager proposed to adopt her. Before long she found herself in an embarrassing position. Her new chief, an old and ill-favoured person, wished to make her his mistress. In order to avoid his advances she looked about for a husband, at the same time resolving most firmly that, come what might, she would not marry unless it seemed certain that her authority would never be disputed. No man of her acquaintance was more likely to fulfil this indispensable condition than one Beauval, who had recently been raised to the dignity of candle-snuffer in the troupe, and who, as the expression of his eyes had often proved, loved her to desperation without daring to avow it. Ever prompt in decision, Mdlle. confessed to him that his undeclared but obvious passion for her was fully reciprocated, and it gave her infinite pleasure to name the happy day. It was to no purpose that the irate Paphetin obtained from the Archbishop of Lyons an order forbidding any priest in his diocese to pronounce the nuptial benediction over her head; married to Beauval she would be, and married to Beauval she was. Paphetin took his disappointment with a good grace. In addition to keeping the young pair in the company, he pro-moted Beauval, who possessed some intelligence, to the rank of speaking-actor. Both Madame Beauval and her husband were now on trial at the Palais Royal, the former, though prone to " giggle" out of season, having proved "un ornament des plus attrayantes de

la scène." Imperfectly educated, she went far to
redeem her deficiencies by a readiness to learn, and
it can hardly be doubted that she played the shrewish
Cléanthis (a character of Molière's invention) to the life.

The next piece offered to the playgoers was at the
Hôtel de Bourgogne, in the shape of Thomas Corneille's
Laodice (February). It did not succeed, for the simple
reason that a hand much stronger than that of the
author was needed to draw such a character as the queen
who dies by her own hand on finding that the man she
is enamoured of is her son. Mdlle. Desœillets represented Laodice, with Floridor as Oronte. "The scene,"
said Thomas Corneille to a friend amongst the audience,
"is in Cappodocia, and to appreciate the picture we
must transport ourselves to that country and enter
into the spirit of its people." "True," said the friend;
"the tragedy is good only to be played on *les lieux.*"
Robinet, in speaking of *Laodice,* apprises us of the
death of Montfleuri, which is said to have been caused
by over-exertion as Orestes in *Andromaque.* In him,
no doubt, the stage lost a fine actor; and it is to be
regretted that he should have sullied his remarkable
career, which began before the *Cid* appeared, by pre-
ferring to the King that hideous charge against Molière.
The vacant place was filled by Juvenon de Lafleur,
described as the first actor who had had what are
called *entrailles*—in other words, the power of moving

an audience by being moved himself. Brought up as a cook, he had been induced by the consciousness of a commanding presence to become a player, and was now beyond the reach of rivalry in Kings, Gascons, and *capitans*. No one could have given better effect to the part he sustained in *Laodice*, that of the Roman ambassador. From the production of this tragedy, too, dates the reputation of a young actress who had joined the company about two years previously, Françoise Jacob de Montfleuri, daughter of the player just deceased. Her first recorded appearance on the stage was in a ballet entitled *Les Amours Déguisés*, danced at Court in 1664. Soon afterwards, apparently against the wishes of her father, she married Matthieu d'Ennebaut, a poor official in Brittany. Finding herself allied to an inveterate gambler, and wisely resolving not to depend upon him for her livelihood, she employed her father's influence to obtain for her a place in the Troupe Royale, with what result I need not say. Earnest, graceful, and clever, Mdlle. d'Ennebaut gave a new charm to secondary characters in tragedy, and from the time she appeared in *Laodice* her position was assured. Nor were her talents limited to the serious; in *L'Amant qui ne flatte point*, which served to introduce Hauteroche as a dramatic author, she gave life to the lifeless. Robinet, that constant frequenter of the green rooms, says he saw no defect in her but one, and that

was a want of tenderness for himself. Her affection
for Matthieu d'Ennebaut, who had accompanied her
to Paris, was not diminished by his mania for the
gaming-table, and it is to be feared that no inconsiderable portion of the money she received had to
be applied to the payment of his losses.

Molière, after producing a good-natured parody by
Subligny of *Andromaque*—a parody which deserves
passing mention as the first work of its kind in
France, and which Racine was weak enough to treat
as an act of desecration—occupied himself with a play
remarkable alike in its character and in its fate. Returning home in triumph from war, the King, " in order
to compensate the Court for the *ennui* occasioned by
his absence," held a magnificent *fête* at Versailles, in
the course of which, by special arrangement, a comedy
by his favourite dramatist, entitled *George Dandin, ou
le Mari Confondu*, was represented in a theatre erected
for the purpose in a secluded portion of the grounds.
Nearly the same in its incidents as *La Jalousie du
Barbouillé*, and consequently not free from an element
of farce, the new piece is lifted into the region of
comedy by fineness of dialogue, character-drawing, and
satirical power. Bitten by the desire to ally himself to
a noble family, George Dandin, a wealthy country-
man (Molière), seeks and wins the hand of Angélique
(Armande), daughter of impoverished offshoots of the

aristocracy, M. and Madame de Sotenville, neither of whom can be credited with the graces associated with good birth (Ducroisy and Hubert). His joy is soon overclouded. Not only does Angélique regard him with undisguised contempt, especially after the elegant Clitandre (Lagrange) pays court to her, but his parents-in-law, forgetting that he has rescued them from pressing indigence, hold no more intercourse with him than is absolutely necessary, pointedly remind him of the inferiority of his rank to theirs, and force him to retract on his knees what the evidence of his own senses shows to be only too well-founded complaints as to his wife's conduct. Angélique, though not positively criminal, is never allowed to engage our sympathies— a sufficient reply to an allegation that the play serves to hold up a noxious example for imitation. Both hearty and unanimous was the applause bestowed by the Court upon Molière's last play. If some of the spectators winced under the ridicule heaped upon the decayed nobility—and many Sotenvilles must have been present—there was the terrible punishment of the *parvenu* to console them. It might have been thought that such a satire would not be well received in Paris, but the event proved quite the contrary. If some of the haunters of the Palais Royal winced under the ridicule heaped upon the mania for social distinc-tion — and many George Dandins must have been present—the soreness so caused was effectually healed by the ludicrous aspect given to the Sotenvilles.

In his next work, *L'Avare*, a five-act comedy in prose, represented for the first time on the 9th September, we have the most typical product of Molière's many-sided genius. In each of his other plays he had given special prominence to one of his qualities as a dramatist; here they are all laid under contribution in about equal degrees. Much of the power revealed in *Don Juan* is displayed side by side with the finest humour, the tenderest sentiment, the most exquisite ridicule, the most searching satire. Indebted to the *Aulularia* for the general conception of the piece, Molière deviated from it in several important respects, and in the result left Plautus far behind. Harpagon is preferable to Euclio, not only as being free from anything like extravagance, but in depth and force of characterization. He is generally regarded as the most vivid embodiment yet in existence of the sordid passion which absorbs his mind. Many of his actions and sayings have passed into proverbs. He is the bourgeois miser who steals the oats from his horses; who is distracted by the suspicion that his children intend to rob him; who from a constitutional objection to the verb "to give" will only say "je vous *prête* le bonjour;" who will sacrifice his daughter to a stupid old man rather than give her a modest dowry; who,

on finding it necessary to entertain ten persons at
supper provides for eight only; who counsels his
gambling son to lend out at good interest the money
he wins; whose love for a young woman yields in
the end to avarice, and who, unlike Euclio, is anxious
to increase as well as hoard what he possesses. Every
scene in which he appears serves to throw fresh light
upon his character. Yet, repulsive as the vice he
represents may be, his presence throws no gloom over
the play, partly because he is held up to derision
as well as hatred, and partly because all his sur-
roundings are treated in the spirit of the liveliest
comedy. For the groundwork of the piece, which
differs from that of the *Aulularia*, we have a double
love intrigue, the personages being numerous enough
to afford employment to the whole of the company.
Many incidents and scraps of dialogue are borrowed
from Plautus and modern Italian farces, but Riccoboni
is sadly deceived in supposing that the first scene in
the second act is copied from the *Dottore Bachelone*,
which had yet to be written. Molière himself, as
may be supposed, played Harpagon, though the increasing weakness of his chest, now shown in a chronic,
hacking cough, rendered him unable, at least without
a dangerous effort, to illustrate the anguish of the
miser on discovering the loss of his treasure. Frosine
(Madeleine Béjart) is made to say to him, " Cela n'est

rien ; votre fluxion ne vous sied point mal, et vous avez grace à tousser." Béjart, who was cast for La Flèche, the valet, was also labouring under an infirmity conspicuous enough to become a part of the play. Not long previously, in the Place Royale, he had surprised two of his friends doing their best to run each other through the body. He impulsively rushed between them, and was so badly wounded in the foot as to make him lame for the rest of his life. "Je ne me plais point à voir ce chien de boiteux-là," says Harpagon of La Flèche ; and from this time, we are told, every country actor who assumed the character deemed it necessary to appear with a sort of wooden leg.

L'Avare, in addition to being singularly bright and genial, was in effect a satire upon a vice not uncommon in Paris at ·that period, especially among the usurers who thrived at the expense of the state and nobles in temporary need of money. Nevertheless, the comedy did not take the public fancy. "I saw you at the performance of *L'Avare* last night," Racine said to Boileau, "and I think you were the only person in the theatre who laughed." "I have too good an opinion of you," replied the satirist, "to suppose that you did not laugh as well, at least in your heart." Unfortunately for Molière, his audience was not exclusively composed of Boileaus. After only nine representations—and these were not consecutive—*L'Avare*

had to be withdrawn. In the course of a few weeks
it was tried again, but with substantially the same
result. "Molière," a grand seigneur remarked, "must
be mad to inflict five acts in prose upon us. He
must take us for boobies. The idea of being entertained by such means!" In this profound criticism,
according to many commentators, a sufficient explanation of the ill-success of *L'Avare* is to be found. The
audience were indisposed from the outset towards a
five-act comedy not written in verse. I see no reason
to endorse the inference. *Le Pédant Joué* and other
prose comedies in five acts had achieved popularity,
and even the superb versification of *Le Misanthrope*
could not have blinded most playgoers to the fact
that Molière did not do justice to his gifts of expression
unless he threw off the fetters of rhyme. Racine's
words to Boileau, perhaps, will afford a key to the
mystery. Intelligent as the audience usually were,
they did not care for the subject of the play, and for
this reason were unable to fully appreciate the force
with which it was treated. Curiously enough, one of
the few admirers of *L'Avare* belonged to the class at
whom Molière had levelled his satire. Delighted at
the plan devised by Harpagon to entertain his ten
guests in the cheapest manner—*i. e.*, by providing
for a less number, by enjoining his servant not to
pass the wine until it had been twice asked for, and,

lastly, by keeping plenty of water on the table—a well-known miser in the parterre declared that he did not begrudge his admission-money, as the piece abounded in excellent lessons of economy.

In no wise discouraged by the comparative failure of *L'Avare,* which showed that the most artistic plays were not necessarily the most successful in the theatre, Molière continued to exert himself in behalf of his beloved *Tartuffe.* Even if that immortal comedy should have only a *succès de curiosité*—and he now had some reason to fear as much—its production would be of advantage to the troupe, every part having been learnt, and of still greater advantage to himself. Louis XIV. had not yet "re-examined" the manuscript; and Molière, too prudent to trouble him with another letter respecting it, seems to have decided to recall the matter to his mind by causing the play to be privately represented before an august assemblage. It should be understood that for some time past he had had a close friend in the great Condé, whose eagle-like face, still unseamed by years, was often to be seen at the hospitable table in the Rue Richelieu or at Auteuil. "Molière," he said one day, "I am sure that my visits interfere with your work. I shall not come to see you again unless you expressly invite me. But I hope that you will come to see me whenever your leisure permits it. You have only to send in your

name by a valet-de-chambre; your visits can never
be ill-timed." Nor did this prove an empty compliment. The Prince invariably received the dramatist
as one of his most honoured guests. "Molière," he used
to say, "is a man of genius, of solid judgment, of wide
erudition. I never tire of his society." In the middle
of September, before *L'Avare* had completed its first
short run, the Comédiens du Roi set out for the ancient
and picturesque château of Chantilly, which now
belonged to the prince, and there played *Tartuffe* before
an audience comprising Monsieur, Madame, and other
personages of a rank exalted enough to give special
interest to the performance. Had not Molière induced
his host to bring them together for the purpose, so
as to remind the King of his promise to Lagrange
and Lathorillière? Be that as it may, his majesty
soon afterwards turned his attention to the piece,
with what result we shall see anon. It is probable
that an incident which occurred at about the same
time was not without some effect upon his mind.
"How is it," he asked Condé, after a performance by
the Italian actors of an irreverent piece entitled
Scaramouche Ermite, "how is it that the people who
are so horrified at *Tartuffe* have nothing to say against
such a thing as this?" "Sire," replied the Prince,
doubtless well pleased to be able to do his friend
a service, "the reason is very simple: they see in

Scaramouche only some ridicule upon what ought to be sacred ; *Tartuffe* satirizes themselves."

Molière had scarcely returned to Paris when he found some of his laurels menaced. Racine, not content with being regarded as the rival of Corneille, suddenly made an excursion into the domain of light satirical comedy by writing *Les Plaideurs*, a clever adaptation of the *Wasps*. Early in the year, it must be premised, he had been dispossessed by legal process of his benefice at Epinay, for the simple reason that he could not summon sufficient resolution to take the *habit*. Brought into contact with advocates, who often exposed themselves to ridicule by their pedantry and wearisome divagations, he resolved to exercise his mordant wit at the expense of law-practice in general, especially as Molière, probably on the principle that " hawks should not peck out hawks' een," was not likely to follow his example. With this view he proceeded to found a piece upon that in which the mania of the ancient Athenians for litigation was so piquantly satirized. In the first instance he simply thought of providing the Italian actors with a string of pleasantries ; but at the suggestion of some friends, who were " anxious to see an *échantillon* of Aristophanes on the French stage," he aimed a point or two higher. Farcical in incident and deficient in humour, *Les Plaideurs* may yet be allowed to take

rank as a comedy, thanks to wit, refined sarcasm,
clever sketches of character, and a by no means
inconsiderable amount of the Attic salt of the original.
In it we find personages soon to become proverbial—
the judge who is so enraptured with his calling that
he sleeps in his robe and cap, the advocate who
opens his address with the creation of the world,
and the countess who seems to have her being only
in the stifling atmosphere of the law courts.   Most
of the piece was written in a tavern on the Place
du Cimetière de Saint Jean, where the wits of Paris,
including Boileau, Lafontaine, Chapelle, and Furetière,
frequently met to kill time.   The scene between
Chicaneau and the Countess was derived from an
incident which occurred in Boileau's elder brother's
house, the enthusiastic litigant of real life being
the Comtesse de Crissé, recently made notorious by
the fact that the Parlement, in sheer self-defence,
had rendered her unable to commence any action
without a certificate from two of its own counsellors.
In order to add to the interest of the piece, the actress
who played Madame de Pimbêche was made up to
resemble this terror of the courts, and the representative of L'Intimé did not omit to mimic the tones
and manners of the best-known lawyers of the time.

Les Plaideurs had a curious fate.   Brought out at
the Hôtel de Bourgogne in November, it evoked little or

no merriment, and in the course of a few days was laid aside. Molière, who was present at the second representation, could not understand the apathy of the audience. " M. Racine's comedy," he said on leaving the theatre, "is admirable ; and those who deride it may well be laughed at themselves." Nor are the causes of this ill-success far to seek. The fine gentlemen in the boxes did not take sufficient interest in the lawyers to enjoy a satire upon them ; the bourgeois in the pit failed to understand most of the allusions scattered over the play. Moreover, the friends of Corneille, with many persons who prized the amenities of life, may have been put in bad humour by a line in the first act. In the *Cid*, it may be remembered, that fine old warrior, Don Diègue, is vividly described as one whose exploits are marked in the lines on his forehead. Racine irreverently parodied the words in speaking of an arrant knave—

Ses rides sur son front gravaient tous ses exploits.

Corneille is said to have been very angry at the liberty thus taken with his verse, and it certainly argued little delicacy of feeling or taste on the part of Racine that he should have shown such disrespect to a man whom he was supposed to have equalled or surpassed. But the verdict of the audience at the Hôtel de Bourgogne was not irreversible. In the following month, for the want of something better, the Troupe Royale performed *Les*

Plaideurs before the King at St. Germain-en-laye.   His
majesty laughed outright; the Court, as a matter of
course, laughed outright also.   The performance over,
the astonished players, instead of passing the night at
the château, set out in a body for Paris to communicate
the news to the author without delay.   Racine was
living in the Faubourg St. Germain, and the arrival
of coaches in that unfashionable quarter, especially in
the small hours of the morning, quickly aroused the
neighbourhood.   Nightcapped heads, we are told, appeared at every window, cold as the weather might be.
The wiseacres soon found a satisfactory explanation of
the incident.   M. Racine, at whose door the coaches had
stopped, had in his last play fallen foul of the judges,
and was now being clapped in prison to be taught better
manners.   And in a few hours, we are assured, all Paris
believed that he was pining in the Conciergerie.   The
truth, of course, soon became known, together with the
fact that the King, far from having M. Racine arrested,
had bestowed upon him another pension, accompanied
by a flattering letter.   In these circumstances, as may
be supposed, the actors lost no time in reviving the
comedy, which proved immensely popular.   Fortunately
for the drama, Racine was not induced by this strange
turn of the scales to suppose that he had the secret of
comedy art.   Evidently perceiving his inferiority here
to Molière, and unwilling, perhaps, to be second to

any one in anything, he thenceforward devoted himself exclusively to the sterner muse.

A retributive fate would seem to have decided that he should not profit very long by the gifts of the actress whom he had lured away from the Palais Royal. Mdlle. Duparc died in the middle of December, just after her new comrades had turned their attention to an admirably versified comedy by Thomas Corneille, *Le Baron d'Albikrac*, and a poor tragedy by the "tender" Quinault, *Pausanias*. It had been said that "her beauty had played for her;" but the effect with which she represented Axiane and Andromaque must have shown that the remark was more piquant than just. That Molière appraised his old comrade at her right value is to be gathered from a scene in the *Impromptu de Versailles :—*

Molière : Pour vous, mademoiselle,—

Mdlle. Duparc : Mon Dieu ! pour moi, je m'acquitterai fort mal de mon personnage, et je ne sais pas pourquoi vous m'avez donné ce rôle de façonnière.

Molière : Mon Dieu, mademoiselle ! voilà comme vous disiez lorsque l'on vous donna celui de la *Critique de L'École des Femmes ;* cependant vous vous en êtes acquittée à merveille, et tout le monde est demeuré d'accord qu'on ne peut pas mieux faire que vous avez fait. Croyez moi, celui-ci sera de même, et vous le jouerez mieux que vous ne pensez.

Mdlle. Duparc : Comment cela se pourrait-il faire ? car il n'y a point de personne au monde qui soit moins façonnière que moi.

Molière : Cela est vrai ; et c'est en quoi vous faites mieux voir que vous êtes une excellente comédienne de bien représenter un personnage qui est si contraire à votre humeur."

Her professional success, however, did not bring her happiness. The dreams of her early life had not been realized ; and the man whom she rejected on account of his worldly position had risen to fame and opulence. It was probably with a feeling of relief that she found herself detached from the scene of his almost unbroken triumphs. Hurt as he may have been by her secession, he now remembered her only as an old and valued comrade, and was not the least affected of the many poets and players who came together at her grave.

The hour to which he had so long looked forward was at hand. Early in 1669, to the consternation and dismay of his devout subjects as a body, the King set aside the decree against the representation of *Tartuffe*, and, as though to mark his sense of the bitter attacks made upon the dramatist, permitted the hypocrite to appear in his original name and garb. The day selected for the reproduction was Tuesday, February 5. The announcement on the bills acted upon Paris like an electric shock ; the approaches to the theatre were quickly blocked up,

and a few minutes after the opening of the doors every
corner in the salle was occupied. Every spectator,
Robinet tells us, ran the risk

> D'être etouffé dans la presse,
> Où l'on oyait crier sans cesse
> " Je suffoque, je n'en puis plus ;
> Hélas, Monsieur Tartuffius,
> Faut-il que de vous voir, l'envie
> Me coûte peut-être la vie ! "

If Molière had any doubts as to the success of *Tartuffe*
as a work of dramatic art they were speedily set at rest.
By a large majority of the audience, it is clear, the
comedy was listened to with mingled admiration and
resentment—admiration of the genius displayed in the
conception and elaboration of the picture, resentment
at the calumnies to which the author had been exposed.
Except in a few unimportant details, *Tartuffe* had
undergone no alteration since its previous representation, and was obviously calculated to promote rather
than injuriously affect the interests of religion. In one
scene, perhaps, the beaux took particular interest.
During the campaign of 1662, Louis XIV. invited the
Bishop of Rhodez, Péréfixe, to join him at supper. The
prelate declined ; it was a fast day, " and he had but
a light repast to make." As soon as he had gone, a
courtier described to the King the character of this light
repast, which consisted of several exquisite dishes.
" Le pauvre homme ! " the King frequently exclaimed,

as the items were named, varying the tone of his voice at each utterance. Molière availed himself of this incident to illustrate the blind infatuation of Orgon for the hypocrite. Returning after two days' absence, the bourgeois asks whether all has gone well during that time. Dorine says that her mistress has been feverish. "And Tartuffe?" "He supped by himself in her presence, very devoutly eating two partridges and half a leg of mutton hashed." "Poor soul!" Dorine goes on to say that her mistress had consented to be bled. "And Tartuffe?" "He took courage like a man; and, fortifying his soul against all evils, to make up for the blood which madame had lost, he drank at déjeuner four good beakers of wine." "Poor soul!" the old dupe again murmurs. Excellently managed, this diverting incident appears like a ray of light upon the surface of the gloomy yet fascinating play. The *dénouement* is somewhat forced and unnatural, but it provided the grateful poet with the means of paying an honourable tribute to the King, whose eyes " se font jour dans tous les cœurs," and who uses his absolute power to crush the hypocrite in the hour of triumph. It was not merely a *succès de curiosité* that *Tartuffe* achieved. No such tumult of applause as that which broke out on the fall of the curtain had yet been heard on the French stage. In this, with the congratulations showered upon him by friends behind the scenes, Molière had some compenssation for the trouble and annoyance he had suffered on account of what he deemed his masterpiece, but he seems to have thought that the advantage had been gained at too high a price. " *Tartuffe,*" he was told, " is really of service to virtue." "That is true," he replied ; " but experience has taught me that it is a dangerous thing to espouse her interests, and at times I reproach myself for having done so."

Tartuffe had the then long run of forty-four evenings, and the company, finding the exchequer full, insisted with one voice that the sum due to Molière as the author should be doubled whenever the piece was played. During the whole of this time, it would appear, he was the object of almost incessant attack out of doors. In one lucubration, *La Critique du Tartuffe,* an attempt was made to represent him as an enemy of the throne as well as of the altar. Robinet declares that the comedy delighted the truly devout among the audience as much as it enraged those in whose image the chief character was created ; but there is reason to believe that the attitude lately assumed towards the dramatist by the religious world in general—by those who were restrained by their scruples from seeing or reading a play—did not undergo an appreciable change. The earnest and eloquent Bourdaloue, preaching on the seventh Sunday after

Easter, attacked *Tartuffe* and its author with considerable vehemence. " As true and false devotion,"
he said, " have many actions in common, it is almost
a necessary consequence that raillery upon the one
should affect the other, that the features imputed
to the second should disfigure the first. And this
has actually occurred. Profane wits have undertaken to censure hypocrisy, thereby bringing true
piety under suspicion. Exposed to laughter in a
public theatre is an imaginary hypocrite, who uses
an exterior of austere piety as a cover for the basest
and most mercenary purposes, who meditates the most
atrocious crimes while he assumes a penitential air.
Does not all this represent an attempt to turn the
most holy things into ridicule ? " If Bourdaloue had
been anxious to prove that he knew next to nothing
of the play so criticized he could hardly have succeeded
better.

How little Molière deserved the blame here thrown
upon him it is unnecessary to say ; but the chief
question raised by the preacher, whether religious
hypocrisy is a fit subject for a dramatist, calls for a
thoughtful reply. " If," writes the author of *Waverley*
in his essay on Molière, " Bourdaloue's arguments were
to be carried to extremity, it would follow as a result
that no vice could be blamed, lest a censure should
arise on its corresponding virtue. In that mode of

reasoning a satire upon avarice would be objectionable as a censure of economy, and the blame applicable to profusion would be proscribed as discrediting generosity. The rash application of satire or ridicule, as the single test of truth, from which there lies no appeal, may doubtless lead to the worst consequences where religion is concerned. To hold up to ridicule the scruples of a conscience really tender and fearful of offence, even if these scruples are stretched, in our estimation, to the verge of absurdity, is, we think, likely to be attended with all the scandal to true religion which is apprehended. But we look in vain to Scripture or in the practice of the best friends of religion in all ages for any warrant to spare such criminals as Tartuffe. No crime is described as more odious to our Lord than that of the hypocrites who make a gain of godliness. They are denounced in a manner which seems to authorize their being held up to detestation by every means that can be taken to expose moral criminals. Ridicule is, we allow, a hazardous weapon, to be used with caution ; yet, when employed in good faith and with honest purpose, it is the most formidable and effectual in a case of this kind. There is much less danger of religion being discredited by the exposure of devoted and self-seeking hypocrisy than in permitting that vice to lurk like a canker in the bosom of society.

Although such exposure may lead men to try more severely the pretensions of such as make peculiar professions of devotion, the separation of the pure gold from the dross must in the end lead to the first being held in higher estimation, and to the worthlessness of the second being exposed to deserved contempt."

By remarkable good fortune, neither of the other theatres suffered very long from the popularity of *Tartuffe*. The players of the Hôtel de Bourgogne found a little mine of wealth in a five-act comedy by Montfleuri, *La Femme Juge et Partie*. Based upon an incident in the life of the Marquis de Fresne, who had sold his wife to a corsair, it had the advantage of a piquant subject, and the acting of Mdlle. d'Ennebaut as the heroine, especially when she appeared in male attire, was attractive enough to disguise the weakness with which the piece was written. Poisson, Hauteroche, Brécourt, and Mdlle. Beauchâteau were in the cast, the first as the unlovely and entertaining Bernadille. *La Femme Juge et Partie* had nearly as many representations as *Tartuffe* itself; and Montfleuri, blinded by vanity to the real causes of his success, came to regard himself in all seriousness as the long-sought rival of Molière. Next, as a reply to the detraction he inevitably experienced, the young dramatist, following the example set in the *Critique de*

L'École des Femmes, wrote *Le Procès de La Femme Juge et Partie,* in which he maintained that his comedy had "bien des beautés, des graces, des appas." In regard to the Théâtre du Marais, the playgoers repaired thither in their hundreds to see a "comédie-pastorale-héroïque" entitled *La Fête de Vénus,* not by reason of any particular excellence in the piece itself, which had been contrived by the Abbé Boyer, but to gaze at and listen to the representative of the tender goddess. I speak of Mdlle. Marie Champmêlé, who had entered the company a short time previously, and who to singular beauty of person united the most musical voice, a keen sense of picturesque movement, and a rare though as yet undeveloped gift for histrionic art.

The early life of the new actress is not without interest. Her father, Claude Desmares, was the son of a President au Parlement de Normandie, and had been disinherited for having married without the consent of his parents. He then found employment at Rouen, where, in 1644, his wife presented him with a daughter, the subject of the present sketch. Poverty was no stranger to that little household ; and Marie Desmares, arrived at woman's estate, resolved to go on the stage. How delightful it would be to represent some of the heroines created by the illustrious Corneïlle ! M. Desmares sternly set his face against

the idea. It was true that she might earn more by
acting than anything else, but the family must not
be degraded. The remonstrance had only a temporary
effect, if any. In a troupe of itinerant players who
came to Rouen was a well-graced youth, Charles
Champmêlé, son of a merchant on the Pont-au-change
in Paris. Mdlle. Desmares chanced to make his
acquaintance; they were clandestinely married, and
when the wanderers left the quaint old city the
bride was one of the number. In 1668, after passing
some time in the country, the young pair, with
Rosimont, an actor of almost Molièrean talent for
impersonating farcical characters, obtained an engagement at the Marais, thanks in great measure to a little
celebrity acquired by the husband. Mdlle. Champmêlé's
acting was still crude and unimpressive; but Laroque,
perceiving in her a world of latent talent, put her
through a course of systematic instruction for the
stage. He had little or no reason to be dissatisfied
with the result. From this time it became clearer and
clearer that another luminary was rising above the
theatrical horizon.

Meanwhile a noteworthy incident had occurred at
the Palais Royal. Having obtained a seat on the
stage, a wealthy but ill-bred person from Limoges,
evidently new to Paris and its ways, thought proper
to insult the Comédiens du Roi in the presence of

their audience. Terrible indeed was the punishment meted out to him. Molière, ever on the watch for an "original," carefully noted the peculiarities of his unwelcome visitor, already of some notoriety in the capital, and soon afterwards brought him on the stage in a three-act farce, *Monsieur de Pourceaugnac.* This monsieur, a Limousin hobbledehoy, impersonated by Molière, appears in Paris to claim the hand of Julie (Mdlle. Molière), which has been promised to him by her father, Oronte (Béjart), but by the lady herself to Eraste (Lagrange). The lovers, with the assistance of Nérine and Sbrigani, two intriguers (Madeleine Béjart and Ducroisy), are not unequal to the emergency. M. de Pourceaugnac, who is not less stupid than the inhabitants of his native province were popularly supposed to be, is made the victim of many tricks and mystifications. He is tempted to believe that Oronte's character is not above suspicion, that Julie is a heartless and self-seeking coquette, and many other dreadful things. He is even delivered as a lunatic into the hands of the doctors, at whom the satire of the dramatist is again levelled with excruciating effect. "If," says Nérine, "he is bent upon matrimony, why doesn't he espouse a Limoges lady, and let Christians alone?" In the end, of course, the poor fellow retires in utter discomfiture, leaving Eraste as master of the situation. Nominally a farce, the piece really belongs to the domain of the most enlivening comedy. In the words of a great critic, it would be an error to assume that more men were capable of writing it than of writing *Le Misanthrope.* For the rest, *M. de Pourceaugnac,* accompanied by dances and songs, the music being provided by Lulli, was played before the Court at Chambord on the 6th October, and at Paris, without the ballets, on the 15th November. According to Robinet, the Limousin whom it took off was half maddened by the hilarity it excited.

> L'original est à Paris,
> En colère autant que surpris
> De s'y voir dépeint de la sorte ;
> Il jure, il tempête, et s'emporte,
> Et veut faire ajourner l'auteur
> En réparation d'honneur
> Tant pour lui que pour sa famille.

His punishment, however, might have been much heavier than it was. Molière infused no ill-nature into the ridicule heaped upon his assailant. Monsieur de Pourceaugnac is a very ludicrous personage, but we are made to like him better than anybody else in the play.

Many eyes were soon to be turned to the Hôtel de Bourgogne, where, in the middle of December, another tragedy by Racine, *Britannicus,* was brought out before a deeply-interested audience, among whom, seated in a box, was the great Corneille himself.

Friends and foes were alike anxious to see how far
the young dramatist would justify the reputation he
had so suddenly achieved. Foreseeing that much
would be expected of him, Racine had taken more
than usual pains with his work, and the result seemed
likely to realize all his hopes. Based upon Tacitus, but
often original in character and incident, *Britannicus*
formed a splendid representation cf Nero and his
Court. It may not be strictly true that "all the
energy of the Roman annalist is here expressed in
verse worthy of Virgil," but the eulogy is not very
extravagant. Nero himself (Floridor) is portrayed with
a vigour which the author often missed in his treatment
of male personages, and anything more winsome and
pathetic than Junie (Mdlle. d'Ennebaut) it would not
be easy to conceive. Every other important character
in the play, too, is finely drawn and contrasted—
the fierce Agrippine (Mdlle. Desœillets), the virtuous
Burrhus (Lafleur), the rascally Narcisse (Hauteroche),
and the generous and ingenuous Britannicus (Brécourt).
No want of sensibility or dramatic skill was betrayed,
and the diction was by far the most refined yet heard
in a French tragedy. Naturally enough, Racine's
partisans were delighted to find he had written such
a play. *Britannicus*, they said, meant nothing less than
a violent death to every other tragic poet. Boileau,
if we may believe Boursault, did all he could to con-

tribute to the hoped-for success, breaking into applause before the curtain rose, and burying his face in his handkerchief during the most pathetic scenes. His interest in the piece, however, was not shared by the bulk of the audience. *Britannicus*, to the profound astonishment of the judicious few, was but coldly received. And the causes of this surprise are obvious enough. Excellent as the play was, it did not equal *Andromaque* in beauty and dramatic interest, and the high-flown expectations of the playgoer were accordingly disappointed. "Do not be disheartened," said Boileau to the author, after suggesting one or two structural alterations, all of which were soon afterwards effected; "it is the best thing you have yet done." Corneille's friends, of course, were overjoyed at his rival's failure; and Racine, in the preface to the first edition of the play, fell foul of his critics, among whom he erroneously included the author of the *Cid*, with all the bitterness which had characterized his letters against Port-Royal.

Louis XIV., struck by six lines put into the mouth of Narcisse—

> Pour toute ambition, pour vertu singulière,
> Il excelle à conduire un char dans la carrière ;
> A disputer des prix indignes de ses mains,
> A se donner lui-même en spectacle aux Romains,
> A venir prodiguer sa voix sur un théâtre,
> A réciter des chants qu'il veut qu'on idolâtre—

abruptly ceased to take part in the Court ballets,
though not before he had figured as Neptune and
Apollo in a luxurious entertainment at St. Germain
in the following February. For this entertainment
Molière wrote *Les Amants Magnifiques*, the story of
which had been devised by the King himself. In
the valley of Tempe, described by Ælian as adorned
by nature with every natural charm, two princes
(Lagrange and Ducroisy) strive to outvie each other
in the splendour of some *fêtes* they give to please
a beautiful princess (Mdlle. Molière), of whom they
are both enamoured, but who bestows her affections
upon an illustrious soldier. Petitot sees in the piece
an elaborate allusion to the passion of Mdlle. de
Montpensier for Lauzun, but a comparison of dates
will show the conjecture to be wrong. Uncongenial
as the subject of *Les Amants Magnifiques* may have
been to Molière, he handled it with appreciable effect,
and the character he himself played has a clear individuality. I speak of Clitidas, the most refined and
witty of Court fools. As has been well remarked, " he
is not a *fou ridicule*, like the jester in the *Princesse
d'Élide*. He avails himself with cleverness and address
of his privilege to say what he pleases." In another
personage there is a little wholesome satire upon
judicial astrology, which, notwithstanding the instruction conveyed to the Académie des Sciences

four years previously, was still a fashionable folly. Each act was introduced by an interlude composed by Lulli, and it was in the first and last of these that the King appeared. *Les Amants Magnifiques*, of course, was applauded to the echo; but Molière, dissatisfied with the work, refused to allow it to be either played at the Palais Royal or printed.

Preceded by *La Comtesse d' Orgueil*, a five-act comedy in verse, by Thomas Corneille, who a short time previously had written a *Mort d'Annibal* to no purpose, the last of Quinault's contributions to the French stage proper, *Bellerophon*, was acted at the Hôtel de Bourgogne. In early manhood, it appears, Tristan's pupil, now a prosperous lawyer, had become attached to a certain Louise Goujon, and doubtless would have become her husband at once if her parents had not prevailed upon her to accept the hand of a rich merchant named Bouret. Four or five years afterwards the latter died, leaving the sum of 40,000 crowns to his widow, who promptly became Madame Quinault. This story is related at length by her second husband in a book bearing the title of *L'Amour sans Faiblesse*— a title which, unless appearances were very deceptive, was not, it is said, exactly justified by the facts. Brought up upon sound principles, Madame held all public amusements in abhorrence, and by this time had persuaded Quinault, though much against his

inclinations, to give up writing for the theatre. Neither
Melpomene nor Thalia could have been greatly discon-
certed by the incident. Except *Astrate*, a harbinger of
the new style of tragedy, and *La Mère Coquette*,
unquestionably a clever comedy, none of Quinault's
plays are known to fame. In his own time, however,
they were highly praised, probably because he chanced
to possess considerable wealth. In the year which
witnessed his abandonment of the drama he obtained
a seat in the Academy, together with the *cordon* of St.
Michel. He owed these honours exclusively to his
work as a dramatist, but Madame Quinault made no
objection to his receiving them. As we shall presently
see, this was not the only strange inconsistency with
which that lady's memory must be reproached.

The production of *Bellerophon* was followed by an
important change in the Troupe Royale. Mdlle.
Desœillets was incurably ill ; and her comrades, fearing that she would not be able to reappear on the
stage, induced Mdlle. Champmêlé to take the vacant
place. Hermione was the character selected for the
new actress's début, which took place on the reopening
of the theatre after Easter. It was an occasion of no
ordinary interest. In two tragedies recently given at
the Marais, *Policrate* and *Les Amours de Vénus et
d'Adonis*, written for her by the Abbé Boyer and
Devisé respectively, she had created an enduring

D 2

impression, if not established her claims to the rank of
a great actress.   Her powers were now to be brought to
a crucial test.   Racine, who knew nothing of her,
determined to spare himself the pain of seeing his
finest character inadequately represented, but was
prevailed upon by some friends to witness the revival.
Mdlle. Champmêlé succeeded in pleasing even this
exacting critic.   The performance over, he hurried to
her room, embraced her with effusion, and overwhelmed
her with praises and thanks.   Mdlle. Desœillets, until
now the queen of the stage, felt that she must give way
to this young and brilliant rival.   "I am no more,"
she mournfully remarked to Floridor.   In a word,
the *débutante* was applauded to the echo, though many
must have thought, as Louis XIV. soon afterwards
put it, that the character of Hermione, to be fully
realized, should be played in the first two acts by
Desœillets and in the rest by Champmêlé.   In other
words, the acting of the former had more subtlety and
finesse but less breadth and fire than that of her successor, whose small dark eyes and cultivated voice
played with passion both stern and tender in the very
spirit of mastery.   Elated to find that such an actress
had arisen, Racine gave her lessons in elocution, at the
same time studying her natural peculiarities with a
view to making them serviceable in any character he
might wish her to represent.   His admiration of her

gifts soon ripened into a warmer sentiment;—she
became his acknowledged mistress. " Racine," writes
Madame de Sévigné, " fait des comédies pour la
Champmêlé; ce n'est pas pour les siècles à venir. Si
jamais il n'est plus jeune, et qu'il cesse d'être amoureux,
ce ne sera plus la même chose." M. Champmêlé, who
had come over with his wife to the Hôtel de Bourgogne, bore his loss with fashionable composure, even
to the extent of holding frequent intercourse with
the author of his dishonour. Mdlle. Desœillets did not
long survive the blow she had received. She died on
the 25th October, in her forty-ninth year. " It is a
great loss that we have suffered," writes Raimond
Poisson ; " Desœillets, though neither young nor
beautiful, was one of the chief ornaments of the stage."
Nor was the praise undeserved. Her acting, if not
very powerful, had all the charm of truth, sensibility,
refinement, and artistic completeness ; and I probably
do her only bare justice in saying that she was the first
in order of time of the long line of great tragic actresses
who have thrown a spell over Parisian playgoers.

CHAPTER II.

1670—1673.

MOLIÈRE, whose malady continued to make very
rapid progress, had now arrived at what may be regarded
as an important point in his career. He saw little or
no encouragement to pursue the new path into which he
had struck six years previously. *Don Juan* had scarcely
appeared when it was rigorously suppressed; *Tartuffe*
had very nearly shared the same fate. Moreover, each
of these comedies had exposed him to the most virulent
calumny, though any pain he may have suffered on this
head was lessened by a conviction that a later age would
do justice to his motives in composing them. Experience
had taught him that between a sportive satire on folly
and an elaborate onslaught on deeply-rooted vice there
was an important difference: the former had the
countenance of the King; the latter aroused so much ire
that his majesty was induced to stop its publication. In
these circumstances, it would seem, Molière, however
tempted he may have been to go on displaying his
powers at their best, seems to have asked himself whether,
for the sake of the little commonwealth of players at the

Palais Royal, whose sole dependence was in him, he
ought not to discontinue the composition of pieces which
his royal master might be prevailed upon to prohibit as
soon as they were learnt.   Had he not done enough
already to secure an enviable place amongst the writers
of the Golden Age ?   He had still many chances of
exercising his wit, his humour, his genial yet searching
satire.   Messieurs the doctors were still ambling on
their mules through the streets of Paris in all the pride
of solemn quackery ; every wealthy plebeian was aping
the tone and bearing of his betters ; the fine ladies of
Paris, who had incited the religious world to regard him
as an " impie digne du feu," had re-delivered themselves
into the hands of the satirist by substituting for
préciosité an affected predilection for all kinds of learning.
Whatever his reasons may have been, Molière henceforward confined himself to his lighter vein, and the
fascinating voice which had spoken to the world in
Don Juan and *Tartuffe* was not to be heard again.

In his next work, *Le Bourgeois Gentilhomme,* the
dramatist once more ridicules the craving among the
wealthy citizens of Paris to get into society.   Monsieur
Jourdain, a retired draper, resolves to make up for the
deficiencies of his education, if he can be said to have
received any at all, and to pose as a man of quality.
He surrounds himself with professors of dancing, music,
fencing, and philosophy.   He arrays himself in clothes

of the most resplendent hues. He is delighted to hear
that his father, far from having been a draper by trade,
as the vulgar supposed, was really a gentleman who
chanced to have a good knowledge of woollen stuffs and
broadcloths, and who, being of an obliging disposition,
chose such articles in the country, had them brought to
Paris, and gave them to his friends for money. Moreover, when Cléonte, an excellent youth, aspires to the
hand of M. Jourdain's daughter Lucile, her father rejects
him on the ground that he is not of noble birth. But
the *bourgeois gentilhomme* is not a person to be angry
with. He is an incarnation of the parvenu spirit in its
most genial aspect. He has an honest belief in the
virtues of rank and education. He is always in good
humour, always satisfied with himself, always of child-
like simplicity. Neither the sharp remonstrances of his
wife, a truly sensible woman, nor the raillery of Nicole,
the waiting-maid, has any effect upon the beaming
complacency with which he struts about in his finery,
makes progress in courtly accomplishments, and learns
that what he has been talking all his life is prose.
His credulity is the pivot upon which the plot chiefly
turns. Disguised as a son of the Grand Seigneur (a
Turkish embassy, by the way, was in Paris at this
moment), Cléonte appears before the delighted bourgeois,
avows a passion for his daughter, and, after investing
him in due form with the dignity of mamamouchi, gains

his consent to the marriage. Neatly dovetailed into the
story is the figure of an impecunious and rascally
nobleman, Dorante, who enriches himself at the expense
of M. Jourdain by promising to advance his interests at
Court. The circumstances surrounding the investiture,
although not without a counterpart in real life, must be
deemed a little too farcical, but have not prevented *Le
Bourgeois Gentilhomme* from taking rank as a masterpiece
of comedy—a distinction it enjoys by reason of its
dialogue, its characters, its unfailing gaiety and humour.

Le Bourgeois Gentilhomme was played at Chambord
on the 14th October, and at Paris in the last week
of November. Before the Court, it should be noted,
each act was accompanied by a ballet, the most
important of all being that in which the Turks accompanying Cléonte to M. Jourdain's house took part,
and in which Lulli, the composer of all the music,
appeared under the name of Chiacaron as the Grand
Muphti. Molière himself played M. Jourdain, supported
by Armande as Lucile, Lagrange as Cléonte, Hubert
as Madame Jourdain, Lathorillière as Dorante, Mdlle.
Beauval as Nicole, Ducroisy as M. Jourdain's instructor
in philosophy, and Mdlle. Debrie as Dorimène, a lady
of quality. Louis XIV., disliking Mdlle. Beauval on
account of her incessant "giggle," suggested that
Nicole should be played by another actress; but
Molière, who had adapted the part to her unfortunate

peculiarity, saved her by saying that there was no
time to make the change proposed.   His philosophy
was brought to a severe test on this occasion.   The
King never relaxed a muscle during the whole of
the performance, and on meeting the dramatist at
supper-time did not utter a word of congratulation.
The courtiers, however disposed they may have been
to enjoy the ridicule heaped upon citizen pretenders
to quality, promptly affected to look down upon
the piece and its author, especially as they had not
forgotten their old grudge against him.   Many were
of opinion that his genius was on the wane ; others
declared he had committed an unpardonable offence
in exhibiting a count as a *chevalier d'industrie ;* while
a distinguished peer, probably the stupid and vicious
Duc de la Feuillade (who, chancing one day to hear
the King express a hope for fine weather, remarked,
" Your majesty has only to command it "), declared
that if such pieces were to be tolerated French comedy
would soon sink to the level of Italian farce.   Moreover,
the dramatist had to shut himself up in his room at
the château to escape unseemly jeers at his expense.
But a peculiar surprise was in store for his censors.
It came upon them after a second performance of the
play.   " M. Molière," the King then said to the
author, who must have personated M. Jourdain in no
very good spirits, " my reason for not speaking to

you the other day of *Le Bourgeois Gentilhomme* was that I feared I had been blinded by the completeness of the acting to any faults it might have. I now see that it is excellent; nothing you have written has diverted me more. Henceforward, too, Mdlle. Beauval," hitherto on trial, "will be a member of your company." In an instant, as may be supposed, the attitude of the courtiers towards the author underwent a change. Many were of opinion that his genius improved with age; others began to admire the adroitness of Dorante as a *chevalier d'industrie;* while a distinguished peer, probably the Duc de la Feuillade, declared that in all M. Molière's comedies there was a *vis comica* which the ancients had never approached. Moreover, the dramatist had to shut himself up in his room to escape a chorus of congratulation. No one who is aware of the servility of the courtiers towards the King, or of the delight he occasionally took in quietly ridiculing the homage he demanded, will doubt the substantial accuracy of the story, strange as it may appear to be. For the rest, *Le Bourgeois Gentilhomme* was received with acclamations at the Palais Royal, not only on account of its intrinsic value, but because, as Grimarest puts it, each wealthy citizen saw in the chief personage a vivid portrait of another. If tradition does not err, M. Jourdain was really one M. Gandouin, a prodigal hatter of the day.

The appearance of this play was contemporaneous
with an event without precedent in theatrical annals.
In the previous spring, it seems, the King's sister-
in-law, the Duchesse d'Orléans, youngest daughter of
Charles I., invited Corneille and Racine to write a
tragedy on the story of Titus and Bérénice without
each other's knowledge, and consequently without the
knowledge of anybody else. Her object in taking
this step was partly to bring the relative merits of the
two dramatists to a decisive test, but still more to see
acted on the stage a little history analogous to that
of her relations with Louis XIV. In a few weeks
from this time she was in the grave; but the
dramatists, both proud of the honour done them,
continued their tasks. Racine was the first in the
field. His *Bérénice*, rehearsed in secret, was· sprung
upon the town on the 21st November, with Floridor
as Tite, Champmêlé as Antiochus, and Mdlle. Champmêlé, of course, as the Judæan heroine. Eight days
afterwards, Corneille's tragedy, entitled *Tite et Bérénice*,
appeared at the Palais Royal, Mdlle. Molière impersonating the chief character, Lathorillière the other
lover, and Baron, who on receipt of an affectionate
letter from Molière had just left the country to resume
his place in the troupe, Antiochus. The astonishment
of the two dramatists on finding they had been
simultaneously engaged upon the same subject, and

that at the instance of the same person, may be well conceived. The result of the inevitable comparison was wholly in Racine's favour. The second *Bérénice* would not do after the first, and soon had to be withdrawn. But the friends of Racine had little reason to exult over his victory. If Henriette d'Angleterre was " the wittiest woman in France," as Burnet calls her, she must also have been one of the most thoughtless. Bérénice might be made to live again in the verse of the young Racine, but not in that of the aged Corneille.

"Had I been consulted in the matter," Boileau said, " Racine would never have undertaken so poor a theme as this." Poor the theme undoubtedly was ; but the great critic, even if he had not been acquainted with the author, must have been constrained to admit, after witnessing two or three of the performances, that it had been handled with remarkable sensibility and art. Condé, being asked what he thought of the piece, replied in the words of Titus,

Chaque jour je la vois,
Et crois toujours la voir pour la première fois,

and the compliment was not unmerited. Racine, it is to be feared, had yet much to learn in the way of worldly wisdom. He testified the utmost resentment on seeing *Bérénice* parodied by the Italian players, and was inclined to quarrel with Chapelle because that bibulous wit,

pressed at a social gathering for his opinion of the piece,
quoted the words of an old song,—

> Marion pleure, Marion crie,
> Marion veut qu'on la marie,—

a burlesque within a narrow compass of the story.   By
the way, what Bérénice says in the fourth act—

> Vous êtes empereur, seigneur, et vous pleurez !

and also in one of the final scenes—

> Vous m'aimez, vous me le soutenez ;
> Et cependant je pars—

was suggested by the speech of Mdlle. de Mancini
when she left Louis XIV.—"Vous m'aimez, vous êtes
roi ; vous pleurez, et je pars ! "   But as the curtain fell
on a performance of the tragedy at Court his majesty
did not appear to be troubled with any painful recol-
lections on the point.   "Ah, Dodart," he said, catching
sight of one of his doctors ; "I was on the point of
sending for you to look after a princess who wants to
die without knowing how."

Corneille's tragedy, I repeat, deservedly failed.   It was
unsympathetic in tone, unskilful in arrangement, and
often obscure in expression.   Baron despairingly asked
his chief whether he could make anything of these lines,—

> Faut-il mourir, Madame, et si proche du terme ?
> Votre illustre inconstance est-elle encore si ferme
> Que les restes d'un feu que j'avais cru si fort
> Puisse dans quatre jours se promettre ma mort ?

Molière frankly confessed that he could not.   "How-

ever," he added, "we need not trouble ourselves about
them; Corneille is coming to supper, and you can then
ask him for an explanation." Corneille arrived; and
Baron, after embracing him in due course, avowed that
he did not catch the meaning of the lines in question.
"Neither do I," said the dramatist, after reading them
with some attention; "nevertheless, recite them as they
are written; persons who do not understand them—"
this was probably intended as a sarcasm against the
Racinians—"may applaud them." Boileau put these
very lines under the second of two heads into which
he divided galimatias—the simple, where an author
knows what he wishes to say, but is unable to make his
readers as wise; and the double, where they fail to understand his meaning because it is not clear to himself.
Corneille, as we may see from two lines he penned,—

Agésilas en foule aurait des spectateurs
Et *Bérénice* enfin trouverait des acteurs,—

was disposed to ascribe his failure to incompetent acting
—a complaint for which there seems to have been little
foundation.

Before we pass from the year now drawing to a close
a few exits and one entrance must be noted. In consequence, no doubt, of the infirmity referred to in *L'Avare*,
Béjart retired on a pension of 1000 livres, which he
enjoyed to the day of his death (1678). He was one of
Molière's oldest and most valued comrades, and had

done good service by his performances of *pères* and
seconds valets.   De Villiers, after having been identified
for some years at the Hôtel de Bourgogne with *comiques*
nobles and third tragedy parts, withdrew at about the
same time.   Endowed with no special gifts for either
acting or dramatic authorship, he must hold for all time
a place in theatrical history, first as one of Molière's
victims in the *Impromptu de Versailles,* and secondly,
as the first Frenchman who brought Don Juan upon
the stage.   His retirement was soon followed by the
death of his wife, who, according to Robinet, played
the principal heroines at the Hôtel de Bourgogne,
probably as a substitute, with good effect.   Béjart's
place at the Palais Royal was not immediately filled,
but on again turning to the Comédiens du Roi we find
among them a recruit in the person of Mdlle. Marotte
Beaupré, for some years previously one of the chief
supports of the Théâtre du Marais.   The daughter of
players, she was born behind the scenes, and from her
infancy had been educated for the boards.   In making
this engagement Molière showed no inconsiderable
moral courage.   Mdlle. was not the gentlest of her
sex.   For example, having quarrelled at the Marais
with a sister-artist, Mdlle. Desurlis, she attacked her
sword in hand, happily without a serious result.   But
then this hot-blooded dame was unrivalled in *ridicules,*
and it was to be expected that a sense of the advantage

of being at the Palais Royal would suffice to keep her
impetuosity within reasonable bounds.

I must now relate an anecdote which for many
reasons should not be passed over. Madeleine Béjart
had touched up an old provincial farce having Sancho
for its hero. It was now revived at the Palais
Royal, the author of *Le Misanthrope* impersonating the
right trusty squire of the knight of La Mancha. In
one of the performances there was an unlucky *contretemps*. Molière, bestriding his donkey in due form,
with his face to the tail, proceeded to the wings a few
minutes before he was wanted. In the words of
Grimarest, the intelligent animal, not knowing its part
by heart, evinced a decided inclination to appear at
once. It was in vain that the rider drew the rein
with all his might; the donkey got nearer and nearer
the stage. Molière, of course, was at his wits' end.
" Baron! Laforêt! here; this execrable brute is determined to go on now!" But the young actor was out
of hearing; Laforêt, the housekeeper, could not render
any assistance, and the other players were before the
audience. Beset in this way, poor Sancho, catching at
one of the wings, allowed the donkey to slip from
between his legs. If he hoped to be in time to turn
its head he was sadly disappointed. In the twinkling
of an eye the animal ambled on the stage, there to
comport itself s it deemed meet. It is not very

difficult to imagine what effect its sudden apparition produced on the spectators in front, but to appreciate all the humour of the incident we must bear in mind that the man who was to have made his bow to the audience of the Palais Royal on that too-clever quadruped was the author of the *Misanthrope* and *Tartuffe*, the grave and erudite and philosophical Molière. *Don Quichotte*, it should be added, did not succeed any better-than Guérin de Bouscal's pieces on the same subject. Cervantes was neither understood nor liked in Paris.

Molière was now to be engaged upon a task more worthy of his powers than the impersonation of Sancho. Louis XIV. requested him to illustrate the legend of Psyche in a tragi-comedy ballet, to be performed in a superb *salle* in the wing recently added by Vigarini to the Tuileries. His majesty wished to see the piece several times before Lent; and the dramatist, finding that he could not finish it in the prescribed time by himself, asked Corneille and Quinault to come to his aid, which they did. It may excite some surprise that Madame Quinault should have allowed her husband to accept the invitation, but the honour of sharing in a work ordered by the King was not to be despised, and in the end she came to the comforting conclusion that in point of moral effect a play with music was very different from one without that accessory. Molière was

responsible for the plot, the prologue, the first act,
and the first scenes of the second and third ; Quinault
contributed all the lyrical matter, except the Italian
plainte, which, like the music, was by Lulli ; Corneille
wrote the rest.   Nor did this literary association fail to
yield good fruit.   *Psyché*, though not a monumental
work, is dignified by a wealth of genuine poetry.
If one of the three dramatists had the advantage over
the others it was Corneille, who, "sec et sévère" as his
genius may have become as he grew old, could enter
into the spirit of the fable so well as to pen the tender
declaration of Psyche to Cupid.   And the charms of
the piece were not to evaporate in the representation.
While trained singers and dancers were called in to give
effect to the interludes, by no means the least conspicuous feature of the entertainment, it was arranged
that Mdlle. Molière and Baron should undertake the
chief characters, with Ducroisy as Jupiter, Mdlle. Debrie
as Vénus, Lathorillière as Psyché's father, Hubert as
Cléomène, Lagrange as Agénor, Mdlle. Beauval as
Cidippe, Mdlle. Beaupré as Aglaure, Molière as Zéphyre
(a comparatively minor part), and Mdlles. Lathorillière
and Ducroisy, youthful daughters of Psyché's father and
Jupiter respectively, as the two Graces.   Lastly, the
decorations, in addition to being artistic in character,
had the recommendation of variety, as they successively
represented heaven, earth, and hell.   Need it be stated

that this delicate little dramatic poem, admirably acted
and mounted, proved a delightful surprise to the Court
when, in the month of January, it was played in the
Tuileries ?

Psyché was to be connected with an incident of deep
personal interest. Nearly five years had elapsed since
Mdlle. Debrie went to Auteuil, and it was hoped that
under her influence Molière had burnt the idol he had
so long adored. But this was not to be. His passion
for the coquette who bore his name was proof against
even the remembrance of the dishonour she had brought
upon him. Her ascendancy over his mind seems to
have increased each time that he met her in the Rue de
Richelieu, at rehearsal, or on the stage. It is probable
that he never appeared with her in scenes more or
less analogous to their own situation—and there were
many such scenes in his plays—without an intensity
of feeling which, if it made his voice husky, must have
added to the force of his acting. Had his wisdom been
equal to his generosity he would have sent her away ;
as it was, moth-like, he continued to hover about the
flame. For example, in *Le Bourgeois Gentilhomme*, not
content with limning her portrait with the lightest and
tenderest hand in the character of Lucile, he identified
himself to some extent with her lover, who, though
persuaded that she has betrayed him, is unable to shake
off his chains—nay, discovers unknown charms in her

acknowledged defects of person and mind. But it was not until *Psyché* appeared that the poet ceased to be master of himself. By the time the curtain fell he was as fervently in love with Armande as when he led her away from the altar in that little Parisian church, or when, the scales having dropped from his eyes, he unbosomed himself to Chapelle in the garden at Auteuil. In anguish hardly to be described, yet unselfishly remembering that mental disquietude would hasten his end, Mdlle. Debrie earnestly urged his wife, if only for the sake of her own interest, to seek a reconciliation with and respect him. Armande went to him in a penitential attitude; and Molière, in the excess of his new-found happiness, had no heart to speak or think of the past. It has been said that at this time Mdlle. Molière was engaged in an intrigue with the once-detested Baron, but the fact that the latter remained in the company will suffice to relieve her memory from the charge. If such an intrigue had existed it could not have escaped the notice of her husband, and would certainly have terminated the young actor's relations with the Palais Royal company in a moment.

In anticipation of the production of *Psyché* at the Palais Royal, Molière, now in the highest spirits, threw off *Les Fourberies de Scapin* (May 24). His need of a novelty at this time must have been very pressing, for in none of his plays did he rely so little on his own

powers of invention as in this. The plot, which turns
on the devices employed by an astute valet to wring
money from a close-fisted father for a prodigal son,
was suggested by the *Phormio*, and was developed
with the aid of details imported from Rotrou's *Sœur*,
Tabarin's farce of *Francisquine*, and other pieces. It
has been said that two of the scenes, with the proverbial expression " Que diable allait-il faire dans cette
galère ? " here reproduced without the adjective, were
taken from *Le Pédant Joué*. As a matter of fact,
however, Molière had originated them in his old farce
of *Gorgibus dans le Sac*, from which they had been
copied by Cirano. " Be these scenes good or bad,"
said the greater dramatist, " they belong to me, and
I retake possession of my property wherever I find
it *(je reprends mon bien où je le trouve)*." It is
supposed that in reply to a charge of plagiarism he
simply said, " Je prends mon bien où je le trouve,"
but the widespread belief among a certain class of
dramatic authors, that the great French comic poet
defended dramatic larceny of the worst kind, has no
foundation in truth. In *Les Fourberies de Scapin* he
improved upon what he did borrow, besides animating
the action and the dialogue with a *verve* quite his own.
Except Mdlle. Debrie, who may have been too ill to
appear, the best players of the troupe were engaged
in the piece, Molière leading off as Scapin. Boileau

witnessed the performance with no very great pleasure.
In conversation, as in the *Art Poétique*, now in pre-
paration, he reproached his friend with having allied
Tabarin to Terence, and declared that the author of
the *Misanthrope* had degraded himself by coming
forward as Scapin. " You forget," Molière replied,
"that I am a manager as well as an author, and am
bound at times to consult the interest of my comrades
at the expense of my own fame." He might have
added that in logic a farce should not be judged as
a comedy. His practical wisdom was amply justified
by the result. The drollery of *Scapin* was more relished
than even the beauty of *Psyché*, which, produced on the
24th July, had thirty-two representations.

Again did the dramatist receive orders to contribute
to the diversions of the Court. The King proposed to
have a *fête* at St. Germain in honour of the arrival
of the Princess of Bavaria, just espoused by Monsieur,
and was desirous that the prettiest of the ballets
already danced there and at Chambord should be
repeated in another play from the hand which had
given him *Les Amants Magnifiques*. Early in December,
just after the political horizon had been darkened by
the hostilities between France and Holland, this project
was realized with princely splendour, the whole of the
Court looking on. Molière's new comedy must have
suffered a little from the ballets it was designed to

introduce, but I am inclined to believe that it excited
no ordinary interest.   In effect, *La Comtesse d Escarbagnas,* as it was called, is a continuation, though in
a light and unambitious form, of the satire he had
launched in *Les Précieuses Ridicules, Le Bourgeois Gentilhomme,* and *Monsieur de Pourceaugnac.*   Madame la
Comtesse (Mdlle. Beaupré) is a raw country lady,
and after a brief visit to Paris returns to her native
province with a mania for fine language, fine manners,
and fine modes of living.   In her, too, the foibles of
country life, or rather what the superfine society of the
capital regarded as such, are pleasantly laughed at.
For one scene of the piece Molière was obviously
indebted to an oft-told anecdote.   Madame de Villar-
ceaux, whose husband lay at the feet of Ninon de
l'Enclos, was very proud of the precocious intelligence
of her eldest little boy, and on one occasion, when
her drawing-room happened to be full, requested his
tutor to ask him some questions likely to reveal his
acquirements.   " M. le Marquis," said the pedagogue,
" quem habuit successorem Belus, rex Assyriorum ? "
" Ninum," was the reply.   Madame was not so proficient in Latin as Molière's friend Roze.   In her
belief the question and answer referred to the too
celebrated Ninon, and her face flushed with anger.
" How dare you," she exclaimed to the astounded
tutor, " speak to my son of the madness of his father ! "

Le Comtesse d'Escarbagnas was preceded by a pastoral, now lost. Molière here appeared as a terrible Turk, aided by Armande, Baron, Mdlle. Debrie, and Lathor-illière. In a few months, reduced to the dimensions of one act by the simple process of omitting the pastoral and the ballets, the piece was transferred to the Palais Royal, to the intense delight of all the patrons of that theatre.

Molière was now to lose sight of an actor whom he knew how to respect, and who, although a member of the Hôtel de Bourgogne troupe, had never countenanced the hostility manifested by his comrades towards their illustrious rival. Floridor, having been seized with what was thought to be a fatal illness, formally renounced, in the presence of the curé of St. Eustache, the profession which he had dignified for more than thirty years. He soon afterwards recovered, but could not be prevailed upon to break his word. That his withdrawal was deeply regretted there can be no doubt. His acting to the last had been distinguished by feeling, natural truth, authority, and refinement; and these qualities, joined to his noble presence and carriage, gave him a hold upon the audience which Mondori himself had not possessed. It is said that from the moment he came upon the stage, if only to say a few words, an unusually deep silence reigned in the theatre. In *Sophonisbe,* among many other examples in point, " he appeared," writes Devisé, " to be really the personage he represented. Every auditor wished him to be constantly on the scene. I can say all these things in his praise without fear of exciting jealousy amongst other players; everybody acknowledges that he is the greatest of the number." Floridor did not long survive his last appearance in the Rue Mauconseil. He died in 1672, presumably between fifty-five and sixty years of age. His closing hours may have been solaced by the remembrance of a career of unbroken success, and yet more, perhaps, by the reflection that he had been the means of lessening the stigma attached to his art. In 1668, having retained the title of *écuyer*, he was called to account by the commissioners appointed to seek out and punish pretenders to good birth; and the King, who held him in high esteem, issued a declaration to the effect that the calling of the player was not incompatible with the quality of a gentleman.

The prosperity of the Troupe Royale, however, was not diminished by the loss they had suffered. Mdlle. Champmêlé, always a host in herself, achieved two remarkable triumphs, first in a tragedy by Racine, *Bajazet* (January 5), and the other in a tragedy by Thomas Corneille, *Ariane* (March 4). In regard to the former, a dramatic episode of Turkish history,

too well known to need recapitulation here, is told
with equal vigour and tenderness. "*Bajazet*," writes
Madame de Sévigné to her daughter, "is a fine piece.
In my humble judgment it will not surpass
Andromaque," and still less "the *divins endroits* of
Corneille. . . The character of Bajazet is cold ; the
manners of the Turks are ill-observed ; the catastrophe
is not well prepared. The piece has nothing that
lifts us out of ourselves, none of those tirades of
Corneille which send a shiver over one's frame." The
author of *Cinna* agreed with this criticism on at
least one point. " M. Racine's personages," he
remarked to Segrais, who sat next to him at one of
the performances, " wear Turkish dresses, but in sentiment are essentially French. I should not say this
to anybody else, as it might be attributed to jealousy."
His criticism was just ; but it must be confessed that his
own *théâtre* is not free from a similar defect. Madame
de Sévigné warmly praises the acting of Mdlle.
Champmêlé as the heroine. " My daughter-in-law "—
a playful glance at the fact that the young Marquis
de Sévigné had been desperately in love with the
lady in question—"appears to me the most wonderful
actress I have seen. She is a thousand times better
than Desœillets ; and I, who am supposed to have
some talent for acting, am not worthy of lighting
the candles when she appears. In reality she is plain ;

and I am not surprised that my son should have
been overwhelmed with disappointment on her being
presented to him.   But when she recites she is
adorable."   *Bajazet* printed, Madame sent her daughter
a copy.   "If I could send La Champmêlé with it,"
she writes, "you would find the tragedy of the best;
without her it loses half its value."   In *Ariane* the
actress created hardly less effect.   The language is
often unworthy of the subject, as when Phèdre, after
surrendering herself to her sister's husband, exclaims—

Je la tue; et c'est vous qui me faites faire.

"Poor Thomas Corneille!" said Boileau, in mocking
tones; "his verses, compared with those of his elder
brother, proves that he is only a cadet de Normandie."
On the other hand, the character of the betrayed and
deserted woman is elaborated with much power, and
was played with the finest effect.   "It is only to enjoy
Champmêlé's acting," writes Madame de Sévigné, "that
I have seen *Ariane*.   It is a poor tragedy; all the characters are execrable.   But when she appears a murmur of
admiration is heard; every one is enthralled, and the
tears of the audience flow at her despair."

In the mean time there was mourning at the Palais
Royal: Madeleine Béjart died on the 17th February,
and Marotte Beaupré, now in the vale of years, had
ceased to play.   Molière could not but have been

deeply affected by the first of these events. Few lives
had been more closely bound up with his than that
of Madeleine Béjart. She had accompanied him into
the country when he became an actor by profession,
and an enduring friendship quickly sprang up between
them. But for her, too, he might never have created
his inimitable soubrettes—the smartly-attired servants
who ridicule the follies of their employers with equal
wit, impudence, and good sense. In playing these
characters Madeleine Béjart was at her best; no other
actress had the same buoyancy of spirits, the same
refined *espièglerie*, the same aptitude for giving due
effect to the clever sentences put into her mouth. On
the day of her death, as we learn from the registers,
"the body of the late Marie Madeleine Béjart, player
of the Troupe du Roi" (residing in the Place du Palais
Royal), "was conveyed to the church of St. Germain
l'Auxerrois, and thence, by permission of the Archbishop, to the church of St. Paul, where it was buried
under the charnel-house," at no great distance from
the grave of Rabelais. "J. B. P. Molière," as we learn
from the registers, was present at the sepulture;
and it may not have been the last occasion on which
he stood with reverent mien before the last resting-place
of one who had shared his aspirations in early life, his
trials as a strolling player, his splendid and bewildering
success.

Madeleine Béjart disappeared from the scene at a
moment when she could ill be spared. Molière had
at length brought his artillery to bear upon a craze
of which mention has already been made, and which
may be described as a survival in a new form of the
affectation he had laughed away in *Les Précieuses.*
Nearly every lady of fashion now deemed it necessary
to be learned in philosophy, metaphysics, mathematics,
Greek, and the niceties of French grammar. The stars
of Mdlle. de Scudéri and Calprenède paled before those
of Plato, Descartes, Nicole, and Vaugelas. If poetry
and romance continued to be read it was simply as
a relief from the strain of sublime and far-reaching
speculation. In a word, Parisian society found itself
overrun with blue-stockings of the most formidable
kind, and it became a question whether the scientific
jargon in vogue was not worse than the inflated
rhetoric of former years. In this folly, which prevailed
to its greatest extent at the Hôtel de Rambouillet,
they were obsequiously imitated, of course, by several
of the men who hovered about them, and to one of
whom I must direct attention. M. l'Abbé Cotin,
according to his own belief, was a very remarkable
man. He seriously regarded himself as the father of
French enigma, as the first of sonnet-writers, and as
a more powerful preacher than Bossuet. He deceived
himself; and in one of Boileau's earlier satires a painful

immortality was conferred upon him. In his consequent exasperation he wrote a pamphlet against his
critic, at the same time heaping gratuitous insults upon
Molière. By doing so, perhaps, he strengthened his
footing at the Hôtel de Rambouillet, where the author
of *Les Précieuses Ridicules* was not loved. Molière
abstained from noticing these attacks; but it presently
occurred to him—and Boileau did not suffer him to
change his mind on the subject—that the Abbé Cotin
might be employed to good purpose as a character
in a comedy designed to throw ridicule upon *préciosité*
in its latest aspect. And such a comedy was now
in rehearsal at the Palais Royal.

Les Femmes Savantes appeared there on the 11th
March. Boileau may well have felt astonished at the
dramatic skill it displayed. Its materials were of the
simplest character, but in point of interest, as of fineness
of ridicule and general workmanship, it was not
unworthy of a place by the side of the *Misanthrope*. The
scene is laid in the house of a sensible citizen,
Chrysale (Molière), the learned ladies being his wife
Philaminte, the most imperious of her sex (Hubert),
Bélise, his sister, who fondly believes that she has the
heart of every man who has seen her (Geneviève Béjart),
and Armande, his daughter, a *bel-esprit solennel* (Mdlle.
Debrie). It must be admitted that this well-contrasted
trio are consistent with themselves. Martime, their

maid-servant, is dismissed because her grammar is not impervious to criticism, and it is to be feared that a lackey with but hazy notions as to the centre of gravity will share her fate. The character designed to represent Cotin was a fashionable pretender to poetry, Trissotin (Lathorillière), who pays court to Philaminte's daughter Henriette, a clever girl (Mdlle. Molière), in the hope of enriching himself. His stage name was originally Tricotin, but as this indicated the original a little too plainly it was changed to that which he now bore, and which, as being equivalent to treble-dyed fool, made matters a little worse. A learned man, he is received with rapture by the learned ladies, who are nearly ready to expire with delight when he reads them some wretched verses of his own—so wretched, in fact, that the audience must have screamed with laughter before he had done. Molière had taken these verses word for word from a forgotten volume of *galantes* by the Abbé himself. Next comes Vadius, an unscrupulous plagiarist from the Greeks and Romans (Ducroisy). Trissotin introduces him as a fine Grecian. "Greek!" exclaims Philaminte; "sister, he knows Greek!" "Niece," says Bélise, "do you hear?—Greek!" "Greek!" says Armande; "ah, how delightful!" The two men beslaver each other with praise, but not for long. Vadius accidentally wounds Trissotin's *amour propre;* a row between them follows; and the Grecian, stung to fury by the

taunts of the other, bounces out of the room. A similar
scene had occurred at the Luxembourg between Cotin
and Ménage—a fact which gave rise to the supposition,
seemingly erroneous, that the latter was the model of
Vadius. In the end, of course, Trissotin and the
savantes are discomfited; Henriette, who pleasantly
satirizes her relatives' mania, pairing off with a lover
(Lagrange). Martine, we are told, was played to the
life by a girl in Molière's domestic service.

The *Femmes Savantes* is said to have met at the outset with a frigid reception, but this statement is not to
be reconciled with the effect which the comedy unquestionably created. Every *bas-bleu* in Paris felt the
ridicule strike home. "Is it to be tolerated," Madame
de Rambouillet indignantly asked Ménage, "that this
miscreant should be permitted to torment us in this
way?" Ménage had the good sense to praise a satire
in which he was supposed to be assailed. "Madame,"
he replied, "I have seen the piece, which is singularly
fine. As for myself, Molière has disavowed any
intention to ridicule me." And he continued to flutter
about the *salons*. Not so the Abbé Cotin. He became
the laughing-stock of Paris. He could not venture to
show his face in either. society or the pulpit. His
friends deserted him in a body. Eventually, overwhelmed by the storm, he abruptly left Paris, never to
be heard of again. He died soon afterwards, and it is

probable that the incident would never have been known
if Devisé had not mentioned it in his *Mercure Galant*—
a periodical established at the beginning of the present
year—and if it had not caused a vacancy at the
Academy.   Then somebody wrote—

> Savez-vous en quoi Cotin
> Diffère de Trissotin ?
> Cotin a fini ses jours ;
> Trissotin vivra toujours.

The empty chair at the Academy fell to the Abbé
Dangeau.   Boileau was at first thought likely to gain
the coveted honour.   " How delightful it would have
been," Bayle once said, " to observe the embarrassment
of Despréaux in delivering the customary eulogy of a
predecessor."   " In truth," remarked the satirist, " I
should have been in a difficult position ; yet, thanks to
the resources of the art of oratory, I could have got
through the ordeal unscathed."   Molière was too large-
hearted to view without pain the consequences of his
satire.   Had he foreseen them, no doubt, he would
have held his hand.   But he had nothing to reproach
himself with.   *Les Femmes Savantes* did not overstep
the bounds of legitimate ridicule, though he may have
drawn nearer to them than was usual with him.   For
the rest, the comedy was repeatedly performed before
the Court at Saint Cloud, there to be treated in the
same way by the King as *Le Bourgeois Gentilhomme*.   If

his majesty hoped that the history of the latter play would be repeated in its entirety on this occasion he was grievously disappointed. The marquises had been made wise by experience.

In the early days of *Les Femmes Savantes* the Spanish players received their dismissal, but a more formidable rival to the French troupes than these foreigners had ever proved, even when they appeared in the original *Don Juan,* was now to arise. Had Mazarin lived twelve years longer he would have died a happier man. *La Toison d' Or* and *Andromède,* with the fanciful pieces which Molière composed at the instance of the King, had created a taste for plays with music, besides showing that French was not so unsuited to lyrical forms as had been alleged. Mindful of all this, the Abbé Perrin persevered with the innovation he had introduced in *La Pastorale* and *Ariadne,* and in the summer of 1669 the King formally gave him leave to establish an "Académie d'opéra en vers François." By this time, in order to gratify a mania for *pièces à machines,* the Marquis de Sourdéac had built a theatre in a tennis court in the Rue Mazarine, near the Luxembourg. M. l'Abbé obtained possession of it at a fixed rent; and here, in 1671, his *Pomone,* set to music by Cambert, was performed by a troupe of singers from the churches of Languedoc. It soon became evident that he was on the high road to fortune. The playgoers went in their

hundreds to listen to the first French opera. But the
cup was rudely dashed from the Abbé's lips. The
Marquis de Sourdéac, impoverished by his outlays in
the theatre, seized the receipts as security for his rent,
and, being remonstrated with by Perrin in terms more
vehement than polite, angrily resolved, in defiance of
the privilege, to assume the direction of so profitable
an enterprise himself. The next opera given in the Rue
Mazarine, *Les Peines et Plaisirs de l'Amour*, written by
Gilbert, was produced under the auspices of this
unscrupulous nobleman. Lulli, envious of the mine of
wealth discovered in the Rue Mazarine, profited by this
quarrel to suggest that the interests of the French opera
would be safer in his hands than those of Perrin, to
whom he was willing to give a small sum. He gained
his point; the King, by *Lettres Patentes* issued in March
1672, gave him the exclusive right of representing
musical pieces, forbade any one to enter the theatre
without paying, and declared that to sing at the
Académie Royale was in no sense derogatory to one's
dignity. Consequently, the founders of the French
opera found themselves put out in the cold in the very
hour of their triumph. Cambert, migrating in disgust
to England, became director of music to Charles II. ;
Perrin, remaining in Paris, sought consolation in working upon elegies, sonnets, and a translation of the *Aeneis*
into heroics.

The history of Jean Baptiste Lulli is worth relating.
By birth a Florentine, he was brought to France in
his boyhood to enter the service of Mdlle. de Montpensier as page, and by reason of his surpassing
ugliness was degraded by that princess to the rank
of scullion. He lost his employment for having
composed a satirical song against his mistress; but
Louis XIV., seeing cleverness in the music, intrusted
him with the formation and superintendence of a
little band of *petits violons.* In that capacity he set
music to the ballets arranged for the diversion of
the Court. His talents as a composer appear to have
been allied to no ordinary impudence. The Secretaires
du Roi au Grand Collége refused to admit him to
their body, on the ground that, having played the
Muphti in *Le Bourgeois Gentilhomme* at Chambord,
he was to be deemed an actor. He pointed out that
he had done so at the instance of the King, but the
argument fell upon deaf ears. He then laid his
grievance before the terrible Louvois, who told him
that the council were justified in their decision.
" What, Monsieur," he exclaimed, " would you, great
and powerful minister though you may be, refuse to
dance before the King if he desired it ? " and Louvois
helplessly gave in. But on one occasion the composer went a little too far. *M. de Pourceaugnac* was
to be played at Court under his superintendence,

and as the curtain did not go up at the appointed
time an impatient message was sent to him by the
King. "Le Roi est le maître," he replied; "il peut
attendre tant qu'il lui plaira." Louis XIV. was gravely
offended. He did not even smile as the piece went
on. Lulli was in an agony of terror. "Feign illness,"
he whispered to Molière; "let me play Pourceaugnac;
it is my last chance." Molière consented; and Lulli,
"to save his majesty from disappointment," magnanim-
ously took the vacant place. He strained every nerve
to be funny, but the King refused to be amused. In the
end, moved to desperation, the unhappy musician, while
fleeing before the apothecaries and their syringes, contrived to fall, seemingly by accident, into the orchestra;
an awful crash proclaimed the ruin of the harpsichord
under his weight, and he clambered back to the
stage with the most rueful of faces. His majesty's
sides shook; and in the end Lulli's offence was over-
looked. Molière, no doubt, was well pleased at the
success of the *ruse*. He had a liking for Lulli, who
was a sprightly story-teller, and who was often to be
found among the little parties at Auteuil. "Now
then, Baptiste, make us laugh," was an adjuration
invariably addressed to him by the host when the
conversation flagged or became a little too serious.

Establishing himself in the Marquis de Sourdéac's
theatre, Lulli, with the aid of Quinault as a librettist,

quickly gave the opera a place in the affections of the
public. It is with some surprise that we find Quinault
again working for the stage, but it fortunately happened
that his wife still held to the opinion that a play
was purged of its unwholesome properties by the
introduction of music—a view which she was not
the first or last person to hold. Lulli failed to wear
his honours meekly. Fortune was unable to change
his birth. He gave himself the most lofty airs. He
proved a veritable Jack-in-office. He loved to make
his power felt. He made his " sanction " indispensable
to everything that was done in the musical world.
According to one memoir he even deemed himself at
liberty to put an affront in the presence of others
upon the man into whose position he had been thrust,
or had thrust himself, and by whose work he was
thriving. In his morbid anxiety to demonstrate his
own importance, too, even the remembrance of the
happy hours he had spent as the guest of Molière could
not restrain him from inflicting a petty annoyance
upon the dramatist. He gave orders that none of
the troupes in Paris, that of the Palais Royal included,
should employ more than two singing voices and six
violins. Molière might have nullified this decree by
simply appealing against it to the King; as it was,
he passed them over in proud silence. He would not
let the world think that this upstart musician had

the power to move him.   But the most amusing
example of Lulli's vanity has yet to be noticed.   It
never occurred to him that his operas might owe their
success to something more than the scores.   He regarded his librettists as mere hacks, as *garçons poëtes*
who merely framed the canvas upon which he was
to paint.   He spoke of Quinault to the company without prefixing " Monsieur " to his name—in other words,
treated him with no more respect than the carpenters
in the theatre.   " Monsieur de Lulli," as the Florentine
took care to have himself called, dwelt in a fool's
paradise.   His music is deservedly forgotten ; the
libretti which Quinault wrote for it have taken a
permanent place in French literature.

Corneille would have done well to enlist his pen
in the service of the opera, as his contributions to
Psyché will prove ; but a total misconception of his own
powers as they now were induced him to keep to the
drama proper.   " The other day," Madame Sévigné
writes to her daughter, " at M. de la Rochefoucauld's,
Corneille read a play which reminds one of what he
used to be, *Pulchérie*.   I wish you had been with me :
you would, perhaps, have shed a little tear ; I shed
more than twenty. . . . .   I am crazy about Corneille ;
in *Pulchérie* you may again see

la main qui crayonna
La mort du grand Pompée et l'âme de Cinna.

Everything must give way to his genius." Elsewhere she bursts out—"Long live our old friend
Corneille! Let us pardon his poor lines in consideration of the divine beauties which lift us out of ourselves. Despréaux says yet more than I do upon this
matter; in a word, it is good taste." Boileau was not
insensible to the merits of Corneille, but it must not
be inferred from this letter that he had ceased to be
an ardent Racinian. Madame de Sévigné had cause
to reconsider her opinion of *Pulchérie* when, in the
month of November, the piece was played at the
Marais. The author had failed to endow the plot
with interest, the language with force, or the
characters, apart from that of an old man who is
amorous of a young girl without exciting ridicule,
with any special individuality. Extolled as the piece
might be by the partisans of the author, it did not
attract the great body of playgoers. "*Pulchérie*,"
writes Madame de Sévigné, "has not succeeded."

But a heavier blow than the failure of this tragi-
comedy was in store for the venerable dramatist and
those who stood by him. Hitherto they had been
able to boast that on his chosen ground he remained
without a rival. Racine's *Mithridate*, brought out at
the Hôtel de Bourgogne in the following January,
must have created some misgivings in their minds
on this point. It was with no less daring a purpose

than to provoke a direct comparison with the author
of *Horace* and *Cinna* that the young poet proceeded
to write the tragedy in question. Mithridates, with
his strength of mind and unfaltering courage, his pride
and resolution, his hatred and dissimulation, was one
of the figures to which only the Corneille of thirty
years before seemed capable of doing justice on the
stage. But the comparison did not prove so direct
as Racine originally intended. The tastes of the play-
going public, to say nothing of the necessity of creating
for Mdlle. Champmêlé a character of tender and
commanding interest, required him to throw an atmosphere of love and jealousy over the play. Accordingly,
devising an intrigue similar to that of *L'Avare,* he
represents Mithridate as consumed by a passion for
Monime, the captive princess, and as having rivals
in the persons of his sons Xipharès and Pharnace.
Monime is an example of womanhood in its purest
and most gracious aspect; and, if tradition may be
trusted, nothing could have been more expressive and
beautiful than Mdlle. Champmêlé's acting, especially in
the utterance of the words, " Seigneur, vous changez de
visage ? " It need hardly be said after this that the
political interest of the tragedy was not very strong,
but the scene where Mithridate enlarges upon his
project of bringing Rome to his feet has a grandeur
which Corneille only had surpassed, and which excused

the partisans of the younger dramatist for believing that he had vanquished Corneille at his best.

Racine now became a member of the Academy, thereby attaining a distinction more and more coveted among Frenchmen as time went on. In the first instance, however, it was proposed that the vacant chair should be assigned to the author of *Don Juan* and *Tartuffe*, though not unless he previously renounced his profession as an actor. Boileau had the privilege of submitting this proposal to his old friend. Nobody seemed to doubt that it would be accepted. Molière could not be insensible to such a mark of esteem, and his chest complaint, aggravated by the fact that since his reconciliation with Armande he had returned to meat diet, furnished him with a sufficient reason for avoiding in future the exertion incident to acting. Yet, to the profound astonishment of Despréaux, he at once declined the offer of the Academy. His sense of honour, he said, left him no alternative in the matter. "Honour!" Boileau sarcastically exclaimed; "prithee tell me what honour there is in blackening your face with moustachios, dressing yourself as a buffoon, and being thrashed on the public stage?" "More than a hundred persons," replied Molière, unmoved by the taunt, "are benefited by my appearing in a piece; and I will not insult a profession which I love, and to which I am so materially indebted, by purchasing personal advantages at the cost of throwing a slur upon it." Boileau, manly as his own nature was, could not appreciate the force of such reasoning in a case like the present. "How strange it is," he afterwards remarked, "that the most ingenious and philosophical censor of human follies should be guilty of one greater than the others!" The Academy, as may be supposed, did not waive the conditions under which their offer to Molière was made, and Racine was elected in his stead. In years to come the Forty did something to atone for the short-sighted-ness of their predecessors. They reverently placed in their hall a bust of the great dramatist-actor. "Nothing," they wrote underneath it, "was wanting to his glory; he was wanting to ours."

His illness daily assumed a graver aspect, but as the shadow of death deepened around him he threw off and played in one of the most vivacious of his comedies. His *Malade Imaginaire*, composed for the diversion of the King on his return from the first campaign in Holland, appeared on the 10th February. In the main it was another broadside against the doctors, if not against the art of healing itself. It ridicules the fear of death and the love of life. M. Argan's hypochon-driacism is nothing less than a mental disease. He takes as much medicine as would meet the requirements of a regiment; and his doctors, needless to say, indus-triously flatter his self-deception. By a fine stroke of

humour, too, his sick fancies are blended with a cautious
frugality. His fond delight in the flowery language in
which the bills against him are drawn up does not
prevent him from cutting them down. "What particularly pleases me in my apothecary," he says, "is that
his charges are so prettily worded. 'Pour refraichir
les entrailles de Monsieur, thirty sous.' Yes, M.
Fleurent; but you must not flay your patients. If you
are not more reasonable I cannot afford to be ill." In
the same spirit he resolves to marry his daughter
Angélique to a pusillanimous medical student, Thomas
Diafoirus, and in the end becomes a doctor himself.
By donning the garb of the Faculty, he is told, he will
cover all deficiencies, as under such a garb folly becomes
wisdom and gibberish learning. In a pleasant interlude,
supplied with music by Charpentier, *vice* Monsieur
Lulli, the hypochondriac goes through a caricature in
macaronic Latin—an idea suggested by Boileau over a
supper at Madame de la Sablière's—of the ceremony
actually observed on the admission of new doctors to
the College. In attacking medical science itself, of
course, Molière was not well advised; but it would be
too much to expect a man in the last stages of an
incurable malady to have much faith in the power
to heal. Fortunately, Argan was not a character which
subjected its representative to a heavy strain, and
Molière acted it with the most whimsical effect. Madame

Beauval and her husband had the next best parts—
Toinette, one of the briskest of soubrettes, who at one
time masquerades as a doctor, thereby importing an
element of farce into what is generally a comedy, and
the Diafoirus already mentioned. The latter appears
to have been cleverly illustrated on the stage. "You
find a good deal of fault with my acting," Madame
Beauval was heard to say behind the scenes to her
manager, "but say nothing to my husband?" "No,"
replied Molière; "M. Beauval has an instinctive comprehension of his part, which I should spoil in attempt-
ing to improve." It is no matter of surprise that the
doctors made "des démarches très-actives auprès de
Louis XIV." to the disadvantage of the play. Paris
again roared at their expense, and *Le Malade Imaginaire*
was extolled by all save them as one of the merriest
of M. Molière's writings.

It was his swan song. Early in the day fixed for the
fourth performance of the piece, the 17th of February,
he was so weak that his wife and Baron united in
urging him not to play. But, as usual, he thought of
others before himself. "How," he asked, "can I refuse
to go on when so many persons' bread depends upon it?
I should reproach myself for the distress I might cause
them, having sufficient strength to prevent it." Nor
was he to be diverted from the resolution he had come
to. Soon after four o'clock, by which time an audience

well disposed to appreciate the new satire against the physicians had filled the theatre to repletion, he again appeared in the high-backed arm-chair of the *malade imaginaire.* His acting showed no falling off in subtlety or humour, but to those who anxiously watched him from the side of the stage it was painfully evident that the comparatively slight exertion it entailed told heavily upon him. How curious must it have seemed to some of them that a man in such a state should be employed in giving expression to the fancies of a mere hypochondriac ! Eventually, in the closing interlude, where Argan takes his oath as a new doctor, swearing to adhere to the remedies approved by antiquity, be they right or wrong, and to ignore modern discovery, there occurred something which he had not set down for himself in the play. The last "juro" had scarcely passed his lips when he was seized with a convulsion. He sought to disguise this by forcing a laugh, but the ring of it was so hard and harsh that many persons among that hilarious assembly in the theatre must have felt a shiver go over their frames. The curtain having been lowered, the stricken dramatist, now a fainting and speechless mass, was tenderly conveyed, first to Baron's lodgings, hard by the Palais Royal, and thence to the house in the Rue Richelieu. In a short time he was able to speak, "My course," he then said, "is run. My wife promised me a drugged pillow to make me sleep : let

me have it.   The only remedies I shrink from are those
which have to be swallowed ; they are enough to rob
one of the little life that remains to me."   In being put
to bed he was seized with a fit of coughing ; blood
streamed from his mouth, and he faintly asked that " les
secours de la religion " might not be denied him.   Baron
and Armande immediately sought out two ecclesiastics
of the parish of St. Eustache, who, however, told
them that the author of *Tartuffe* was not· a person fit
to receive the last consolations.   The next priest applied
to had a better sense of his duties, but he arrived only
in time to see Molière die in the arms of two sisters of
Mercy to whom he had long given shelter during their
Lenten visits to Paris, and who, by what may strike
many as a suggestive coincidence, had chanced to knock
at his door as the ecclesiastics of St. Eustache were
refusing to soothe his last moments.   He was not to
be wholly deprived of the consolation the Church was
asked to afford him.

It is no mere figure of speech to say that his death
cast gloom over many a hearth.   For there is no
doubt that this swarthy, thick-featured, neatly-dressed
man, so grave in mien, so refined and unassuming in
manner, so self-respecting in his intercourse with rank,
so observant of all that passed under his eyes, so full
of the milk of human kindness, so ready to acknowledge
the merits of others and undervalue his own, so frank

and cordial with his chosen friends, so whimsical in
the contrast presented between his sedate demeanour
and the gleams of humour which shot from beneath
his heavy black brows, had created an ineffaceable
impression upon the hearts and minds of those
who knew him, whether at Court, in *salons*, at the
theatre, or in his home. Louis XIV. was as much
grieved as the hardness of his nature would permit;
Corneille may well have felt that his old age had
been deprived of another great solace; the kindly
Lafontaine wrote tender verse in praise of the dead;
Chapelle took his loss so much to heart that for some
hours his life was in danger; Boileau, albeit not used to
the melting mood, burst into tears; Condé, receiving
from some poetaster an ill-turned epitaph on the author
of *Tartuffe,* said a thing which in cooler moments he
must have regretted—" Would that it had been his
fate to write yours ! "   As for the players of the Palais
Royal, it was no ordinary blow they suffered by the
event.   Irritated as at times they may have been by
the impossibility of pleasing him at rehearsal—and his
judgment and taste were too fine to be easily satisfied—
they held his name in grateful veneration, not only
because his genius brought them prosperity, but as a
result of the brotherly feeling he had manifested
towards them.   It was not forgotten that he had
given them more than a due share of the profits of

their commonwealth, had elected to remain one of themselves instead of becoming their titular chief, had often been content to play comparatively trifling parts, and in their interest had worked when prudence counselled him to rest. His charity, too, was on too large a scale not to be sorely missed. For instance, hearing one day that a comedian whom he had employed in the country, by name Mondorge, was waiting downstairs in the hope of receiving pecuniary assistance, he immediately called him up, welcomed him as an old comrade, and talked with him of bygone times. "How much needs he, think you?" he whispered to Baron aside. "Four pistoles," was the reply. "Well," said Molière, "give him four pistoles as from me; add twenty as from yourself; let him also have a good stage coat." To no one, however, was his death a matter of more poignant affliction than an aged domestic, Laforêt. I have somewhere seen it stated that she had been in his father's service; perhaps she was the Lisette who had smiled upon his juvenile essays in the art of mimicry. Finding that what diverted her invariably diverted the public, he read his lighter pieces to her before they were produced, and if any passage he intended to be comic did not make her laugh he took care to improve it forthwith. He once attempted to palm off the *Noce du Village* upon her as a new production of his own, but had not got very far with

the reading when the good dame began to maintain
that, whatever he might say to the contrary, such
rubbish as that could never have emanated from his
pen.

By the Parisians in general—by the lively world
he had lived in and portrayed and amused—the news
of his death was received with a feeling of profound
regret.   Every playgoer must have been consciously
his debtor, and many of them were able to perceive
that in him a fine original genius had passed away.
The accuracy of that estimate is not open to question.
As a rule, it is true, he was content, as Shakspere had
been, to work with second-hand materials, though the
pieces in which he relied almost exclusively upon his
own powers of invention, such as *Tartuffe* and *Le Bourgeois Gentilhomme*, are not inferior in dramatic interest
to any of their companions.   In his search for subjects
he seems to have traversed the whole field of ancient,
mediæval, and latter-day literature.   His library, in
addition to the Greek and Roman classics, included
nearly two hundred and fifty volumes of French,
Italian, and Spanish plays,—and I have no doubt that
he had waded through them all for suggestions as to
plot and detail   But—again like Shakspere—he was
no servile plagiarist.   His works bear the same relation
to their sources as Macbeth bears to the weird legend
on which it was based.   He transmuted comparatively

G 2

base metal into fine gold. Everything he borrowed
was recast in a mould peculiar to himself, was to
assume a form and colour which he alone could impart.
In truth, he brought to his work a combination of
qualities previously unequalled out of England. He
had high creative power, a wide knowledge of mankind,
genuine wit, humour both rich and dry, spontaneous
gaiety, felicity of expression, the gift of satire without
bitterness, no inconsiderable command of pathos and
tenderness, unpedantic scholarship, a dramatic skill
that never failed him except in *dénouements*, and
last, but not least, an all-controlling good sense.
Employing these gifts in the spirit of an artist, he
applied himself in the main to the delineation of
everyday character, either repelling or sympathetic.
It would not be easy to overrate the importance and
value of the result. Despite a tendency to sacrifice
the relieving tints of real life to a clear and telling
portraiture of some particular trait, his leading personages, be their costume what it may, are illustrative of
human nature in its eternal aspects, besides standing
out with a dramatic force and vividness that may well
fascinate the most unphilosophical reader or observer.
He passed and repassed from one extreme of character
to another, now pouring a matchless stream of ridicule
upon the ridiculous, anon dealing in a sympathetic
spirit with the affections of the heart, and anon darting

a ray of light upon the deepest mysteries of life. His
range was large enough to include such different specimens of our kind as Don Juan and Célimène, Tartuffe
and the soubrettes, M. Jourdain and Agnès. In saying
this, perhaps, we come to the limits of his power. He
could not invest comedy with an aureole of poetry, and
even the depth of *Le Festin de Pierre* and the fine
sensibility of the *Misanthrope* will not justify the
assumption that tragedy was within his reach. For
these reasons, as in his partial neglect of the many-
sidedness of character, he loses by comparison with
Shakspere ; but in general excellence upon his chosen
ground, the representation of the true, he has never
had, and is never likely to have, an equal. Nor did
he fail to make an industrious use of his strength.
It might be thought that a man in his circumstances—
obliged to appear on the stage three or four times a
week, laden with the cares of theatrical management,
sought after by irresistibly attractive society, and long
a prey to ill-health and domestic affliction—would have
had but little time or inclination to write. In the
space of fourteen years, as it was, he produced no fewer
than twenty-eight plays, most of them of the first
order. His productiveness is explained by various circumstances ; he loved work for its own sake, recognized
the necessity of bringing out novelties in rapid succession, habitually sought refuge from sorrow and

annoyance in fresh literary enterprises, did not trouble
his head with wine, and was seldom at a loss for ideas
or words.   In the composition of verse, we are told,
this

> Rare et fameux esprit, dont la facile veine,
> Ignore en écrivant le travail et la peine,

felt so little difficulty that he would prepare the rough
drafts of his prose plays in neatly rhymed lines—a
story which Boileau's half serious request,

> Enseigne-moi, Molière, où tu trouves la rime,

does nought to discredit.   This exceptional facility was
increased by the fact that he regarded purity and elegance
of diction as of less importance than matter.   "If I
tried to make my verses as good as yours," he said to
Boileau, "I should spend more hours over them than
I can spare."   Nevertheless, his dialogues, especially
those in prose, are models of nervous, graceful, sparkling
French ; and *Le Misanthrope*, to which he gave the
leisure of nine months, has a chaste beauty of style
which Boileau himself could not approach.   And the
influence he exercised over the public mind was all
on the side of good.   Judged by the standard of his
own age, his plays contain nothing which, dying, he
could have wished to blot.   In his liveliest mood he
is at pains to convey a beneficial lesson, sometimes at
the risk of appearing a little too didactic.   He broke his

lance full in the visor of evils and follies rampant under
his eyes—religious hypocrisy, avarice, *préciosité*, medical quackery, insincerity of speech, the pride of the
nobles, the affectation of learning, the pretensions of
the wealthy bourgeoisie, the belief in judicial astrology,
and the narrow system upon which women in his time
were educated,—and succeeded in modifying all. His
treatment of even an ephemeral madness, however,
possesses undying interest, for the simple reason that,
as I have already said, he penetrates beneath the surface
of things. Universal truth, arrayed in a more or less
fascinating guise, is present throughout his work; and
this, aided by acting at once natural and expressive—
so expressive in fact that, according to Perrault, a
simple gesture in him had more meaning than could
be conveyed in half-an-hour's conversation—served to
establish on a solid basis the school of comedy introduced
by Corneille. "Name the writer who has conferred the
greatest lustre on my time," Louis XIV. once said to
Boileau. "Sire, c'est Molière," was the unhesitating
reply. In these simple words, it is often remarked,
the verdict of posterity was anticipated. Unless I am
greatly mistaken, posterity goes a step or two further.
It is not enough to say that Molière was a head and
shoulders above Bossuet and Fénélon, Corneille and
Racine, Lafontaine and Boileau. It would not be
enough to say that his is the most colossal figure that

French literary history can exhibit. He conquered for himself a place among the poets who have created a real world in the region of fiction; and that place, I take it, puts him between Shakspere and Cervantes.

Yet, incredible as it may seem, the remains of this great and high-minded man were laid to rest with less reverence than would have been paid to those of a pauper.   Most of the clergy, Bossuet not excepted, seized upon the circumstances attending his death as a means of affixing an additional stigma to the stage. For example, contrary to the spirit and letter of their Master's teaching, they maintained that, having been overtaken by mortal illness during his performance, he was to be regarded as an object of Divine displeasure; and the curé of St. Eustache, with the hearty concurrence of the reigning Archbishop of Paris, Harlai de Champvallon, who was to fall a victim to debauchery of the worst kind, took advantage of the fact that the player had died without the technical consolations of religion to refuse him a Christian burial. " What! " exclaimed Armande, now aroused to a partial sense of the dignity of the name she bore, " can they offer such an insult to a memory which in Greece would have been honoured with altars ? "   In this mood, but wisely covering her indignation under an appearance of profound respect, she addressed a petition to " Monseigneur l'illustrissime et reuerendis-

sime Archeuesque de Paris," praying him to let her
husband be interred in his parish church, St. Eustache,
" dans les voyes ordinaires et accoutumées," as he had
died a true Christian, and had not long previously
received the sacrament at the hands of one of the
priests at St. Germain.   Monseigneur appears to have
turned a deaf ear to her appeal, for soon afterwards
we find her repeating it in person to the King at
Versailles.   Her chief argument, though unanswerable,
was hardly well chosen.   " If," she said, " my husband
was criminal for acting, it should not be forgotten
that his criminality was often countenanced by royalty
itself."   To make matters worse, the curé of Auteuil, who
accompanied her for the purpose of bearing testimony
to the " bonnes mœurs " of the deceased, and of whom,
perhaps, the King had never heard, began to defend
his orthodoxy from some imputations lately cast upon
it.   His majesty, annoyed with both his visitors,
abruptly terminated the interview, remarking that the
matter did not rest with him.   In heart, as may be
supposed, he made a different reply, and in a few hours
the Archbishop received an intimation that the King
wished the order against a decent inhumation to be
withdrawn.   Harlai, to do him justice, was a fanatic
rather than a courtier.   He would not be entirely
diverted from his resolution.   Accordingly, having
feigned to satisfy himself that the statements in the

petition were true, he consented to allow two priests
to take part in the ceremony, though only on the
understanding that the body should not be removed
at any hour during the day, presented at any church,
borne through the streets with any pomp, or interred
within any sacred walls. On the character of these
stipulations it is quite unnecessary to dwell. Armande,
evidently believing that she had nothing further to
hope for from the King, resigned herself to the Archbishop's modified decision, and the best resting-place
that could be found for her dead husband in such
circumstances was the ground set apart behind the
Chapelle St. Joseph, in the Rue Montmartre, for
the bodies of felons and suicides and unchristened
children.

On the evening of the 21st February, as the
church bells in the old city struck the hour of nine,
the funeral procession set forth. The coffin, hidden
under a large pall, was preceded by two priests and six
enfants bleus, the latter with tapers, and was followed
by more than a hundred friends, some holding lighted
torches over their heads. Among the mourners, of course,
were Boileau, Lafontaine, Chapelle, and the players of the
Palais Royal. It was feared that a rabble in front of
the house intended to offer some indignity to the remains
of the author of *Tartuffe*, but a *largesse* of a hundred
pistoles, judiciously flung to them from the windows

by Mdlle. Molière, induced them to forego any such
design. In deep silence, unbroken by the chant usually
heard on such occasions, the procession slowly passed
up the Rue Richelieu into the Rue Montmartre,
the whole of the way being lined with spectators.
Inside the burial-ground, " a hemmed-in yard, pestifer-
ous and obscene, whence malignant diseases were communicated by the dead to the living," the scene, as in
the streets, was weirdly picturesque and impressive;
the stars shone brightly in the deep winter night, and
the lurid glare of the torches carried by the mourners
assembled round the open grave served to show that
the enclosure was densely crowded. The last rites
were too much maimed to occupy many minutes.
Without a syllable of prayer from the two priests,
who had simply to look on, the coffin was lowered
into the ground, there to lie undisturbed for nearly a
hundred and fifty years.

If the clergy had foreseen the consequences of their
intolerance in this case they might have taken a
different course. In the first place, what they had
denied to the illustrious dead was spontaneously supplied by the laity. Many a benison was breathed over
his remains, as may be inferred from the fact that in
a few hours innumerable masses for the repose of his
soul were ordered by persons to whom he was unknown
except as a dramatist and player. In almost every

quarter, moreover, the policy of the Church was openly
and sternly reprobated.

> Puisque à Paris on dénie
> La terre après le trépas
> A ceux qui pendant leur vie
> Ont joué la comédie,
> Pourquoi ne jette-t-on pas
> Les bigots à la voirie ?
> Ils sont dans le même cas.

So wrote Chapelle ; and the feeling underlying the
lines soon came to be shared by thousands. Indeed,
there can be little doubt that the blow aimed at the
theatre in the name of religion recoiled with terrible
effect upon her own head. Hitherto she had reigned
supreme ; henceforward, the example of the Court notwithstanding, she had to cope with an anti-clerical
spirit of hourly-increasing intensity. It may not be
too much to suppose that this spirit was largely
strengthened, if not absolutely generated, by the
spectacle exhibited in the graveyard off the Rue
Montmartre on that February night in 1673.

CHAPTER III.

1673—1680.

MOLIÈRE had not been dead many weeks when the existence of the Comédiens du Roi as a separate company was exposed to imminent danger. Naturally enough, the management of the theatre devolved upon his wife, who re-opened her doors on the 24th of February, wisely brought Rosimont from the Marais to fill the place of her husband as an actor, and looked forward to the future in the most hopeful spirit. Before long, however, the ground began to slip from under her feet. Covetous of laurels as a tragic actor, the fast-rising Baron, accompanied by Lathorillière and the Beauvals, migrated to the Hôtel de Bourgogne; while Monsieur Lulli, as the result of another Court intrigue, obtained the King's permission to make the Théâtre du Palais Royal the home of French opera. Mdlle. Molière and her associates accordingly found themselves left without a stage to act upon.

Louis XIV. probably intended to provide a new theatre for the ousted players; but Mdlle. Molière,

knowing that more than one of the number would
suffer from any delay in his doing so, determined,
with a courage and self-reliance hardly to be expected
in so young a woman, to take the task upon herself.
In possession of her husband's savings, which amounted
to about 40,000 livres, a considerable sum in those
days, she agreed with the Marquis de Sourdéac and
M. Champeron—subject, of course, to the approval of
the King—to buy their theatre in the Rue Mazarine,
with all appointments, for 30,000 livres, 14,000 to
be paid at once, and the remainder by instalments
of fifty livres on each representation given there. In
a *contre-lettre* of the same date, May 23, the Marquis
and Champeron waived their claims to the balance
in consideration of being allowed to share in the
expenses and profits of the troupe.

His majesty, probably well-pleased to find that
Mdlle. Molière had saved him some trouble, immediately sanctioned these agreements, and, as though to
atone for the loss he had inflicted upon the actors
by ejecting them from the Palais Royal, evinced a
practical interest in the success of the enterprise.
The chief members of the troupe at the Marais at
present were Laroque, Verneuil, Mdlle. Auzillon, Dupin,
Dauvilliers, Madame Dupin, Guérin d'Etriché, Mdlle.
Dauvilliers, and Mdlle. Guiot. Dupin, a son of M.
Dulandas, Lieutenant-Général of La Rochelle, had

married Louise Jacob de Montfleuri, sister of Mdlle.
de Ennebaut, and, in company with his wife, a singularly pretty woman, who filled the *grands rôles tragiques
et comiques* well enough to make her auditors forget
at times that she lisped and spoke through the nose,
had had a rough provincial training. It is said that
their début was made at the Court of Hanover.
Dauvilliers had no advantage of person, but in tragedy
he manifested something like genius—a genius which,
as we shall see, was "near allied to madness." His
wife, Victoire Françoise, was a daughter of Raimond
Poisson, whose cleverness she inherited. Guérin
d'Etriché distinguished himself in lighter comedy,
and Verneuil, a brother of Lagrange, as valets. Thus
constituted, the troupe continued to fill a large space
in the public eye, although the pieces they brought
out were of no very high merit. It was now the
King's good-will and pleasure that they should join
Mdlle. Molière in the Rue Mazarine, and that the
Théâtre du Marais, which had survived the theatrical
vicissitudes of nearly eighty years, should be finally
closed.

The decree of the Lieutenant-Général de Police in
this matter was issued towards the end of June.
The Comédiens du Roi, formerly of the Palais Royal,
received permission to play in comedies and other *divertissements honnétes* in the Rue Mazarine, to transport

thither from their old theatre all the paraphernalia
that belonged to them, and to post their announcements
at the corners of the streets and squares in the city
and fauxbourgs of Paris. No persons, whoever they
might be, should assemble before or near the doors,
carry firearms of any description, force a way in, draw
a sword, or create a disturbance, under pain of being
treated as breakers of the public peace. If pages and
lackeys caused disorder they would meet with an
exemplary punishment, besides having to pay a fine
of two hundred livres to the Hôpital-Général. In
the event of their services being required, the police
of the quarter should repair to the spot, and should
be assisted by the citizens in restoring tranquillity
and bringing the offenders to justice. The comedians
of the Marais, too, were prohibited from playing in
either that or any other part of Paris ; and in order
that no one should be able to plead ignorance of
this regulation, the present order should be posted
in conspicuous places. " Fait et ordonné par Messire
Gabriel-Nicolas de la Reynie, Conseiller du Roi en
ses conseils d'Etat et privé, Maître des Requêtes
ordinaires de son Hôtel, et Lieutenant de Police de
la Ville, Prevôté et Vicomté de Paris, le Vendredi,
23 June, 1673 : signé, De la Renie, De Riantz
(Procureur du Roi), Sagot, greffier."

Established in their new quarters to the south of the

Seine, the united companies, with Mdlle. Molière at
their head, opened the campaign on the 9th of July
with a performance of *Tartuffe*. " The Troupe du Roi,"
writes Chappuzeau, " are at present so well assorted,
so strong in number of actors and actresses known to
fame, and so well-assured of the support of the most
celebrated authors," Corneille and Racine excepted,
" that nothing less than a magnificent success can be
expected to await them. Moreover, they are established
in an excellent locality, and have a stage large and
deep enough to allow the most elaborate machinery to
be worked. This admirable company, which is formed
of the remains of two others, have appeared before the
public, and the large audience brought together at
the first performance, as on succeeding days, must be
regarded as of good augury. In these few words I
have related the results of the first efforts of the two
troupes, now collectively called the 'Troupe du
Roi,' as we may see from an inscription in gold
letters on a black marble tablet over the door of their
hôtel."

In the perennial comedies of Molière the players
found a wide field for the exercise of their talents,
but the demand for novelties was not unheeded by the
shrewd and far-sighted manageress. Thomas Corneille,
in conjunction with Montfleuri, wrote a piece of the
oddest construction, *Le Comédien Poëte*, which appeared

at the theatre in the Rue Mazarine—or, as it was usually called, the Théâtre de Guénégaud, the street of that name being close at hand—on the 10th of November, and was played eighteen times. Damon, the son of a wealthy merchant, profits by the absence of his father to enter upon an extravagant course of life. He has a liking for spectacles, and is having an opera played under the paternal roof when the merchant unexpectedly returns. In this emergency the latter is told and induced to believe that the house is habited by demons. Then one of the players refuses to go on with his part, and a comedy by himself, with a conventional love-plot, is perforce substituted for the opera. *Le Comédien Poëte* brought its authors 660 livres each. Thomas Corneille was not so fortunate with his next essay in tragedy, *La Mort d'Achille* (December 29), although it had been lauded by the Duc de Richelieu in society as superior to *Ariane*, and had been puffed by Devisé in the *Mercure*.

By way of meeting this rivalry, the Troupe Royale, while utilizing the talents of their new recruits in the old repertory, fixed their attention on an untried dramatist. Many loungers in the *salon* of the Maréchal de Luxembourg in Paris found their chief pleasure in listening to his secretary, whom he treated as a valued friend. I speak of a young ecclesiastic from

Provence, Gaspard Abeille. He was a wit; and the turns he gave to the expression of his already furrowed face in telling a story was in itself a thing to see. It is true that he had no taste for pruriency or ill-natured satire, but in spite of this drawback he was pronounced a delightful companion. Entirely mistaking the bent of his talents, he wrote a tragedy, *Argélie*, for the Hôtel de Bourgogne, where it was now produced. His heroine, at least as far as the catastrophe is concerned, was Thargelia, a name which he thought it expedient to modify. For a time the success of the play was more than doubtful. One of the actresses, owing to a loss of memory, was so long in replying to the question,

Vous souvient-il, ma sœur, du feu roi notre père ?

that an auditor cried, "Ma foi! s'il m'en souvient, il ne m'en souvient guère," and the burst of laughter which naturally followed was not likely to assist the Abbé in the serious impression he desired to create. Nevertheless, *Argélie* was played to the end, remained in the bills several nights, and eventually—an unlucky line or two having been judiciously blotted out— appeared in all the bravery of print.

Encouraged by the success of *Argélie*, the same players allowed another aspirant to dramatic honours, Nicolas Pradon, to have a chance. The company may be excused if they did not profoundly admire the

new-comer.   His demeanour was awkward and vulgar;
his dress sadly needed a brushing; his thin pale face,
with its shifty dark eyes, had a rather sinister look.
In regard to his early life—a subject upon which he
observed some reticence—nothing was known save that
he came into the world at Rouen about 1644, and had
just settled in Paris to push his fortunes as a writer.
It may be assumed, however, that his parents were
in only humble circumstances, as he had received but
little education.   His ignorance was a fertile source
of merriment to literary men in Paris.   Boileau asserts
in his tenth *Epître* that the unfortunate young man
had spoken of "metaphor" and "metonymy" as
chemical terms.   Nor would this appear to be an
invention.   "M. Pradon," said the elder Prince de
Conti to him one evening, "you have spoken of an
Asiatic city as being in Europe."   "I beg your high-
ness to excuse me," was the reply; "I am not well
read in chronology."   By dint of laborious self-improve-
ment, however, he acquired some facility in the construction of verse, and the ambition to distinguish
himself as a dramatist took possession of his mind.
His first tragedy, founded upon the legend of Pyramus
and Thisbe—a legend which, as he had good reason
to know, had been successfully treated by Théophile
—was now played at the Hôtel de Bourgogne.

Before long he found himself famous.   Not that

this *Pirame et Thisbé* displayed any particular merit.
On the contrary, the least critical spectator, favourably
impressed as he may have been by isolated passages,
must have seen in it a proof that the author was hopelessly destitute of imagination, dramatic skill, energy
of thought, and the power of drawing a character.   But
then it answered the purpose of an influential little
cabal to extol the new writer to the skies.   Racine
had made a swarm of enemies at Court, where, like
Boileau, he had long been well known.   His demeanour
was usually marked by a cold and almost haughty
reserve.   His sarcastic wit had been too freely exercised
not to inflict many ever-open wounds.   His ingratitude
towards the Solitaries of Port Royal had rendered him
an object of dislike to more than one of their most
uncompromising opponents.   His triumphs in the
theatre led the worshippers of Corneille to regard him
in the light of something like a personal foe.   Last,
but not least, he continued to make steady progress
in royal favour, and the most coveted dignities in the
way of State employment might be within his reach.
Nor did all the ill-feeling excited against him fail
to take a tangible form.   The Duchesse de Bouillon,
niece of Mazarin, and Madame Deshoulières, the " tenth
Muse," organized a cabal to lower his prestige as a
dramatist, with the ultimate end of at once lessening
his influence at Court and of wounding his ever-sus-

ceptible vanity. It was at this moment that the new
Pirame et Thisbé appeared. Might not the fiat go
forth that the author had at one bound attained the
first place among living dramatists, Corneille alone
excepted? Numerically strong, the cabal eagerly acted
upon the suggestion. In and out of season, at Versailles and in Paris, it was declared that the genius
of Racine had been overshadowed by that of Pradon.
Pirame and Thisbé accordingly obtained a factitious
celebrity, and the shabby poet from Rouen found
himself the hero of the hour. It is at least to the
credit of his shrewdness and address that any astonishment he may have felt at this sudden elevation was
skilfully concealed. He did not demur to the verdict
which assigned to him a higher rank than the author
of *Andromaque* and *Bérénice.*

Racine was weak enough to show that his persecutors had cut him to the quick, but in the course of
a few weeks their enjoyment of his annoyance was
qualified by a very different feeling. Early in February,
while the cry against him was at its height, his *Iphigénie* appeared at the Hôtel de Bourgogne, with Mdlle.
Champmêlé as the young Greek virgin. He had recast
Euripides' noble tragedy in a new mould, deepening
the interest at the expense of the essential spirit of
the original, and discarding the catastrophe in favour
of one based upon the legend as it is recorded by

Pausanias.   Iphigénie must be sacrificed at the altar
before the breezes required to bear the Greek fleet
from Aulis to the Phrygian shore will set in, but at
the eleventh hour it is found that another princess
of the name is the victim intended by the gods.
Inferior to the old play, though in no very marked
degree, *Iphigénie* went beyond anything Racine had
yet achieved.   *Andromaque* itself does not exhibit so
powerful a command over the springs of human sensibility as that with which he portrays the resignation
of Iphigénie to her seemingly inevitable fate, the
terrible anguish of Clytemnestre, and the strife of con-
tending feelings in the heart of Agamemnon.   Mdlle.
Champmêlé's acting, too, was not unworthy of the
play.   " Never," writes Boileau—

> " Jamais Iphigénie, en Aulide immolée,
>   N'a coûté tant de pleurs à la Grèce assemblée,
>   Que dans l'heureux spectacle à nos yeux étalé,
>   En a fait, sous son nom, verser la Champmêlé ; "

a tribute of which the poet's mistress may well have
been proud.   Louis XIV., fresh from yet another little
war, had the tragedy represented before him in the
orangery at Versailles, where, in the words of Félibien,
it received " de toute la Cour l'estime qu'ont toujours
eu les pièces du Sieur Racine."   In the face of such
a triumph, as may be supposed, the cabal were temporarily silenced.   Ridicule of Racine was just now likely

to do more harm than good to those who indulged
in it.

More than one pleasant reminiscence of Molière must
have been awakened by performances given at the
two theatres during the summer. The Troupe Royale,
as though to make graceful reparation for the bitterness they had manifested towards him eleven years
previously, played in a little piece written by Brécourt,
his sometime comrade, in honour of his memory.
L'Ombre de Molière may have been suggested by
a perusal of the *Dialogues of the Dead.* The shades
of Molière's chief victims assail him in the presence
of Pluto, who, however, places him between Terence
and Plautus. "Molière," we are incidentally told,
"was what the character of his plays would suggest
—estimable, judicious, humane, frank, generous." It
must have been with a curious feeling that Villiers,
the most conspicuous figure on the side of the Troupe
Royale in the warfare of 1663, listened to these words.
Then Mdlle. Molière revived *Le Malade Imaginaire,*
which, Rosimont playing Argan, ran for thirty-one
evenings. In the second of two one-act comedies
contrived by Hauteroche for the Hôtel de Bourgogne—
Crispin Musicien and Crispin Médecin—he was obviously
tempted by the success of this revival to deride the
doctors in his own way. The derision was at best
very mild, although the Duc d'Orléans relished it

so much that he had the play repeated before him in
the course of a *féte* at Saint Ouen. It was not for
Hauteroche to bend the bow of Molière.

In the autumn the long career of Corneille as a
dramatist came to a final close. Boileau had recently
completed his *Art Poétique*, in which he formulated
the principles underlying his criticism, and which,
doing more than its prototype, the *Ars Poetica*, became
a general "profession de foi littéraire." In one chant
he pointedly referred to " le Corneille et du *Cid* et
d'*Horace*." The aged dramatist seems to have been
much pained by the distinction thus drawn. He
could not bring himself to admit the large difference
between his earlier and later work. "Ne suis-je pas
toujours Corneille ? " he almost plaintively asked. In
this spirit—this disinclination to admit that his
intellectual energies were declining—he proceeded to
write another tragedy for the Hôtel de Bourgogne.
He at first thought of introducing Usanguey on the
stage, but the hero on whom his choice eventually
fell was one of the greatest of Parthian warriors,
the ill-fated Surenas. By undertaking this task, as it
proved, he exposed himself to a twofold mortification.
It was not without visible reluctance that the players
put *Suréna* in rehearsal; the audience, predisposed as
many were in his favour, listened to the piece in
frigid silence. In truth, he had failed to do justice

to his theme, and the few noble images scattered over the versification had only the proverbial effect of lightning on a murky night. His faith in himself was left unshaken by this new failure; yet, resentful of what he deemed the ingratitude of the playgoers, and anxious, perhaps, to avoid the ᵗ humiliation of having a piece rejected, he finally ceased to work for the stage.

Corneille continued to live in the Rue d'Argenteuil, and his uncouth but impressive figure was not an unfamiliar object in the streets of Paris and at first representations of noteworthy plays. It was a comparatively sad old age that awaited the man who had spread the fame of the French drama throughout Europe. His wife, the Marie de Lamperière of the Richelieu days, was in her grave; his third son, the pride of his declining years, had lost his life at the head of a party of cavalry at the siege of Graves; his younger daughter, Marguérite, had taken the veil. He could not but remember that his once splendid career had closed in gloom and disaster; and his pension, almost the only means of living now left to him, was neither adequate to his requirements nor regularly paid. In these circumstances, as may be supposed, his brusqueness of manner and speech, which had all along withstood the influence of Parisian society, became more pronounced than ever,—to the great regret, it would

seem, of one who liked to look in upon and have
a glass with him, M. François Arouet, a rising young
notary. But life had not yet lost its charms in the
eyes of the broken-spirited poet. He received more
than one proof that the authority acquired by the
new school of tragedy did not prevent the growth of
his own fame. Six of his best plays were represented
at Versailles by royal command. He conceived a
tender interest in his sister's son, Bernard Le Bouvier
de Fontenelle, at present in his eighteenth year, but
already distinguished by a turn for study and a
sobriety of thought and demeanour which led his
preceptors, the Jesuits at Rouen, to hope that he would
become one of themselves—a hope not destined to be
gratified, as on leaving them he became a student of
law. Above all, Thomas Corneille and his wife resided
under the same roof; and the lapse of time served only
to strengthen the ties by which the two brothers had
so long been united.

If the retired dramatist went to one theatre more
than another it was to that in the Rue Mazarine, for
Mdlle. Molière, mindful of the success of *Timocrate*
and the merit of *Ariane*, to say nothing of the magic
of his surname, evinced a preference for anything
Thomas Corneille might write. M. Corneille de l'Ile,
as the latter was still called, now brought her two
plays—*Don César d'Avalos* and *Circé*. The first was

a failure, but the leader of the company did not allow this circumstance to deter her from making arrangements for the production of the second with all the spectacular effect of which it was susceptible. Hereupon a serious division among the troupe became manifest. Dauvilliers and Dupin, supported by their wives, refused to share in what they regarded as an extravagant outlay, and Mdlle. Molière undertook the responsibility of dismissing them from their employments. Before long, however, they were reinstated in the company, doubtless as the result of a little friendly mediation. Events showed that Mdlle. Molière knew her business better than her refractory associates. Embellished with changes of scenery and music by Charpentier, this tragedy, in which the loves of Glaucus and Scylla, with the sad fate brought upon the latter by the jealousy of Circé, are set forth, met with a success out of all proportion to its dramatic and poetical excellences, high as they unquestionably were. "During the first six weeks," writes Devisé, who fashioned the divertissements, "the house was filled by midday." No part of the work was sung, but Monsieur Lulli, by virtue of the privilege he enjoyed, betrayed his annoyance at the popularity of *Circé* by forbidding the players to employ any singers or dancers. In due time the author applied for the " surplus de ses parts de *Circé*," which amounted to about 700 livres. As the Register has it, "the company, wishing to satisfy M. Corneille, who was an author of merit, and to receive other pieces of his composition, decided to present him with sixty louis," then 780 livres. Dramatic authorship, it is clear, was becoming a profitable employment.

Circé was to be associated with what may be described as a curious anticipation of the story of the Diamond Necklace. During one of the performances, a well-dressed man, having contrived to obtain the privilege of a seat on the stage, went up to Mdlle. Molière at one of the wings with the air of an ardent and favoured lover. "Never," he whispered, "have you appeared more beautiful in my eyes than this evening; and if I had not been your slave before I should be so now." Armande, who had never seen him before, turned away without making a reply. But when the play was over he followed her to her room, where a servant was waiting to undress her. "May I speak freely before this girl?" he asked. "Excuse me, Monsieur," the actress haughtily replied; "there are no secrets between us, and you are at liberty to explain your intrusion before everybody." The stranger's face flushed with anger. "I could understand this treatment," he said, "if I had done anything to displease you; as it is, I have nothing to reproach myself with. You fail to keep an appoint-

ment you have made with me, and when I seek you
out, fearing that you have met with some accident,
you treat me as the vilest of men." And he loaded
her with bitter reproaches. Mdlle. Molière looked at
him in utter stupefaction. He was not drunk, nor
did he seem to be out of his mind. "Monsieur," she
said, "what on earth induces you to suppose that
you have ever spoken to me before?" "Mon Dieu!"
exclaimed the stranger in a fury, "how can you have
the audacity to say that to me after what has passed
between us? I respect every woman; but you are
unworthy of that respect when, after having given
me twenty rendezvous, you ask me whether I know
you." "Bring the company here," said Mdlle. Molière
to her maid. "Do so," cried the stranger, "and I
only wish that all Paris could be present with them
to witness your shame." Several players entered the
room, there to find both their leader and the stranger
quivering with rage. Without waiting for the lady
to speak, the stranger hotly told them that after
repeatedly accompanying him to a questionable place
she now disclaimed his acquaintance—"nay," he said,
"the necklace she is now wearing is one of the presents
I have made her," and he snatched it from her neck.
He would have done well to keep his hands to himself.
Mdlle. Molière instantly sent for the guardians of the
peace, and the stranger, declaring that he would hold

her up to the scorn of the whole world, was marched
off to prison for the night.

His statements to the authorities served to deepen
rather than unravel the mystery. He was M. Lescot,
a Président at Grenoble, and had come to Paris for
a too-brief holiday. He had become enamoured of
Mdlle. Molière after seeing her in one or two performances at the Théâtre du Guénégaud, but had not
been able to obtain a presentation to her. Now, he
was in the habit of going rather frequently to the
house of a woman named Ledoux, " dont le métier
ordinaire était de faire plaisir au public." He apprised
her of his anxiety to become acquainted with Mdlle.
Molière, adding that he would liberally reward any one
who brought her to him. "I do not know Mdlle.
Molière," said Ledoux, " but I know a person who
has great influence over her, and if you call upon
me again in a few days you may hear some good
news." In the result, the charming actress saw him
under the roof of Ledoux, and an *entente cordiale*
immediately sprang up between them. He nearly
emptied his purse into Ledoux's lap, but the only
present which Mdlle. Molière would accept from him
was a jewelled necklace of ordinary pattern, purchased
in her presence at a shop on the Quai des Orfévres.
He was positively forbidden to speak to her at the
theatre, as her comrades, jealous of her growing

popularity, to say nothing of the position she held
in the troupe, would be only too ready to adopt the
worst interpretation of the relations which subsisted
between them.   But one afternoon she failed to keep
a promise to meet him after dinner, and his anxiety
to know what had become of her was so intense
that all the remonstrances of Ledoux could not restrain
him from going to the theatre.   In doing so he flattered
himself with the belief that a *petit emportement de
passion* would rather please than offend her.   He
was mistaken; she coldly disclaimed his acquaintance, and in a fit of exasperation he snatched from
her the present hereinbefore mentioned.   Her own
statement would complete the story.

Mdlle. Molière no sooner heard of this deposition
than she instituted proceedings against him for defam-
ation of character.   Even in those loose times she
could not afford to let the world believe that he had
truth on his side.   But it was not so easy to vindicate
herself as she at first imagined.   The jeweller on the
Quai des Orfévres had no hesitation in swearing that
she was the person for whom and with whom the
Président bought the necklace, and Ledoux was found
to have fled from the city when the scene in the
dressing-room at the theatre became known.   Mdlle.
Molière, as may be supposed, was in despair.   Everybody would think that she had been in the pay of

the keeper of a house of ill repute, and how could the King allow such a person to remain in one of his theatrical companies? In the course of a few days, however, the cloud passed from over her head. Hunted down by the police, Ledoux confessed that she had palmed off upon the Président as Mdlle. Molière a girl named Tourelle, who bore an astonishingly close resemblance to the charming actress in both appearance and voice, and was able to imitate her languishing air and other peculiarities to perfection. Tourelle herself, arrested directly afterwards, subscribed to this confession, though well aware that the imposture would cost her dear. The prisoners were whipped half-naked along the Rue Mazarine by the public executioner; while the unhappy Président, cured of his passion for Mdlle. Molière by the compensation he was required to make her, allowed himself to be driven out of Paris by as merciless a storm of laughter as ever fell to the lot of a human being.

In *L'Inconnu*, a comedy by Thomas Corneille and Devisé, played soon afterwards at the Théâtre du Guénégaud, there is an allusion to this strange little history. Of "matière galante," *L'Inconnu*, like *Circé*, was "mêlée d'ornements et de musique," and a run of twenty-eight evenings showed that such extraneous attractions were not without commercial value. Early in the previous year, before the subject of Racine's last

great essay had been bruited abroad, the author of
Virginie Romaine, after a silence of thirty years as a
poet, composed, in conjunction with one Coras, an
Iphigénie en Aulide in imitation of, but immeasurably
inferior to, that of Euripides. In the spring of this
year it was produced by the Comédiens du Roi, serving
to deepen rather than qualify the impression created
by its predecessor. Racine was above rivalry; yet,
with characteristic ill-nature, he sought to aggravate
the discomfiture of the authors by publishing a biting
epigram against them :—

> Entre Leclerc, et son ami Coras,
>   Tous deux auteurs, rimans de compagnie,
> N'a pas longtemps s'ourdirent grands débats
>   Sur le propos de leur *Iphigénie :*
> Coras lui dit, la pièce est de mon crû ;
>   Leclerc répond, elle est mienne, et non votre ;
> Mais aussitôt que l'ouvrage a paru,
>   Plus n'ont voulu l'avoir fait l'un ni l'autre.

The edge of the lines, it should be added, was a little
blunted by the fact that in the preface to the tragedy,
published after the performance, Leclerc took pains
to show that the lion's share of the work had been
performed by himself. Better success attended the
introduction of a *Coriolan* by the Abbé Abeille, but
it was in comedy— in *Le Volontaire,* the last of a series
of overstrained farces by Rosimont, and in *Le Triomphe
des Dames,* a fanciful comedy by Thomas Corneille—that

the company, now poorer by the death of Laroque, were at their best.

Parisian society was at this moment aglow with expectation respecting what promised to be a memorable contest in the dramatic world. " In a conversation at Madame de la Fayette's," the Abbé de Saint Pierre tells us, " M. Racine contended that it was in the power of a great poet to make the darkest crimes appear more or less excusable—nay, to arouse compassion for the criminals themselves. Even Medea and Phædra, he thought, might become objects of pity rather than horror upon the stage. His hearers,. however, were inclined to dissent from this view, if not to turn it into ridicule." In order to convince them of their error, as well as to measure his strength once more against that of Euripides, the dramatist took the fierce passion of Phædra for her stepson as the subject of a tragedy. His intention soon became known in the *salons;* and his enemies, recovering from the depressing effect upon their minds of the success of *Iphigénie,* again assumed a hostile attitude towards him. Having persuaded a good many persons that a *Tamerlane* by their friend Pradon, the most important novelty lately favoured by the players of the Hôtel de Bourgogne, had raised him to the first place among living dramatists, which was not exactly the case, they urged him to tear any laurels that might still rest on the brow of Racine by

adopting the same story; the suggestion was complacently adopted, and the keenest interest in the result
of the impending duel immediately became manifest in
nearly all quarters.

In less than three months the two *Phèdres* were in
a presentable shape.   As the bells were ringing out
the old year the Troupe Royale went through their
last rehearsal of Racine's tragedy, which was played for
the first time on the following day.   Mdlle. Champmêlé
was the heroine, supported by Baron as Hippolyte and
Mdlle. d'Ennebaut as Aricie.   An unwelcome surprise
fell upon the company as the curtain rose.   The theatre
was half-deserted.   Instructed by experience, the cabal,
instead of seeking by yawns and giggling to weaken
any impression which the piece might create, had
previously bought the best seats, though only to leave
them unoccupied.   It was in vain that the author's
friends struggled against the effect of this stratagem;
the dreary aspect of the house threw a chill over most
of those present, and the performance concluded in
comparative silence.   When, two days afterwards, on
the 3rd of January, Pradon's *Phèdre* was brought
forward at the Théâtre du Guénégaud—the leading
character, originally offered to but wisely declined by
Mdlle. Debrie, being in charge of Madame Dupin—the
scene was very different.   The *salle* presented a most
enlivening appearance.   The cabal, having purchased

most of the places, had repaired thither in their dozens, and any expression of disgust on the part of Racinians in the parterre was promptly drowned in roars of applause. Moreover, these tactics were pursued at each theatre for the first six representations, though at a cost of no less than 15,000 livres. How the contrast thus effected was turned to account need hardly be pointed out   The many-headed public, it was alleged, had decided upon the comparative merits of the two dramatists. M. Racine might be a clever man, but one must not suppose that he was worthy even to unbuckle M. Pradon's shoes.

Nor did the work of the cabal end here. Great pains were taken to give wide currency to a sonnet which Mdlle. Deshoulières had composed after a little supper with Pradon and other friends, and in which, as we shall see, the *Phèdre* of the Hôtel de Bourgogne was turned into burlesque :—

> Dans un fauteuil doré, Phèdre, tremblante et blême,
>   Dit des vers où, d'abord, personne n'entend rien ;
>   Sa nourrice lui fait un sermon fort Chrétien,
> Contre l'affreux dessein d'attenter sur soi-même.
>
> Hippolyte la haït presque autant qu'elle l'aime,
>   Rien ne change son cœur ni son chaste maintien ;
>   La nourrice l'accuse ; elle s'en punit bien ;
> Thésée a pour son fils une rigueur extrême.
>
> Une grosse Aricie au teint rouge, aux crins blonds,
> N'est-là que pour montrer deux enormes tetons,

Que, malgré sa froideur, Hippolyte idolâtre.
Il meurt enfin, traîné par ses coursiers ingrats ;
Et Phèdre, après avoir pris de la mort-aux-rats,
Vient, en se confessant, mourir sur le théâtre.

It was commonly believed that this sonnet had been written by the Duc de Nevers ; and the Comte de Fiesque and the Chevalier de Nantouillet, with other friends of Racine, secretly turned it against that dabbler in verse as follows :—

Dans un palais doré, Damon, jaloux et blême,
    Fait des vers où jamais personne n'entend rien ;
    Il n'est ni courtisan, ni guerrier, ni Chrétien,
Et souvent pour rimer il s'enferme lui-même.

La muse, par malheur, le haït autant qu'elle l'aime,
    Il a d'un franc poëte et l'air et le maintien,
    Il veut juger de tout, et n'en juge pas bien,
Il a pour le Phœbus une tendresse extrême.

Une sœur vagabonde, aux crins plus noirs que blonds,
    Va partout l'univers promener deux tetons,

Dont, malgré son pays, Damon est idolâtre,
    Il se tue à rimer pour des lecteurs ingrats,
    L'Enéïde, a son gout, est de la mort-aux-rats ;
Et, selon lui, Pradon est le roi du théâtre.

The "sœur vagabonde" was the ill-starred Duchesse de Mazarin.

Naturally enough, the Duc de Nevers was greatly irritated by this response. Not doubting that Racine and Boileau were its authors, he loudly proclaimed his intention to send them to their last account at the first opportunity, and, probably to embitter the few

hours left to them on earth, wrote a sonnet in the
same measure :—

> Racine et Despréaux, l'air triste et le teint blême,
>   Viennent demander grâce et ne confessent rien,
>   Il faut leur pardonner, parce qu'on est Chrétien,
> Mais on sait ce qu'on doit au public, à soi-même.
>
> Damon, pour l'intérêt de cette sœur qu'il aime,
>   Doit de ces scélérats châtier le maintien,
>   Car il serait blâmé de tous les gens de bien,
> S'il ne punissait pas leur insolence extrême.
>
> Ce fut une furie, aux crins plus noirs que blonds,
>   *   *   *   *   *
>
> Ce sonnet qu'en secret leur cabale idolâtre.
>   Vous en serez punis, satirique ingrats,
>   Non pas en trahison, d'un fou de mort-aux-rats,
> Mais de coups de bâton, donnés en plein théâtre.

The Duc, who was not remarkable for physical
courage, soon had reason to reconsider his heroic resolution. The great Condé came to the protection of the
threatened poets. "Messieurs," said his son Henri-Jules
to them, "M. le Prince begs you will come to his
Hôtel, no matter whether you have written the lines or
not. If you are innocent he will not let you suffer; in
the other case he will take care that the authors of so
agreeable a sonnet shall be exposed to no danger or
annoyance." Condé followed this up by declaring that
he should take to himself any insult offered to MM.
Racine and Despréaux, in whose friendship he felt
honoured. The Comte de Fiesque and the Chevalier de

Nantouillet simultaneously avowed their culpability,
adding that they were quite ready to afford satisfaction
to M. le Duc de Nevers if he deemed himself aggrieved.
In these circumstances the Duc discovered that the
verses were not so offensive as he had supposed;
"indeed," said he, with a ghastly affectation of good
temper, "I am much less aggrieved than amused."
Racine and Boileau accordingly found themselves able
to go out without fear of hired bravos, and an incident
which for a time kept the *salons* in a ferment of excitement was at length brought to what many persons
thought a premature and unsatisfactory close.

Not so the history of the *Phèdres.* The cabal soon
had the mortification to perceive that they had gone
to infinite trouble and expense without accomplishing
their purpose. Notwithstanding their ingenious device,
Pradon's tragedy became an object of general contempt,
Racine's of more enthusiastic admiration than any of
his previous essays had won. In each instance the
verdict of the playgoers has been endorsed by succeeding ages. If Pradon's *Phèdre* be remembered now it
is simply by reason of its temporary association with
that which it was originally held to have eclipsed, and
in which the genius of Jean Racine reached its culmin-
ating point. It is only in the tragedies of Shakspere
and the graver comedies of Molière that we can find
any character worthy of comparison with Phèdre. In

the Greek and Roman tragedies on the same subject, where the death of Hippolytus is treated as the chief source of interest, the miserable wife of Theseus engages little or no sympathy. Her passion for the young warrior is essentially material, and in covering him with infamy she acts of her own free will. Racine represents her in a finer light—as a woman struggling with all the energy of a high and noble nature against the illicit yearnings instilled into her by Aphrodite, as loathing herself with increasing intensity as she sinks lower and lower into the abyss of guilt, as refusing to accuse Hippolyte until she has been craftily goaded to frenzy by the nurse, and finally as a prey to bitter though unavailing remorse. It was a great original conception, worked out with all the force that could be imparted to it by analytic insight, imaginative art, and beauty of diction. Inferior to Euripides in *Iphigénie*, Racine here surpassed his model, besides furnishing the French stage with the finest tragic character, though not the finest play, yet seen upon it. Mdlle. Champmêlé may have done much at the outset to make the merits of *Phèdre* appreciated; as the daughter of Minos and Pasiphaë, indeed, she is said to have risen to the summit of her reputation.

As the proudest achievement in a memorable career, though rather as a portrait than an elaborately-composed picture, Racine's tragedy bears some analogy

to *Don Juan*, which was announced at the Théâtre de
Guénégaud as soon as Pradon's piece had been withdrawn.   Molière would have found it difficult to recognize his handiwork in the play as it was now revived.
For, at the instance of Armande, Thomas Corneille had
turned the nervous and flexible prose of the original
into more or less stilted verse, at the same time
deferring to over-nice susceptibilities so far as to elimi-
nate or soften many passages essential to the really
blameless purpose of the author.   The document relating
to the transaction is still preserved :—" Je soussigné,
confesse avoir reçu de la Trouppe, en deux payements,
la somme de 2,200 livres, tant pour moi que pour M^r.
de Corneille, de la quelle somme je suis créancière avec
lad. Trouppe, et dont elle est demeurée d'accord pour
l'achat de la pièce du *Festin de Pierre*, qui m'appartenoit,
et que j'ai fait mettre en vers par led. Sieur Corneille. . .
Fait à Paris ce 3 Juillet 1677.   Signé, Armande-
Grésinde-Claire-Elizabeth Béjart."   Devisé, who, to do
him justice, was never to be trusted as a dramatic
critic, especially when anything done by his friend
Thomas Corneille was under consideration, had nothing
but praise for this mutilation of *Don Juan*.   " Formerly,"
he writes, " one could not say all he thought of this
piece, owing to speeches which offended the scrupulous.
In its present form it is entirely free from such drawbacks, and in the process of being changed from verse

into prose has acquired new beauties without losing any
of the old.   It has proved exceedingly popular, and
doubtless would have remained on the bills much longer
if the players, who are more pious than one is usually
inclined to think, had not voluntarily taken the publication of the jubilee as an order to shut their theatre."
It is grievous to see that the posthumous fame of Molière
should have suffered at the hands of the woman who
owed to him fortune, social distinction, and an illustrious
name.

Mdlle. Molière's next step was to accept a new
tragedy by Pradon, *Electre.*   In all probability it would
not succeed, but the players would at least be repaid for
their pains by the patronage of the coterie at the Hôtel
de Nevers.   Her expectations on this head were not
justified by the event.   The cabal, alive to the
ridiculous nature of the position in which they had
placed themselves, abandoned Pradon to his fate as a
dramatist—nay, ceased to show any desire for his
society.   Deprived of their support, *Electre* fell most
ingloriously, and had the unenviable distinction of being
the first piece which a French audience hissed.   In
the midd'e of the pit, with his face half-buried in a
cloak, was the unhappy author himself, who, failing to
understand why his *Phèdre* had produced so poor an
effect after the sixth performance, had gone thither
with a friend to hear the criticisms passed upon his

work. When the hisses "came full volley home" he stamped his foot with rage. "Monsieur," said his companion, "you may be recognized; do not let it be said that you are crushed by this reverse; hiss like the others." Pradon, perceiving that the doom of the play was sealed, grimly followed the advice. Near him stood a mousquetaire on duty in the theatre. "What is the meaning of this noise," the latter angrily asked him; "the piece is a fine one, and the author is a man of consideration at Court." "I shall hiss as long as I like," was the haughty reply. The mousquetaire did not possess an even temper. He tore off the poet's peruke, doubled it up, and hurled it to the side of the theatre. Pradon fiercely flew at the admirer of the play, and in a few moments, bleeding from a wound he had received in a scuffle that ensued, was hurried into the street.

By a noteworthy coincidence, two dramatists were now separately at work upon the story of Queen Elizabeth's last favourite, each in emulation of Calprenède's tragedy upon that very grateful theme. "The troupe of the Hôtel de Bourgogne," writes Devisé at the end of the year, "will give on the lendemain des Rois the first representation of the *Comte d'Essex*, by M. Corneille the younger. It is said that we have nothing more touching than this piece." Nor was the rumour entirely at fault. If not a production of the first order, the new *Comte d'Essex* had a dignity and pathos which

its predecessor had missed, and which, deepened by the
acting of Mdlle. Champmêlé as Elizabeth, reduced many
hardened playgoers to a lachrymose condition.   In the
old *Comte d'Essex*, it should be remarked, a good deal
turns upon the ring given by the Queen to the hero.
Corneille, to the amazement of the Ethereges and
Sedleys who periodically descended upon Paris like a
swarm of butterflies, ignored the incident altogether, as
he was "convinced that it had been invented by M.
de–Calprenède."   Courageously enough, the Comédiens
du Roi soon afterwards brought out a *Comte d Essex* by
the Abbé Boyer, though only to shelve it on the eighth
representation.   It was substantially a rearrangement
of the 1638 piece,· but in fairness to the unluckiest of
dramatic authors I must add that where he deviated
from the original it was generally for the better,
excellent as in many respects that original was.

More than a year elapsed before either of the theatres
obtained a remunerative novelty.   "M. Abeille's
Lyncée," says the *Mercure Galant* on the 28th February,
"appeared three days ago" at the Hôtel de Bourgogne.
"It was extraordinarily applauded. The lines are
beautiful, the thoughts brilliant." M. Devisé must
have written this upon hearsay only; the piece was not
well received, and its versification is detestable.   Next
came a tragedy, *Anne de Bretagne*, by a young writer
from Avignon, Louis Ferrier, who had drawn upon

himself the wrath of the Inquisition in that city by declaring in a juvenile poem that

L'amour pour les mortels est le souverain bien,

and who had recently arrived in Paris to act as tutor to the Chevalier de Longueville. It had long been said that French history could not furnish a dramatist with other than commonplace subjects. Ferrier thought to prove the contrary, but his *Anne de Bretagne* was not supported by the skill required to make the innovation acceptable. After a silence of many years, Boursault, erroneously believing that his *forte* lay in tragedy, wrote for the Théâtre de Guénégaud a *Princesse de Clèves*, which fell at the second performance. In *La Troade*, an imitation by Pradon of Seneca's tragedy, that curious fusion of two subjects treated separately by Euripides, the Troupe Royale met with hardly greater success, all that was impressive in the original having been spoilt by inharmonious episodes and tawdry versification. Racine, unmindful of what he owed to himself, administered two distinct kicks to the moribund play, one in a sonnet turning its story into ridicule, after the manner of Madame Deshoulière's lines upon *Phèdre*, and the other in an acrid epigram. I quote the conclusion of the former :

En vain Baron attend le brouhaha,
Point n'oserait en faire lacabale ;
Un chacun bâille, ou s'endort, ou s'en va.

Baron, it should be mentioned, was the Pyrrhus.

Noteworthy events in connexion with the theatres
occurred during the next Easter. Mdlle. Champmêlé
and her husband, as a consequence of some dissensions
with their comrades, passed over to the Comédiens
du Roi, who naturally received them with open arms.
By a contract signed on the 12th April, the company, " in gratitude," awarded them, in addition to a
full share each, an annual allowance of 1000 livres.
The gloom cast over the Hôtel de Bourgogne by this
double secession was intensified by the deaths of
two valued actors—Lafleur and Lathorillièrc. Excellent
tragedy kings, they both appeared to advantage in
comedy, the former as Gascons and *capitans*, the latter
as peasants. It is said that Lathorillière's end was
hastened by the chagrin he experienced on learning
that one of his daughters had clandestinely married
an obscure young provincial actor, Florent Carton
Dancourt. In no wise ashamed of the profession, he
had yet hoped, perhaps, that his sons-in-law would
be of a social rank at least equal to that which he
had abandoned on becoming a member of Molière's
company. In regard to the Théâtre du Guénégaud,
the players there, in solemn conclave assembled,
dismissed Mdlle. Auzillon for inefficiency, but agreed
to give her a pension of 750 livres. The unfortunate
actress instantly went to law against them, though
for what precise object it is not easy to say. Hubert

and Lagrange were interrogated on the subject before the Commissaire de la Maire, and the dispute was finally terminated by Parliamentary decree to the effect that the pension should be increased to 1000 livres.

The Troupe Royale, as may be supposed, lost no time in endeavouring to recover its former strength. Mdlle. Françoise Cordon, known at the theatre as Mdlle. Bélonde, was brought forward to fill the place of the great Champmêlé. A native of Paris, she had played for some time in the far south, and M. le Maréchal Duc de Vivonne was so impressed by her acting at Marseilles in *Ariane* that he spoke of her at the Hôtel de Bourgogne. Her success admitted of no doubt. Corneille hailed her as a worthy representative of his Pauline. Devisé says that few actresses had ended their careers amidst such applause as she drew down at the outset. Nevertheless, she failed to take a high position, as only two or three characters were within her grasp. For comedy, on the other hand, the troupe secured a player of unequalled versatility and humour in Jean Baptiste Raisin, younger son of the inventor of the wonderful spinet. His parents dead, he reconstituted the Troupe du Dauphin, which now enjoyed a national reputation. This reputation was probably due in a large measure to his own talents. He shone in every department of comedy. He transformed himself with wonderful completeness into the tender and libertine coxcomb, the crabbed old man, the sprightly and audacious valet, the impetuous Gascon, the romantic lover, or the loutish peasant. He was " a veritable Proteus, not only in each character he played, but in each scene of the character." His fine humour, his ease of movement, his elaborate though concealed art, the workings of his mobile face and bright dark eyes,—all this could make the spectators forget that he was not above the middle height. Inimitable as a story-teller, he soon found his society in wide request, and much of his time appears to have been wasted in boon conviviality. He was accompanied to the Hôtel de Bourgogne by his wife, *née* Pitel, an expressive young actress, who had recently played before the Court of Charles II. under the eye of her father, and by a brother-in-law, Jean Devilliers, excellent in all " parts de travestissement." Another new face in the troupe is that of the " young King," Jean de Latuillerie, son of the late M. Lafleur,—a strikingly handsome youth the best horseman and tennis player of his day, and as much petted by Court ladies as his contemporary Kynaston was in London.

Mdlle. Champmêlé brought good fortune with her to the Théâtre du Guénégaud. I am not able to state with certainty that she appeared in a *Germanicus* by Boursault, but as the piece met with a " considerable success," though it was only the unattractive *Princesse de Clèves* of the previous year in a different dress, we may reasonably assume that she did. The production of this "novelty" gave rise to a most unfortunate incident. In the course of a meeting at the Academy, we are told, "Corneille spoke highly of M. Boursault's *Germanicus*, even to the extent of saying that it wanted only the name of M. Racine," in whose hearing he spoke, "to be deemed a great work." Boursault dwells upon this utterance with amusing complacency. To him, he said, it was "extremely gratifying" to find a man so famous as M. Corneille "pronouncing *Germanicus* to be worthy of so great a name as that of M. Racine." He had but little cause to shake hands with himself so vigorously. Corneille had simply indulged in a little pleasantry at the expense of his illustrious rival, as *Germanicus* is at best an indifferent work. Racine, mistaking Corneille's intention in the remark, made some bitter and sarcastic retort ; high words between the authors of the *Cid* and *Phèdre* followed, and the coolness which had subsisted between them since the preface to *Britannicus* appeared was so far increased that they did not speak to each other again. Racine would have been well-advised if he had laughed off what was clearly nothing more than a little raillery, but his *amour propre* was too deep and sensitive to be under the control of his better judgment.

Mdlle. Molière—or, as we must henceforward call her, Mdlle. Guérin d'Etriché, as she had lately espoused the player of that name, who soon brought her under submission to his powerful will—now produced as well-timed a *pièce de circonstance* as has ever been devised. Imported from Italy, the practice of slow-poisoning, notwithstanding the terrible punishment meted out to the Marquise de Brinvilliers in the Place de Grève three years previously, had become a mania among all classes and conditions of persons. Hatred and avarice alike resorted to it. Husbands murdered their wives, wives their husbands, children their parents, hosts their guests. It was with a shudder that the priest left the confessional; every prison in the country was crowded with persons accused of this particular crime; the stake blazed for scores of victims. " I begin to fear," writes Madame de Sévigné, " that French-man and poisoner will become synonymous terms." Early in the present year, alive to the enormity of the evil, the King established the Chambre Ardente, endowing it with extraordinary powers for the detection and punishment of offenders. This court succeeded in hunting down two old women named Lavoisin and Lavigoreux, who for some years had pursued the trade of poison-sellers under cover of telling fortunes. In a list of the customers of the former was the name of Racine's enemy, the redoubtable Duchesse de Bouillon.

Brought before the Chambre Ardente, she satisfactorily
proved that her only object in going to Lavoisin's house
was to get a glimpse of futurity, and especially of the
Devil. " And have you ever been gratified by a sight
of his Satanic majesty ? " asked the President of the
Court, a little ill-favoured old man. " I see him now,"
the lady replied, fixing her eyes upon the questioner ;
" he is in the form of an ugly fellow in the robes of a
Councillor of State." M. le Président did not think
it necessary to pursue the inquiry any further.   Lavoisin
and Lavigoreux, after a long examination, were burnt
alive in the Place de Grève, their hands having previously
been pierced with a red-hot iron and cut off.   During
their trial, as may be supposed, Paris found nothing
else to speak of ; and Mdlle. Guérin, with unimpeachable
sagacity, resolved to have a piece in which Lavoisin
should be a prominent personage.   Devisé received
the commission, but after dashing off a score or more of
disconnected scenes he sought the aid of Thomas Corneille.   The result of this collaboration was a comedy
in five acts, *La Devineresse.*   Brought out in November,
with Hubert as Lavoisin, here named Madame Jobin, it
ran for forty-seven evenings, the clear profits amounting
to nearly 47,000 livres.

At this time the players of the Hôtel de Bourgogne
experienced a long succession of disasters. *Statira*, a
tragedy by Pradon, hardly survived its first represent-

ation.   Ferrier, losing faith in the dramatic value of
French history, concocted an *Adraste,* which failed so
dismally that he resolved to "quit the loathed stage."
In *Genséric,* a partly historical play, Madame Deshoulières, described by Boileau as

> une précieuse,
> Reste de ces esprits jadis si renommés
> Que d'un coup de son art Molière a diffamés,

was equally unfortunate.   Her talents were restricted
to the lighter walks of poetry, and as the piece appeared
without the writer's name it was deprived of any
adventitious interest that might have been conferred
upon it by her rare personal beauty, the romantic story
of her youth, her devotion to her husband at a time
when such devotion was held in more ridicule than
respect, and the fame she had deservedly won by her
pastorals and odes.   The Duc de Nevers having been
popularly accused of writing *Genséric,* she at once took
the burden of its ill-success upon her own shoulders—a
course which more than one dramatist in like case had
not had the courage to adopt.   It is sorry work to
"make war upon women" in any circumstances ; but
Racine, not forgetting her share in the attempt to
disparage his *Phèdre,* sealed her discomfiture in a sonnet
concluding with these lines :—

> Auteur de qualité,
> Vous vous cachez en donnant cet ouvrage.
> C'est fort bien fait de se cacher ainsi ;
> Mais pour agir en personne bien sage
> Il nous fallait cacher la pièce aussi.

The Comédiens du Roi continued to prosper. The Abbé Boyer introduced to them a young advocate from Toulouse, M. Pader Assézan, the son of a painter much esteemed in the south. Having favourably distinguished himself at the Jeux Floraux, even to the extent of becoming a master thereof, the stranger had ventured to make an essay in tragedy, *Agamemnon*, and had come to Paris in the hope that before he returned it would be represented by the most renowned players in the kingdom. The Abbé did not omit to add that he had materially improved the versification. In the result, *Agamemnon* was produced on the 12th March, and when Assézan reappeared in Toulouse it was with the satisfaction of knowing that he had not written in vain. Not long afterwards, evidently satisfied that his young friend would never be seen in Paris again, the Abbé had the effrontery to claim the piece as his own. And now comes another untried author, Jean de Lachapelle, a gentleman of Bourges. Of good birth, he was acting as secrétaire des commandements to the Prince de Conti, and had just bought the post of Receveur Général des Finances at la Rochelle. His sympathies, however, were really with poetry, to which much of his ample leisure was devoted. He was possessed by the idea that he might surpass Racine as a tragic dramatist by imitating him ; but it was in two trifles—*La Bassette* and *Les Carrosses d'Orléans*—that he first presented himself to the public. "The latter piece," he airily writes, "has been written simply to relieve the tedium of a rather long journey, during which I endured all the *ennui* and inconveniences familiar to travellers by the coach."

By this time, to the astonishment and dismay of the town in general and of the Troupe Royale in particular, Racine had definitively abandoned the profession which he adopted with so much ardour in his youth. Soon after the production of *Phèdre*, thanks to the mediation of Boileau, he effected a reconciliation with the theatre-hating Port Royalists, who, aided by as much remorse for his ingratitude towards them as the coldness of his sympathies would permit him to feel, obtained a complete ascendancy over his mind. The impressions he had received from their teaching came back to him with added force, and we are assured that he would have become a Carthusian friar if his friends, convinced that the rigours of ecclesiastical life would be more than irksome to one of his temperament, had not prevailed upon him to marry. His choice fell upon Catherine de Romanet, a person of birth and a little fortune, described by the *Mercure Galant* as "amiable," but religious to the point of bigotry. It is said that she never knew her husband's plays except by their names—plays which, whatever may be thought of his personal character, were defaced by no unholy or impure thought, could not but strengthen every worthy resolution in their hearers, and had already been accepted by the world as some of the noblest efforts of human genius. In his new-born pietism, with such a woman by his side, the poet naturally began to ask himself whether he had not committed a crime in the eyes of God by working for the theatre. Had not the drama been condemned by most of the luminaries of the Church? More than one circumstance served to confirm him in this self-immolating mood. He felt that he could add nothing to the fame he had won by his last tragedy. Still a prey to morbid vanity, even to the extent of confessing that a page of covetable praise would not console him for a syllable of depreciation, he shrank from the prospect of facing a renewal of the hostility aroused against him by his success, his pride, and his epigrams. Before the appearance of Mdlle. de Romanet on the scene, his mistress, the only actress then capable of impersonating his heroines with good effect, transferred her affections to the Comte de Clermont-Tonnerre, and the ridicule consequently brought upon the discarded lover made him disposed to punish her inconstancy by ceasing to lay such characters as Iphigénie and Phèdre at her feet. Lastly, at the instance of Madame de Montespan, whose good opinion he had been careful to win, he became joint historio-grapher royal with Boileau, and the task that now awaited him was arduous and delicate enough to claim undivided attention. Rumour had long credited him with an intention to write an *Alceste*, but it was now made known that henceforward he would be prevented by religious scruples from treating that or any other subject for the stage. Many of his contemporaries questioned the reality of this conversion, seeing that he continued to be an obsequious courtier, to participate freely in the frivolities of Versailles, and to exercise his caustic wit in verses against even necessitous gleaners in the field where he had reaped so abundant a harvest. "I have been told," Boileau once remarked, "that Racine is my superior as a satirist; he certainly surpasses me in bitterness." On the other hand, this voluntary abandonment of the stage by a man like the author of *Phèdre*—hungry for distinction, proud of success, and still in full possession of his genius—is not to be adequately explained by anything short of fanaticism, though his conduct was often at variance with the spirit and letter of the faith he now held in such profound and self-sacrificing reverence.

CHAPTER IV.

1680—1684.

RACINE's abdication of the throne of dramatic poetry
was nearly coincident with a sweeping change in the
conditions under which the players had previously
appeared before the public—in other words, with the
formation of what is known as the Théâtre Français.
Louis XIV., it must be premised, had a love of unity
for its own sake, regarded State aid as essential to the
interests of literature and art, and was determined that
every means of influencing the opinion of his subjects
should be under the immediate control of the Court.
In the summer of 1680, mindful of the power acquired
by the drama, he suddenly applied these ideas to the
theatre as it existed in Paris. He issued an order to
the effect that the two troupes should form themselves
into one, take up their quarters at the playhouse in
the Rue Mazarine, and be allotted a subvention of
12,000 livres a year (first paid in 1682). No other
actors would be allowed to ply their vocation in the
town or fauxbourgs without his majesty's express permission, but the Italian comedians, who had played

alternately with Mdlle. Molière's company at the Théâtre
Guénégaud since 1673, would migrate to the Hôtel
de Bourgogne.　In the *lettre de cachet* on the subject,
signed at Versailles on the 22nd October by Louis
himself, with Colbert and Scellé as witnesses, we
are told that the object of the union of the two
troupes was to "render the representations of comedies
more complete, and to afford the players the means of
perfecting themselves" in their art.

Louis XIV. himself took the trouble to constitute
the troupe and determine how each member of it should
be remunerated.　The players retained were Baron,
Mdlle. Champmêlé and her husband, Poisson, Mdlle.
Beauval, Dauvilliers, Mdlle. Guérin (Molière), Lagrange,
Mdlle. Bélonde, Hubert, Mdlle. Debrie, Latuillerie,
Mdlle. de Ennebaut, Rosimont, Mdlle. Dupin, Hauteroche, Mdlle. Guiot, Guérin, Ducroisy, Mdlle. Raisin,
Raisin, Mdlle. Ducroisy, Devilliers, Verneuil, Mdlle.
Lagrange, Beauval, and Mdlle. Baron.　The receipts of
the theatre, after all expenses had been paid, were, with
the sum given by the King, to be divided into twenty-
three parts.　The first eighteen of the players named
were to receive each a part, the next six a half-part,
and the last three a quarter of a part.　The unallot-
ted portion was probably set apart for a special
expense.　This regulation seems to have been just
enough except in one case, that of Ducroisy.　The actor

who had been selected by Molière to play Tartuffe, and had acquitted himself of his task to general satisfaction, must have better merited a full share than Latuillerie or Guérin.

Before proceeding to deal with the achievements of the united companies we must bid adieu to four players who, as may be seen from the above list, had either retired or been dismissed—Dupin, Victoire Françoise Poisson, and Mdlle. de Lathorillière. The first—to the last a poor actor—had a pension of 500 livres, which, joined to some property bequeathed to him by a brother, enabled him to pass the rest of his life in comfort. His wife, Louise Jacob de Mont-fleuri, whom he married when he had spent all his patrimony, and who induced him to go on the stage, remained, as we have said, at the theatre. Victoire Poisson (Madame Dauvilliers) withdrew on account of a painful malady—a cancer in the nose, which sadly disfigured her once pretty face. From this time until 1718, however, she acted as prompter at the theatre, and the sight of her must have awakened many pleasant memories in the minds of old playgoers behind the scenes. She died at Saint-Germain-en-laye in 1733. Her sister Catherine, the wife of Latuillerie, became a widow eight years after leaving the theatre. Even then, although past youth, she was one of the toasts of the town; and a gentleman of the house of Coiflin,

receiving a challenge to a duel, and not being possessed
of sufficient courage to accept it, espoused her in the
hope—which was not disappointed—that her credit
would be sufficient to save him. His adversary must
have relented before he saw the lady or her portrait.

"To-day," runs an entry in the registers of the
Théâtre du Guénégaud for the 25th August, "the
union of the two troupes has been accomplished,
MM. of the Hôtel de Bourgogne representing with us
Phèdre and *Les Carrosses d'Orléans.*" The audience
was unusually large, and as one public favourite
after another appeared on the scene the air was rent
with acclamations. "The one troupe of French comedians," writes Devisé, "plays every day instead of
three or four times a week, and the large crowds it
attracts to the Théâtre de Guénégaud shows how much
it is esteemed. It is about to give some representations of *L'Inconnu,*" by M. Thomas Corneille, "and as
it is composed of a large number of actors there is
reason to believe that this comedy will be played with
admirable effect." Elsewhere Devisé says,—"You will,
no doubt, be surprised to hear that the two troupes
have received the King's orders to roll themselves into
one, and that the Hôtel de Bourgogne is given up
to the Italians. This event can only serve to augment
the numerous assemblies we have seen for so many
years in the Rue Mazarine."

The united companies proved attractive enough in
the masterpieces of the French drama, but all their
talent could not save from condemnation the first
two new tragedies they brought out. The Abbé Abeille
had written a *Soliman,* and now, in order to prove that
his failures had been due to a cabal, had it played as
the work of Latuillerie. The *ruse* did not succeed ;
the pit quickly recognised in the verse the hand of
the real author, and *Soliman,* though favoured by the
players, was soon consigned to the shelf. Next comes
Zaïde, a spiritless imitation of Racine, by Lachapelle,
with an original but not very interesting plot. " The
author of *Phèdre,*" it has been remarked, "formed
a school, as have great painters ; but he was a Raphael
who did not make a Giulio Romano." Even Mdlle.
Champmêlé, with the support of Baron, Dauvilliers,
Beauval, Hubert, Guérin, Devilliers, and Mdlle. Ducroisy, could not make anything of *Zaïde,* which,
however, was soon afterwards played before the King
at Saint-Germain-en-laye.

Yet another disappointment was in store for the
Théâtre Français. Fontenelle, cured of any taste he
may have had for the law by the failure of the first case
placed in his hands, resolved to trouble himself with
nothing but literature ; and a tragedy from his pen,
entitled *Aspar,* was now accepted in the Rue Mazarine.
Devisé, prompted by Thomas Corneille, sounded the

praises of the new poet in no uncertain voice. Inherit-
ing the genius of his uncle, the author of the *Cid* and
Cinna, M. de Fontenelle, the *Mercure* thought, would
at once leave all the younger dramatists behind, if not
become the monarch of the scene. The consequences of
this puff need hardly be stated. Extravagant expectations as to the quality of *Aspar* were aroused, and the
play was so far beneath them as to become an object
of popular derision. Racine, imagining that the letter
in the *Mercure* was an elaborate sneer at himself, swelled
the chorus against the inoffensive author by means of a
bitter epigram. In the house of a veteran actor, we are
here told, a controversy arose as to which dramatist
had first caused an audience to hiss. Boyer was the
" favourite " with some ; others wished to lay a wager
on Pradon. Eventually the host interposed :—

> Boyer apprit au parterre à bâiller ;
> Quant à Pradon, si j'ai bonne mémoire,
> Pommes sur lui volerent largement ;
> Mais quand sifflets prirent commencement,
> C'est (j'y jouais, j'en suis témoin fidèle)
> C'est à l'*Aspar* du Sieur de Fontenelle.

The unenviable distinction thus ascribed to Fontenelle
had been acquired by Pradon, but it suited the ill-
natured purpose of the satirist to allege what he must
have known to be untrue.

Unsuccessful as a tragic dramatist, M. de Fontenelle
now essayed his powers in comedy. *La Comète*, a small

piece in prose (January 29), was from his pen, although produced under the name of Devisé.   The plot, it need hardly be said, had reference to the comet of the previous year, which, by the swiftness of its progress and the enormous train of light it threw off, had created a feeling little short of awe and terror.   An astrologer, believing that the celestial wanderer exercises a malign influence, postpones the marriage of his daughter until it has disappeared, but while he is observing it from a neighbouring house with the Comtesse de Soustignan, who is as mad as a March hare about it, the lovers elope.   *La Comète* was not very diverting except in one scene, and then only by reason of the fact that in an explanation of Descartes' system the author betrayed the most curious ignorance thereof.   Fontenelle was so mortified by his second failure that he never wrote another play, probably on the ground that either success or failure had a perniciously exciting effect upon a dramatic author.   The world, however, had reason to congratulate itself that *La Comète* was written.   Piqued at the jeers with which the " Cartesian scene " had been received, he devoted himself to the study of exact sciences, and his pleasant *Entretiens sur la Pluralité des Mondes*, published a few years afterwards, was the result.

   La Comète gave place to a five-act comedy by Thomas Corneille and Devisé, *La Pierre Philosophale*, mixed with spectacle and dances. This, in its turn, was followed by a number of poor pieces, one of which, *Hercule*, was written by the Abbé Abeille under the name of Latuillerie. The company, jealous of some honour which the latter acquired as the author, thought fit to reveal the deception, but could not induce him to lay aside his borrowed feathers. He promptly printed the play, remarking in the preface that "the Abbé was possibly as dismayed to find that his works were ascribed to M. de Latuillerie as M. de Latuillerie was proud to find that they were good enough to be ascribed to his learned friend." Such a success as the Abbé pined for in vain was won by Lachapelle in his *Cléopatre* (January 1682). Baron and Mdlle. Champmêlé, as Antoine and the Egyptian Queen, turned to excellent account some fine scenes prepared for them, and a moving description of the battle of Actium deservedly became the talk of the town. The triumphant poet, I must add, had no doubt that this play would carry his name down to the latest posterity, as a letter he addressed to the Prince de Conti at this time would show.

The next new tragedy, *Zélonide Princesse de Sparte* (February 4), served to introduce another Abbé of dramatic tastes to the audience. This was Charles Claude Genest, a young poet of the age of forty-seven. His origin and early life are wrapped in obscurity, but I find that by reason of his gaiety and wit he had won the regard of the Duchesse d'Orléans, who made him her almoner and Abbé de Saint Vilmer. He devoted himself with singular ardour to his duties, dividing his leisure between pleasure and literary pursuits. His *Principes de la Philosophie de Descartes* is in many respects a clever work. It has been suggested that if he had addressed himself exclusively to the drama he would have risen to a proud eminence. I see no reason to entertain any such opinion. He could not devise an interesting plot, create characters, nor write dramatic verse. By a not uncommon freak of fashion, however, most of his plays, as we shall see, had what in their day were regarded as long runs. *Zélonide*, perhaps the poorest of all, was performed seventeen times.

In *Le Parisien*, a five-act comedy by Champmêlé, Mdlle. Molière achieved one of her most remarkable triumphs. The author, in order to oblige her, had added to the *dramatis personae* an Italian girl who sings in her native tongue, and the part was acted by Armande with equal spirit and ease. The fact that three-fourths of the audience did not understand a word she said seemed to augment their delight. But for her, I think, the piece would have failed, as it is made up only of some stale devices employed by a valet to hoodwink his master's father.

Mdlle. Molière was also seen in a revival of Pierre Corneille's *Andromède*, the *pièce de résistance* of the summer. Pegasus was on this occasion represented by a real horse, the first ever brought on the Paris stage. Right well did the animal play its part in the piece. It impatiently pawed the ground, snorted, reared itself on its hind legs, and generally manifested a "noble ardour." This may well be believed, for the poor brute had been brought to the verge of starvation, and when it appeared on the stage a man stationed himself at the side thereof with a basket of oats to irritate it. *Le Bourgeois Gentilhomme*, with more songs and ballets than usual, was revived on the 8th August to celebrate the birth of the Duc de Bourgogne, admission being free. The *Mercure Galant* informs us that the audience—a very large one —testified their delight by holding a sort of "concert" among themselves at the beginning and the end of the play, and that their choruses of "Vive le Roi!" each lasted nearly a quarter of an hour. Nevertheless, "all passed off very quietly."

The players, as has been seen, had pandered a little during the summer to the lower tastes of the audience, but as the year drew to a close they returned to their usual track by producing the Abbé Boyer's *Artaxerxe*. Not that this tragedy was in any sense worthy of the pains they bestowed upon it. It was

inherently feeble, and, to the intense mortification
of the author, was quickly laid aside. It possessed,
however, one good quality—it relied for success upon
purely legitimate means. The same remark applies
to a five-act comedy in verse, *La Rapinière, ou
l'Intéressé* (December 4). The author was Jacques
Robbé, the most enthusiastic of living geographers.
The piece had eighteen representations, the audience
on one occasion being so dense that a man who had
drawn his sword upon a thief in the parterre could
not lower his arm after doing so, and until the act
closed he was to be seen in a mirth-moving position.
Believing that his success was due rather to accident
than merit, Robbé did not again send a piece to
the theatre—a sign of uncommon prudence and self-
command. In this he presented a direct contrast to
Lachapelle, who, inflamed by the applause bestowed
upon his *Cléopatre*, now brought out a *Téléphonte*
(December 26). The story of Merope is here turned
to good account, but the heroine is not so much
Merope herself as the mistress of her persecuted son.

If, as was not improbably the case, Lachapelle
imagined that he had now gained the first place amongst
practising French dramatists, the illusion was abruptly
dispelled. Not the least conspicuous of the wits who
resorted to Raisin's house was Jean Galbert Campistron,
a young man fresh from Toulouse, where his family

—one entitled to call itself "noble"—had been established since the middle of the previous century.   From
his boyhood he had aspired to distinction as a poet,
and his father, a Procureur Général des Eaux et
Forêts, had sent him to Paris in the hope that a little
intercourse with the world would serve to get such idle
notions out of his head.   This step, it need hardly be
said, had the reverse of the effect intended.   Jean
Galbert became an inveterate playgoer, arrived at
the conclusion that the drama was at once the best
and the pleasantest form of poetical expression, and
at last, aided by the counsels of Racine, whose acquaintance he fortunately chanced to make, wrote a *Virginie*.
It is said that while at work upon it he was dangerously
wounded in a duel.   Jean Raisin, another of his
friends, took the tragedy to the theatre in the Rue
Mazarine, where it was played for the first time on
the 13th February 1683.   "I was so young (only
twenty-six) when I composed *Virginie*," he remarked
some years afterwards, "that I am always astonished
I should have had the temerity to begin and the power
and happiness to finish it.   Its success, though indifferent, did not allow me to despair."   Here, as in other
instances, the poet scarcely did himself justice.   *Virginie*
did not disappear from the bills until the 4th March,
although the Duchesse de Bouillon, learning that the
author was befriended by Racine, loudly deprecated

it to the advantage of *Téléphonte*. Nor was the
piece undeserving of the little run it enjoyed. The
impressive Roman story is rather artistically told ;
and if the versification is over long the defect is to
a large extent redeemed by interesting situations and
well-drawn characters. In appearance, I may add,
Campistron hardly fulfilled the popular idea of a poet :
his figure was thickset, his face flat and round, his nose
remarkably broad. It is said that he had an invincible
repugnance to letter-writing, and, probably in order to
save himself from unnecessary trouble on this head, made
his handwriting almost undecipherable. From what I
have read of his character he seems to have been one
of the best disposed of men. Mindful, for example, of
his obligations to Raisin, in whose house he now lived,
he resolved that all the heroines in his plays should
be played by that actor's wife, and even the advantage
of having some of them in the hands of Mdlle. Champmêlé
could not induce him to alter his mind on that point.

Devisé, chancing to pass through the Rue Mazarine
one morning in the spring of this year, was amazed to
find that the company intended to play a piece called
Le Mercure Galant, ou la Comédie sans Titre. Evidently
fearing that it was a more or less stinging satire upon
himself, he immediately posted to Versailles and lodged
a protest against the proposed performance. It was
scandalous, he urged, that a print like the *Mercure*

should be exposed to unmerited ridicule. The Court
authorities referred the matter to the Lieutenant-General
of Police, who, after sending to the players for and
looking over the MS., declared that the piece was too
good to be suppressed, but that, out of deference to M.
Devisé, the first title should be discarded.   The fears
of the accomplished editor proved all but groundless.
He figured, it is true, as one of the characters, but not
in an unflattering light.   The author, while indulging
in a little sly and genial humour at his expense, represented him as a disinterested and otherwise excellent
man.   Indeed, one might believe that as the object of
the comedy was unfolded Devisé listened with considerable satisfaction.   For that object was to hold up to
derision a number of well-born poetasters whose effusions
were printed in the *Mercure* to the exclusion of really
meritorious things.   During the absence of the editor his
place is taken by the hero, and the scribblers in question,
caricatured under other names, come in one by one.
Devisé was too good a judge of literary excellence to
approve all he printed, but the fear of giving offence
in high quarters frequently induced him to favour the
sorriest trash, and the *Comédie Sans Titre*, by putting
his persecutors to confusion, was one which he may
have wished but did not dare to write.   Perhaps—
startling thought—he was all along in collusion with
the author, the request for the suppression of the piece

being made for no other purpose than to throw dust in
the eyes of the world. However that may be, it is
nearly certain that he had no hand in writing the
comedy, which, although attributed at the time to
Raimond Poisson, was written by Boursault in his
most distinctive style.

The favour with which Corneille's *Andromède* had just
been received now induced the players to revive his
Toison d'Or. The original prologue having reference
to the King's marriage, they asked Lachapelle to
furnish them with one more suitable to the year of
grace 1683, and, on his doing so, instructed an actor
to present him at his residence with fifteen louis d'or
in return for his trouble. It seems to me that they
should have endeavoured to induce Corneille to undertake the task. On the 30th July, just after Lachapelle's prologue had been spoken for the tenth time,
a mounted messenger arrived with news of the Queen's
death. The performance was accordingly stopped,
the money taken at the doors returned, and the
theatre closed until further orders. The period of
public mourning over, the company deputed Dauvilliers
and Lagrange to wait upon the royal widower at
Fontainebleau to learn his pleasure in reference to
them, and in the result the theatre was re-opened on
the 22nd August with *Rodogune* and the *Comtesse
d'Escarbagnas*. Not long afterwards, at midnight, in

one of his cabinets at Versailles, the King was married
to the widow of Scarron, who some years previously
had become governess to the children of Madame de
Montespan, and, under the title of the Marquise de
Maintenon, had won at least the esteem of the King
without making any sacrifices inconsistent with her
self-respect. The event was kept a profound secret,
but was generally assumed to have taken place. The
influence which Madame de Maintenon exercised over
her royal husband was generally for good. The
beautiful and lively Françoise d'Aubigne of times gone
by had become austerely devout, and under her sway
the Court all but relieved itself from the taint of
licentiousness. Her unworldliness, however, seems in
one or two instances to have carried her a little too
far. From the hour of her ascendancy, for instance,
the drama was not so largely honoured at Court as
it had been.

Boursault now made another essay in tragedy,
courageously selecting the story of ill-starred Mary
Queen of Scots for his theme. The piece did not
succeed, but at the same time the author had reason to
congratulate himself upon having written it. The Duc
d'Aignan, to whom it was dedicated, presented him with
a hundred louis in five instalments, delivered to him
in due form by a liveried servant. The Abbé Genest's
Pénélope (22 January 1684), though unfavourably

received, is full of beauties of detail—-a fact of which
we should not be aware if a copy of it had not been
printed in Holland as by Lafontaine. The verdict at
first pronounced upon it was eventually reversed, and
the author, who had intended to suppress it, then
laid it at the feet of the Duchesse d'Orléans. The
players next produced Campistron's second tragedy,
Arminius (February 19), the author at the same time
astutely printing it with a dedicatory epistle to the
dreaded Duchesse de Bouillon. In arrangement and
writing the piece is excellent, but the characters,
are far from clearly drawn. Flattered by the homage
rendered to her by the author, the Duchesse de
Bouillon abruptly became one of the most fervent
admirers of his stage work,—and *Arminius* proved
more successful than its merits deserved. In *Ragotin*,
the next novelty, the great Lafontaine dramatized a
considerable portion of the perennial *Roman Comique*,
while Hauteroche, in *Le Cocher Supposé*, turned to good
account a little comedy by Antonio de Mendoca.
During the run of this latter piece some dissension arose
behind the scenes, owing to a refusal on the part of the
majority of the company to allot the principal character
in *La Femme Juge et Partie* to Mdlle. Raisin, who
thought herself entitled to it. Campistron, in order to
console her, wrote his comedy *L'Amante Amant,* in which,
as in Montfleuri's piece, the heroine appears as a gay

cavalier. Brightly written, though so indelicate that
the author afterwards disavowed it, and strengthened
by the spirited acting of Mdlle. Raisin, now, of course,
on her mettle, *L'Amante Amant* took the fancy of the
town. Mdlle. Guiot, hitherto regarded as a mediocre
player, also did good service here. Brécourt's *Timon*
(August 13) is an undramatic dramatization of Lucien's
dialogue, but was represented seventeen times.

More changes in the company have to be chronicled.
Not long previously Hauteroche had retired from the
stage. His example was now followed by Verneuil, an
adequate representative of utility parts. The period of
his retirement was marked by several débuts. Jacques
Raisin, the elder of the organist's two sons, was received
for second and third tragic parts, in which he displayed
more judgment than talent. Extremely tall and thin,
solemn in manner, and of secluded habits, he presented
a direct contrast to his brother, to whose influence he
was doubtless indebted for his advancement. The only
diversion he permitted himself was the composition of
music for pieces requiring it. Pierre Lenoir de Lathorillière, Molière's last pupil, was also received for
second tragedy parts and lovers in comedy. Hard work
in the provinces had developed in him rare qualities as
an actor, and if his figure was not above the middle
height he redeemed the disadvantage by his fine open
countenance, a fine voice, and lively and agreeable

expression. The original Louison in *Le Malade Imaginaire*, Mdlle. Pitel, now Madame Bertrand, became a
confidant; while a Madame Desbrosses, though good
only in *caractères*, was accepted for tragedy.

By this time Michel Baron had more than realized
the rich promise of his youth. He had become the
most prominent member of the company, the Louis
XIV. of the scene. It was not simply that constant
practice and study had enabled this Apollo-like player
to demean himself with ease and dignity, to clearly
indicate a condition of mind by facial expression
alone, and to attune his voice to almost every variety
of passion and sentiment. His power of execution
matured, he was found to have special qualifications
for the profession which Molière had encouraged him to
adopt,—imagination, sensibility, calculating judgment,
originality of thought, and a keen appreciation of what
is striking in language, incident, and character. His
versatility, too, was sufficiently wide to make him
successful in all parts save those which demanded a
flow of rich humour. He could forcibly realize the
dissembled hatred of Mithridate and the chivalric
warmth of the Cid, the magnanimity of Auguste and
the gaiety of Dorante, the stern patriotism of the elder
Horace and the jealousy of Arnolphe, the tenderness of
a lover and the airs of contemporary men of quality.
Numerous as his impersonations were, each is said to

have been individualized with the utmost completeness,
even where a marked distinction of tone was supposed
to be unattainable.   Both Alceste and Arnolphe are
educated Parisians, but their representative made his
audience feel that the first was a gentleman and the
other a citizen.   In such achievements, perhaps, he
was aided by a greater attention to detail than his predecessors had thought necessary.   He gave the least
important lines their full meaning, and would fill up
his intervals of silence by appropriate and eloquent by-
play.   French theatrical history contains many proofs
of the effect he produced by a gesture, a look, or an
inflexion of voice, often in passages previously deemed
unimportant.   For instance, by his delivery of the
words in *Mithridate*—

Vous, le Pont, vous, Colchos, confiés à vos soins—

he vividly portrayed the different feelings with which
the King regards Xipharès and Pharnace.   Nor did the
actor aim at originality for its own sake.   His new
readings were generally acute, suggestive, and in character.   Far from treating the speech of the younger
Horace to Curiace when the latter is chosen to meet the
Roman champions—

Albe vous a nommé ; je vous ne connais plus—

as an ebullition of savage and unrelenting ferocity,
after the manner hitherto favoured, he relieved the

stern determination of the patriot with a touch of the
sadness which the termination of a life-long friendship
might be expected to induce.   In Pyrrhus, on saying
to Andromaque,

Madame, en l'embrassant, songez à le sauver,

he substituted a pathetic expression of interest and
pity for the menacing air here assumed by Floridor;
" by the impressive movement with which he accompanied the words *en l'embrassant,*" we are told, " he
seemed even to take Astyanax by the hands and present
him to his mother."   Next to its deep poetry, indeed,
the most conspicuous feature of his acting was what
Molière had implanted in his mind—a high regard
for natural truth.   He declaimed with as much simplicity as the character of French tragic verse would
allow; his deportment was easy, unlaboured, and unaffected.   For the narrow etiquette observed by other
players he had nothing but contempt.   " My comrades,"
he once said, " contend that even in bursts of passion
I ought not to let my arms go above my head.   But
if passion would take them there I shall let them go.
Passion knows more about it than the rules."   In the
same spirit he would turn his back to the audience—
certainly a daring innovation — and lay his hand
familiarly upon the shoulder of the personage with
whom he was supposed to be conversing.   In brief,

he sought to give his acting the appearance of spontaneity instead of studied elaboration, and to this end
would prepare himself for any violent scene by working
himself into a fever of excitement behind the scenes.
It was said of him by a contemporary,

> Du vrai, du pathétique il a fixé le ton :
> De son art enchanteur l'illusion divine
> Prétait un nouveau lustre aux beautés de Racine,
>   Un voile aux défauts de Pradon.

Eulogy could hardly go further than this, but there
is sufficient evidence to show that it was fairly deserved.
Baron was one of the few actors who have been fitted
in both mind and body for the highest walk of their
calling, and it may be doubted whether any of them
have surpassed him in the power of moving the sympathies of an audience.

It is not only by his achievements on the stage that
Baron merits notice. Idolized by the public, caressed
by society, and studied by most of his fellow-men,
clergymen not excepted, as a model of bearing and
elocution, he conceived a somewhat extravagant idea
of the importance of his art, and a still more extravagant idea of his own talents. His self-assertion was
loud and persistent enough to pass into a proverb.
" Every player worthy of the name," he seriously said,
" ought to be born in a palace and nursed in the lap
of a queen. In both ancient and modern times, I find,

nature has produced many great men of all sorts save
one.   Since the dawn of history the world has seen
only two great actors—Roscius and myself.   Every
century has its Cæsar ; two thousand years are required
to produce a Baron."   Egregious as his vanity was,
however, it did not hinder him from adopting a good
suggestion.   In Mithridate, before replying to the
excuses of the two princes, it was long his custom to
assume an air of deep reflection.   One of his comrades
held this reflectiveness to be misplaced.   "Mithridates," said the critic, "ought to reply to his sons on
appearing with them, for such a man as he was would
perceive the true aspect of the most important affairs
in a moment."   Baron, struck by the force of the
argument, promptly made the needed change in his
performance—a proof that the artist was stronger than
the man.   But even as a man he put forth irresistible
claims to our respect.   He had the spirit to practically
resent any insolence to which a member of the company might be subjected behind the scenes by the coxcombs assembled there ; he was also open-handed to a
fault.   In the *salons*, continuing the work begun by
others, he did much to soften the stigma which the
Church cast upon the histrionic profession ; his manners
were indicative of good breeding, and the education
given him by Molière, of whom he spoke with filial
tenderness and reverence, had more than atoned for

the neglect he suffered in his orphan boyhood. He found personal friends in men by no means disposed to make their friendship cheap.

It was just as Baron reached the zenith of his power that the venerable figure of Corneille disappeared from the theatre of life. In the records of the poet's closing days we have a striking instance of the contrast occasionally presented between the public position and private circumstances of the man of genius. His fame, thanks in some measure to the controversy provoked by the appearance of Racine, now stood at a higher point than it had previously reached. By all classes of his fellow-countrymen, from the King down to the workman, it was felt that he more than merited the epithet of "le grand." He could not stir out of his dingy abode in the Rue d'Argenteuil without receiving marks of respect from persons with whom he had never exchanged a word, but who numbered the *Cid* and *Polyeucte* among the dearest treasures of their memories. One evening, having unexpectedly appeared in a box at the theatre after a long absence, he became the object of a remarkable demonstration ; the players interrupted the performance to pay him homage, and the whole of the audience, which included Condé and other illustrious personages, rose at and warmly cheered him. Yet the recipient of these almost royal honours was just then in extreme destitution. His pension from the Court, at no time regularly paid, had been temporarily stopped, and only the precarious earnings of his brother as a play-writer and journalist stood between him and absolute starvation. "Yesterday," writes a citizen of Rouen from Paris, "I saw our old friend Corneille. Considering his age," seventy-eight, "I think he is pretty well. He asked me to remember him to you. In the afternoon we went out, and in the Rue de la Parcheminerie he entered a cobbler's shop to have a few stitches put into his boot. He sat down meanwhile on a plank; I sat beside him. The boot mended, he gave the cobbler all he had—three pieces of money. On our return I offered him my purse, but he would neither accept it nor any portion of it. I was truly grieved to see such a man reduced to such misery." The pride shown in the rejection of the proffered money probably led the old poet to disguise that misery as much as he could. Presently, however, the truth came to the knowledge of Boileau, who at once brought it to the notice of the King. "Sire," he said, possibly with a vein of sarcasm traversing the elaborate deference of his manner, "a little bread for the great Corneille! Let him have my pension; I should be ashamed to receive it if he were in want." His majesty, of course, did not adopt this generous suggestion. He sent Corneille two hundred louis, at the same time resolving that the suspended pension should not be withheld in future. The *largesse* came too late. Forty-eight hours after it was received, on the night of the 30th September, the author of the *Cid*, enfeebled in both mind and body by age and privation, passed away in the presence of all the surviving members of his family, by whom his remains were laid to rest in the church—then unfinished—of St. Roch.

The finest of the tributes laid upon the grave of the illustrious dramatist came from a quarter whence it could have been least expected. He was succeeded at the Academy by his brother; and Racine, anxious to soften the reproach he had brought upon himself by his unprovoked insolence towards the living, appeared at the reception of the new member to do honour to the dead. "In what state," he said in the course of his address, which had previously been read and approved by the King, "was the French stage when Corneille began to work? It was without order, regularity, taste, morals, characters, or a perception of true dramatic beauty. Most of its subjects were extravagant enough to be destitute of all probability; its language depended for effect chiefly upon miserable quibbling. Every rule of art, every rule of self-respect and decency, was constantly violated. In this infancy, or rather chaos, of dramatic poetry in France, Corneille, after endeavouring for some time to strike into a higher path, was impelled

by an exceptional genius to bring reason upon the scene,
—reason accompanied by all the majesty and embellish-
ments of which our language is susceptible,—and
combined the semblance of truth with the marvellous.
He went far ahead of his rivals, the majority of whom,
no longer daring to struggle with him for the prize,
vainly tried to depreciate the merit they were unable to
equal. Indeed, where can we find a poet uniting in
himself so many rare gifts as art, force, judgment, and
imagination? How noble his subjects; how energetic
his pictures of passion; how grave his sentiments;
how dignified and varied his characters! His heroes are
always what they ought to be, always uniform with
themselves, always differing from one another. Magnificent in expression, he could yet descend at will to
the most simple *naïvetés* of comedy, where he was
likewise inimitable. Lastly—and this was his most
distinctive characteristic—he had a certain power and
elevation which lifted us out of ourselves, even to the
extent of blinding us to his faults, if faults he can be
said to have had. He was born for the glory of his
country; his masterpieces will ever be on the lips
of men. He is to be compared, I do not say with
the tragic poetry of ancient Rome, since Rome was
confessedly not very fortunate in this branch of letters,
but with Æschylus, Sophocles, and Euripides, who were
no less honoured by the Athenians than Themistocles,

Pericles, and Alcibiades." In some respects, it must be pointed out, the orator went a little too far in his praise. He unduly depreciated the antiquities of the French stage ; and it would be as unreasonable to say that Corneille was a master of the French language as to hold that he was great in the painting of anything but exalted heroism. With these exceptions, however, we must subscribe on all points to the glowing eulogy just quoted,—an eulogy which might well have been inscribed in letters of gold upon the simple slab placed over his remains. In a rather narrow circle of art he had risen to a high level ; his best things, as Saintsbury has remarked, are second to none.

CHAPTER V.

1684—1689.

MINDFUL of the influence acquired by Baron in and out of the theatre, the dramatists of the day, with hardly one exception, employed their gifts to promote his interests—and with them, of course, their own. Especially successful in this way were Lachapelle and Campistron. "In all his pieces," the *Mercure* says, "the former has devised brilliant scenes for M. Baron, who finds in them a means of increasing his already high reputation." Devisé is here speaking of an *Ajax*, which appeared on December 27. The author, with a curious mixture of pride and modesty, declared the "great soul" of Condé had been touched by the image of the hero in "these hurried lines;" but as the tragedy was not printed—certainly a significant circumstance—we are justified in supposing that any effect it created was due almost wholly to the genius of the actor. His performance of such a character must have gratified the eye and the ear, even if what he had to say did not very profoundly agitate the heart or the head. In regard to Campistron, we find him producing an

Andronic (February 8).   Devisé tells us that it succeeded at Court as well as in Paris, drawing tears from the most unsympathetic of auditors.   Delighted with the piece, the young Dauphiness requested the Duc de Villeroi to present the author to her, and from that moment displayed a warm interest in his welfare.   In the face of such facts, perhaps, the old procureur at Toulouse ceased to maintain that his son had taken a deplorable course in life.   The plot of *Andronic* was originally suggested by the conspiracy of Don Carlos, as related by the Abbé de Saint Réal in his *Histoire Espagnole.*   The King, however, objected to this subject being treated, and Campistron was obliged to seek elsewhere for an event similar to that which he had treated.   " In the annals of Constantinople," he writes, " I fortunately found what I wished.   The characters of Calo-Jean, Andronic, and Irène find counterparts in the work of M. de Saint Réal ; and the circumstances," apart from the manner in which Calo-Jean's son is put to death, " are precisely the same."   History, indeed, had repeated itself in this instance with remarkable precision ; and the playgoers were not deprived of a tragedy which, as the representative of the hero made them feel, had considerable interest and pathos.

Dissatisfied with the characters devised for him by contemporary dramatists, and not content, perhaps, with the laurels he had won as an actor, Baron himself began

to write. His first essay was a prose comedy in three
acts, *Le Rendezvous des Tuileries, ou Le Coquet Trompé*
(March 3). If, contrary to his expectations, the world
declined to accept him as a Molière in embryo, or even
as a writer of more than ordinary talents, his new
ambition was not inexcusable. High intelligence and
long experience of the stage had made him acquainted
with the chief principles of dramatic effect, and his
intercourse with the lively society of his day furnished
him with hints by which he knew how to profit. The
Rendezvous des Tuileries merely shows a young lady
proving the infidelity of a nominal lover by means of a
pretended appointment—certainly no very novel or
interesting story. On the other hand, the dialogue is
not without animation, and the leading figures, notably
those of a coquette and a pert waiting-maid, have a
degree of freshness hardly to be looked for in the
treatment of well-worn materials. It is worthy of
mention that in his prologue the author gives us a few
satirical sketches of the Comédiens du Roi (not sparing
himself), and of the coxcombs who, ensconced on the
stage, hissed or applauded a play as the shallowest
caprice might dictate.

Another clever actor-dramatist vanished from the
scene. The irascible Brécourt was to share the fate of
Mondori and Montfleuri. In a representation of *Timon*
he exerted himself so violently as to break a blood-

vessel, and at the end of February 1685 his comrades
had to lament his death. His plays were soon forgotten,
but his impersonations of kings and heroes, to say
nothing of his Harpagon and Pourceaugnac, were long
remembered. His versatility, perhaps, was never more
conclusively shown than when, not long before his death,
he played in *Bérénice* and the *Noce du Village* on the
same evening. The audience could hardly believe that
the two characters had been in the hands of one man.
Brécourt to the last retained the esteem of the King, on
account both of his special talents as a comedy actor
(" this man," his majesty used to say, " might make a
stone laugh ") and the admirable coolness and bravery
he had displayed at a critical moment in the foresta t
Fontainebleau twenty-seven years before.

Mdlle. Debrie, whom Molière might have described
as " the best and truest friend he ever had," now went
into private life. Her hold upon the town seems to
have become stronger as she passed into the vale of
years. Not long before her retirement her comrades
induced her to give up Agnès in *L'Ecole des Femmes*
to a much younger actress, Mdlle. Ducroisy. But the
parterre would not consent to the substitution, even for
one night. From the moment the new Agnès appeared
on the stage there was such a tumult that hardly a word
of the piece could be heard. The company promptly
sent for Mdlle. Debrie, who, without doffing her private

dress (there was no time to do so) reassumed her usual
place in the comedy. The applause which greeted her
was loud enough to be heard a long distance. No one
after that disputed her right to the part, although it
seemed strange that a girl of seventeen should be
represented by a woman of sixty-four. It must be
confessed, however, that time had dealt gently—very
gently—with her. Her impersonations in the *grand
tragique* and the *noble comique* may have fallen off
towards the end in power, but not in earnestness,
feeling, or grace. In the evening of her life, which
closed in 1706, her characteristic generosity and self-
denial shone forth in their highest lustre. Her nature
was not soured by the remembrance of the misery
of her early days or the unrealized aspirations of her
maturer womanhood. Much of her modest income
went in works of charity, and the woman to whom
Molière owed the little happiness he experienced was
regretted by others than her fellow-players and the
frequenters of the theatre.

Hubert, another valuable member of Molière's
company, resigned at the same time. "M. Hubert,"
writes Devisé, "has requested permission to retire.
He was the original representative of several parts
created by Molière, and being in possession of the
meaning of this famous author, by whom he had been
educated for the stage, he played them to perfection.

No actor has ever done so much for (*porté si loin*) the characters he possessed. His Bélise in *Les Femmes Savantes,* his Madame Jourdain in *Le Bourgeois Gentil-homme,* his Madame Jobin in *La Devineresse,"* and also, I may add, his Comtesse d'Escarbagnas and Madame Pernelle, " elicited the applause of all Paris. He gained admiration, too, as the Vicomte in *L'Inconnu* as well as in doctors and *marquis ridicules."* Hubert, who died in 1700, was the last male representative of women on the Paris stage. His characters in this walk were transferred to Madame Beauval, in whose hands they lost but little of the effect imparted to them by her predecessor.

Raimond Poisson was the next to retire, although his career had extended over little more than thirty years. It was as an actor rather than an author that he was regretted by the play-going public. His plays exhibit only faint traces of the infectious gaiety which is said to have distinguished his acting. Both on and off the stage he was held in high esteem ; indeed, one of the sons born to him was held at the baptismal font by no less a person than Colbert. This son having attained man's estate, Raimond proceeded to exert his influence with the minister for purely worldly purposes, and after many failures was ushered into his presence at a moment when he was surrounded by friends. " Monseigneur," he said, " I am anxious to read to you a few verses I have written upon you." The great statesman was alarmed; he had no taste for flattery, and Raimond's effusions were notoriously dull. "No, no," he exclaimed; "your incense is too overpowering." "Monseigneur," said the player, "I assure you that if you deign to hear what I have written you will suffer no headache." The company with one voice politely expressed a wish to have the lines, and Colbert reluctantly gave way. Poisson began—

> Ce grand Ministre de la paix,
> Colbert, que la France révére
> Dont le nom ne mourra jamais—

"Poisson," interrupted the minister, "you are not keeping your word; give over." "One moment, Monseigneur," returned the poet—

> Eh bien, tenez, c'est mon compère :
> Fier d'un honneur si peu commun,
> On est surpris si je m'étonne
> Que de deux mille emplois qu'il donne
> Mon fils n'en puisse obtenir un.

Colbert good-humouredly laughed, and forthwith M. Poisson fils was made a Contrôleur Général des Aides. The King, too, would have gone a little out of his way to oblige the creator of Crispin on the stage. In 1676 one of the player's daughters gave her hand and heart to a valet favoured by the King, and the marriage contract was signed in the presence of his majesty and all the royal family. "Poisson," remarked the King on hearing of the player's death, which occurred in 1690, "was certainly a clever actor." "Yes," bluntly replied M. Boileau, overhearing the remark, "as Don Japhet he certainly was ; but he shone only in Scarron's wretched pieces." The King was visibly annoyed, not only because he liked Poisson, but chiefly because the author of the wretched pieces was the first husband of Madame de Maintenon. "Really," said Racine to his maladroit friend, "I cannot appear at Court with you again if you are so imprudent." "No doubt I was wrong," said the satirist ; "but where is the man who has never said a foolish thing ? "

With Raimond Poisson disappeared three actresses— Mdlle. d'Ennebaut, Mdlle. Dupin, and Mdlle. Guiot. The first, Françoise Jacob de Montfleuri, was extremely popular in all kinds of characters. Roxane and Junie found in her a sympathetic and forcible represent- ative ; as a woman in male attire she played with equal spirit and delicacy. Her husband never conquered his passion for the gaming-table, but in spite of this draw- back to her happiness she lived until 1708. Mdlle. Dupin (Louise Jacob de Montfleuri) was by no means so attractive as her sister Françoise, whom she survived a little more than a year. Mdlle. Guiot, whom Guérin had deserted for Mdlle. Molière, did not leave the theatre on abandoning the stage. For the sum of three livres per day she undertook the custody of the money taken at the doors. In this capacity she embezzled many small sums received for and on account of the company, although the usual pension had been allotted to her. In 1691, finding herself on the point of death, and apprehensive for the first time of the consequences hereafter of her breach of trust, she made a will restoring to her comrades a large portion of the misappropriated money, appointing them her executors, and beseeching them to have pity on her dependants, pray for the repose of her soul, and give her a decent but unostentatious burial. Three of her relatives contested the will, which, however, was decisively upheld at law.

These retirements were still the talk of the taverns of Paris when four new players were received. Nicolas Desmares, with his wife, Anne d'Ennebaut, daughter of Françoise Jacob de Montfleuri, had passed some years in a French troupe attached to the Court of Copenhagen, and one of his children was held at the baptismal font by the King and Queen themselves. Now, at the instance of his sister, the great Champmêlé, Louis XIV. invited him to appear at the Comédie Française, where he was received without début—a rare compliment—on the 27th March. His range was limited to peasants, but within it he was above competition. Mdlle. Beauval, too, exerted her influence with similar success, though not to so much advantage to the theatre, on behalf of a nephew named Durieu, the husband of Anne Pitel. In

Florent Carton Dancourt, the next new-comer, we
recognize the youth who a few years previously had run
away with and married Thérèse Lenoir de Lathorillière,
thereby hastening the end of her father. It is difficult
to comprehend the old player's reasons for objecting so
strongly to the match. Dancourt was of good birth,
had been well educated, and was qualifying himself for
a respected profession. Descended on his mother's side
from the Badées, he was born on the 1st November
1661, the same day as le grand Dauphin, and was
brought up by the Jesuits. Père Delarue, his regent,
spared no pains to induce him to join the order, but on
arriving at man's estate he turned his atttention to the
law. It was while studying for this profession that he
wooed and won Lathorillière's daughter. Soon afterwards he appeared on the stage with good success;
the doors of the Comédie Française were thrown
open to him, and he became a Comédien du Roi. So
also did his wife, who in *amoureuses* quickly showed that
she had inherited the histrionic talents of her family.
Monotonous and cold in tragedy, Dancourt was admirable in the *haut comique* and *rôles à manteau*, thanks to
natural gaiety and quickness. His figure was elegant,
his countenance noble, his tone that of a well-bred man
of the world. His elocution, too, was so excellent that
many dramatic authors resolved that from this time
nobody else should read their works to the company.

Père Delarue, in his regret that such a man should be lost to the order, severely reproached him for having gone on the stage. " Ma foi ! " replied the actor, " I cannot see, father, why you should blame me. Is there much difference between a comédien du Pape and a comédien du Roi ? "

The claim of the players to that dignity was strengthened by new regulations issued at this time as to the Comédie. The King, more alive than ever to the power of the drama as a means of influencing public opinion, assigned the care of the two theatres in Paris to the Dauphiness, ostensibly " pour faire plaisir à cette Princesse," but really, as may be supposed, to bring them as much as possible under the domination of the Court. It is not improbable that the form in which *Andronic* was first written suggested the advisability of this measure. Madame la Dauphine, " after making due inquiries," drew up an interesting series of regulations in regard to the Comédie. The troupe was always to consist of a number of players sufficient to adequately play a piece in the Maisons Royales when his majesty wished to be so amused. They would receive their orders from the Premiers Gentilhommes de la Chambre through the medium of the Intendants and Contrôleurs de l'Argenterie et des Menus. The profits of the theatre, as before, would be divided into twenty-three parts. Champmêlé, Baron,

Dauvilliers, Latuillerie, Lagrange, Poisson, Devilliers, and the younger Raisin would each receive one part without charge.   Guérin, Rosimont, and the elder Raisin would have the same on payment, the first two of 571f. and 18f. each, and the last of 1000 livres. Lecomte, Lathorillière, Ducroisy, Beauval, Desmares, and Dancourt received each a half-part, the last-named actor on payment of 285 livres.   This left nine parts to be distributed among the actresses.   Those who received one without charge were Champmêlé, Bélondé, Beauval, Raisin, Guérin (Mdlle. Molière) and Poisson; and half-shares were allotted to Lagrange, Baron, Bertrand, Desbrosses, Dancourt, and Durieu.   If an actor or actress should die, or wish to retire, the First Gentleman of the Chamber should report the same to the Dauphiness, in order that the parts vacated might be re-allotted.   The contract of 1681 should be observed to the letter, any difficulties arising under it being inquired into and reported by the afore-said Intendent and Contrôleur to the First Gentle-man, who would settle the matter as he thought right.   The pensions awarded to retired players were to be paid in full, as was the 500 livres due every year to the Marquis de Sourdéac.   The casts of pieces were to continue as arranged by the authors, but for the good of the service and the convenience of the troupe all the characters should be understudied by those who

in the estimation of the company as a body should be
the most capable of filling them. The characters of
new plays should also be distributed by the authors
and doubled. In order to prevent disputes, no piece
was to be played without the consent of the whole
company, and in order to preserve peace in the theatre
all quarrels in business among the players should
be adjusted by the First Gentleman as he thought
fit. Such, stripped of its verbiage, was the new regulation—one "fait et arrêté par nous, Duc de St.
Aignan, Pair de France, chevalier des ordres du Roi,
et Premier Gentilhomme de la Chambre, suivant l'ordre
que nous en avons reçu de Madame la Dauphine. A
Versailles, 3 April, 1685. Collationné à l'original par
moi, Intendant et Contrôleur Général de l'Argenterie
et affaires de la Chambre du Roi : signé, Dussé."

This decree was certainly made known before Lent
ended ; and the players, delighted by such a proof
of royal countenance and protection, which seemed to
presage a change in the attitude of the Church towards
their profession, probably reopened the theatre in the
Rue Mazarine in the best spirits. The first novelty
they brought out was a three-act comedy by Dancourt,
who, like Baron, aspired to something more than the
May-fly stories of the stage. Nor did this aspiration
prove empty. *Le Notaire Obligeant*, or, as the piece
soon afterwards came to be called, *Les Fonds Perdus*,

diverts us in spite of its plot, which is needlessly
disagreeable. The everlasting valet and soubrette are
here concerned with a father in love with his son's
mistress and a mother desirous of espousing the lover
of her daughter. Incredible as it may seem, the next
new piece, *Le Florentin*, a comedy in one act, was a
bitter attack by the good-natured Lafontaine on Lulli.
The composer, it appears, had employed the fabulist
to write the libretto of an opera, but on its completion,
deeming it hopelessly unsuited to his purpose, declined
to accept or pay for it. Lafontaine besought Madame
de Thiange to use her influence at Court to make
Lulli abide by his agreement.

> Deux mots de votre bouche et belle et bien disante
> Feraient des merveilles pour moi,

he told her. Madame complied with the request, but
a glance at the book convinced the King that Lulli was
not to blame. Irritated at finding that all his labour
had been thrown away, Lafontaine wrote the story and
the comedy of *Le Florentin*, in which Lulli is satirized
with more asperity than effect. The comedy was saved
from failure only by a pleasant scene between the Florentin and his ward, charmingly played by Mdlle. Raisin.
Angélique et Médor, which followed, is a parody of
Lulli and Quinault's opera of *Roland*, at this time the
chief attraction at the rival theatre.

   This brings us to the autumn, when the company,

as though required to prove that it consisted of a
number of players sufficient to divert his majesty in
one of the Maisons Royales, were commanded to give
performances at Fontainebleau.   During their visit
here Dancourt was particularly remarked by the Court,
both as an actor and as a dramatist.   The King com-
plimented him upon his histrionic talents, expressed
a wish to hear at first hand the romantic story of his
abandonment of the law for the stage, and finally
requested him to read his plays in the royal cabinet.
The actor's trepidation, joined to the high temperature
of the room, where a large fire was burning, soon made
him too faint to continue ; and the King, guessing the
cause of his indisposition, considerately led him to and
opened one of the windows.   On another occasion, after
mass, he spoke to the King on " some matters relating
to the Comédie."   Etiquette required him to walk back-
wards, which he did.   The King, suddenly looking up,
saw they were within only a few feet of a staircase.
" Have a care, Dancourt," he exclaimed, starting forward
and catching the actor by the arm, " else you will fall."
It is said that the courtiers present, who had been
deterred by etiquette from apprising Dancourt of his
danger, thought this an act of phenomenal condescen-
sion on the part of the King.   " It must be admitted,"
Louis said with a gracious smile, ·· that you plead
your cause well.   Your request is complied with."

The nature of the request soon became evident. On the 29th October, "at the instance of the company," the Dauphiness added to the regulations of the previous spring a few clauses by virtue of which promotion at the Comédie could be secured only by a money-payment. The actor who succeeded to a whole part should pay 4400 livres to his predecessor, or, if the vacancy had been caused by death, to his predecessor's widow and heirs. The tax upon three-parts of a share would be 3300 livres, and upon a half-share 2200 livres. In case of death, the sum would be paid two months afterwards by the troupe, which would then proceed to reimburse itself. Those who voluntarily left the company, or received orders to withdraw, should enjoy the ordinary pension of 1000 livres to the end of their lives over and above the value of their shares, in consideration of the services they should have rendered and the contributions they should have made to the expenses of the said company. In order that these regulations might be well established, Madame la Dauphine ordered that the players should "have in good form a contract setting them forth, so as to ensure to the whole of the company the benefits they conferred." No doubt this tax pressed rather heavily upon beginners, but it did not make them poorer in the end if they lived long enough to earn a full share and the right to repose.

Unfortunately for the theatre, another decree emanated from Versailles at about the same moment. The players were to lose a considerable section of their regular audience. Louis XIV., at the instance of the Church in France, gradually crowned a long series of regulations against the Protestants by revoking the Edict under which they had enjoyed freedom of worship. Madame de Maintenon might have saved him from so dire a mistake, but a fear lest àny intervention on her part should be ascribed to a lingering sympathy with her former creed induced her to look on in silence. It was ordered that all Huguenot places of worship should be destroyed, that all unconverted ministers found in France fifteen days after the date of the measure should be sent to the galleys, and that the property of those who persisted in the exercise of their religion should be confiscated. Nor was the King content with merely issuing the decree. He sent troops in nearly all directions to enforce it. Nothing was heard in Paris except accounts of children being dragged from their parents and shut up in convents, of girls being ravished by the pitiless soldiery, of refractory Huguenots being stripped of their possessions, sent to the stake or the wheel, or murdered outright. For a time it seemed that these severities would have the desired effect. Multitudes of French Protestants, impelled by either terror or positive torture, agreed to forswear the faith of their forefathers. In the space of twenty-four hours, we are told, one might frequently have seen a strong man brave the rack, consent in his agony to abjure, and then be taken to the altar by the common executioner. The Roman hierarchy went into transports of delight at the large number of conversions thus effected. Bossuet gleefully remarked that the churches of the true faith were too small to hold them. But, after all, only a portion of the Protestant body were gathered to the Romish fold. Nearly half a million of them contrived to escape to other countries, although orders had been received at the seaports and on the frontiers to turn them back. Some entered the service of the hereditary foes of France; some sent forth from the press at the Hague a shoal of pamphlets of a nature to inflame the mind of Protestant Europe against the government of the Grand Monarque; some settled in the East-end of London, gave a new impulse to the commercial prosperity of England, and, by their recitals of the sufferings they had endured, materially added to the forces which hurled James II. from his throne. By revoking the Edict of Nantes, indeed, Louis XIV. at once weakened himself and strengthened his enemies at a moment when he could ill afford to do so. The priesthood had even less to congratulate themselves upon. Religion was extensively confounded with the cruelties perpetrated in her name, and the hostility she had encountered since the burial of Molière assumed a more and more threatening form.

Nearly four months elapsed before success again rewarded the enterprise of the players. *Les Façons du Temps*, a five-act comedy in verse (December 13), did not long remain before the public, its dramatic value being very slight. The author was Saintyon, a descendant of one of the butchers who figured so conspicuously in the civil wars of the fifteenth century. Cultured, shrewd, observant, and witty, he might have made a name at the theatre if he had not given his heart to philosophical inquiry, and if, moreover, a naturally timid disposition had not led him to shrink from rather than court publicity. Practised dramatists were no less unfortunate than the unpractised. Campistron's *Alcibiade* (December 28), which bears a strong resemblance to Duryer's *Thémistocle* in point of plot and characters, was produced only to be withdrawn, notwithstanding a fine impersonation of the hero; and by writing *Le Baron des Fondrières* (January 14), Thomas Corneille, the author of *Timocrate*, came to share with Pradon and Fontenelle the unenviable distinction of having a piece hissed. Baron, however, came to the rescue with *L'Homme à Bonne Fortune* (January 30), one of those comedies which no one interested in stage matters could pass over. The chief character, the Marquis de Moncade, is a gay, witty, and, as the title

of the piece would suggest, a too-successful Lothario ;
and the author, it need hardly be stated, was by no
means displeased to find it accepted as a portrait of
himself. The plot is decidedly interesting, and some
faults of style in the dialogue are redeemed by considerable vivacity. Baron himself, of course, played Moncade,
supported by Mdlle. Raisin, Mdlle. Guérin, Mdlle.
Dancourt, Mdlle. Durieu, Mdlle. Beauval, the brothers
Raisin, Guérin, and Desmares. The part of the little
chevalier, afterwards done away with, was undertaken
by a boy of tender years, Etienne Baron, a son of the
author. The merits of the play being incontestable,
Baron's enemies—and his overweening vanity had raised
up many against him—insisted that he had not written
it at all. One ascribed it to Subligny, the author of
La Folle Querelle, and another to a M. d'Alègre. I do
not think there was any foundation for these imputations. Subligny never claimed a share of the laurels, and
it is permissible to doubt whether " M. d'Alègre " ever
existed. On the other hand, *L'Homme à Bonne Fortune*
is precisely such a comedy as might be written by a
man who, if without the graces of style, had a practical
knowledge of the stage and the best society of his time,
—and such a man was Baron.

Pader d'Assezan, the friend of Boyer, now came to
Paris with an *Antigone*, which appeared on the 14th
March. It received high praise, especially from the

Dauphiness, and seems to have been a work of more than average excellence. The author soon afterwards returned to Toulouse, where he died ten years afterwards. Far greater success than one-act pieces usually met with was gained by *Merlin Dragon* (April 14). The writer was M. Desmares, formerly "officier chez le grand Condé." His Merlin is a valet of a new kind, and will often be imitated by other dramatists. In order to prevent a marriage he disguises himself as a dragoon ; hence the title of the piece. M. Desmares was better known to the company than any playgoer of his time. It was only in the theatre that he seemed to have his being. Four or five times every week he was to be seen in a particular place on the stage—a somewhat ill-favoured person, with long and extremely white hair. He never wore a wig, certainly a proof of rare moral courage. Proud of his success as a dramatist, he would not risk the result of a second piece, and accordingly, although thirty years elapsed before death snatched him from the stage, *Merlin Dragon* is the only piece standing to his credit with posterity. It was followed by *Le Niais de Sologne*, a one-act comedy by Jacques Raisin, and *Renaud et Armide*, a lively parody of the opera which, thanks to music by Lulli, a libretto by Quinault, and the singing of Mdlle. Lerochois, had just caught the public ear.

Paul Poisson, son of Raimond Poisson, had entered

the service of Monsieur the King's brother, but now
abandoned it for the stage.   In the characters made
famous by his father he achieved great success, notwithstanding an inherited tendency to stutter.   He had
scarcely well-established himself at the Comédie when
an equally clever actor was removed from the scene.
Rosimont had fallen a victim to excessive drinking,
and the proprietor of his favourite tavern, who had
received from him about eight hundred livres a year,
lifted up his voice and wept on receiving the news.
It should be added, however, that Rosimont never
allowed his "pleasure" to interfere with his business.
He had always been sober enough at rehearsals and
during performance to get through his work well.
His death was too sudden to allow him time to renounce
his profession, but as he had been a man of letters as
well as an actor, and had at least assisted in compiling
the *Vies des Saints*, his comrades ventured to hope that
some honour would be paid to his remains.   The priesthood, however, were inflexible ; and an actor who had
so often delighted the King in the Maisons Royales
was interred at night without any religious ceremony,
without any prayer save what an old comrade may have
breathed over his remains, in that portion of the burial-
ground of St. Sulpice which had been set apart for the
mortal remains of unbaptized children.

Campistron became more than usually conspicuous

this year. The libertine Duc de Vendôme had invited
the Dauphin to Anet, and was anxious that a new
opera should be played there during the royal visit.
He accordingly enlisted the services of Lulli, and,
finding that Quinault had laid down the pen for ever,
besought Racine to write the libretto. The illustrious
poet excused himself, at the same time suggesting that
the task should be allotted to Campistron. This
suggestion was promptly acted upon; the young
dramatist hastened to confer with Lulli, and the result
of their joint labours was the musical pastoral of *Acis
et Galatée*—the last work, as it proved, of the maestro.
The projected *fête*, which cost M. le [Duc a hundred
thousand livres, a sum he could ill spare, had all
possible success. The graceful château erected by
Diane de Poitiers in place of the old manor-house of
the De Brézes was the scene during a whole week
of an almost incessant round of gaiety. Now a
hunting-party is issuing from the gateway; now the
grounds are alive with fair dames and gallant cavaliers;
now high wassail is held in the banqueting-hall. The
company was decidedly of a mixed character. M. le
Duc and his titled guests were surrounded by men of
letters, musicians, and the singers and dancers brought
from Paris to give due effect to the opera. Distinguished
poets recited unpublished verses at every repast. The
witty Abbé de Chaulieu sang the praises of inconstancy;

Lafare, in reply to the Princesse de Conti, maintained that men of that time loved more and better than those of old. These verses wcre by no means too delicate, but the presence of the Dauphiness and other ladies of high station saved the *fête* from degenerating into an orgie. "As," says Lafare in his *Mémoires,* "M. le Grand Prieur, the Abbé Chaulieu, and myself had each a mistress at the opera, ill-natured people said that we had induced M. de Vendôme to spend 100,000 livres to divert ourselves and our damsels ; but we had higher objects than that." We may admit the latter statement without dismissing the accusation which called it forth. M. le Duc and his companions were not merely desirous that a work of musical and poetical genius should be produced on the occasion, but that they attached great importance to the new pastoral I have no doubt. In no respect could *Acis et Galatée* have fallen below their just expectations, and the still youthful author of the verse was rewarded with applause, thanks, and a hundred louis. Probably he was quite content with the guerdon, but on his return to Paris Champmêlé and Raisin emphatically declared that he had been underpaid. He was eventually prevailed upon to write a letter on the subject to the Duc, who, as an additional recompense, made him his principal secretary.

The poet accordingly took up his residence at Anet,

and there, surrounded by souvenirs of the illicit loves
of Henri II. and Diane de Poitiers—souvenirs not
excluded from the chapel itself—completed a tragedy
derived from Parthian history. *Phraate* appeared at
the Comédie Française on the 26th December. No
little sensation was created among the audience by
some of the passages, in which the tyranny and vices
and prodigality of kings were assailed with great spirit.
The audience, recovering from its surprise, immediately
divided into hostile sections. Those who did not approve
all the proceedings of the Grand Monarque were
naturally delighted ; others declared that the audacious
author ought to be clapped in the Bastille. The players
were for retaining the piece in the bills ; but Campistron,
terrified by the storm he had raised, induced the
Dauphiness—doubtless assuring her that he had simply
complied with the exigencies of his subject, and that
nothing had been further from his thoughts than an
attack, directly or indirectly, upon the prince who had
done so much for France as the King—to order its
withdrawal, which she did. How far the "allusions"
were intentional or otherwise I am unable to say, as
the author had the wit to destroy the MS. as soon as
possible. The Duc de Vendôme, it should be added,
did not dispense with the services of his dangerous
secretary—nay, seemed from this time to hold him in
higher regard than before. Even Campistron's uncon-

querable repugnance to letter-writing did not qualify
this feeling. "Don't let me disturb you," he good-
humouredly remarked to the dramatist, surprising him
in the act of burning a basketful of letters ; "I see
you are occupied in making replies."

Phraate was still being talked of when two more
novelties by Baron were given—*La Coquette et la Fausse
Prude*, a comedy in five acts, and *Géta*, a tragedy.   The
actor's claim to the authorship was vehemently denied
out of doors.   The *Coquette* was ascribed to Subligny,
Géta to a certain Nicolas de Péchantré.   The comedy
obviously emanated from the same pen as *L'Homme à
Bonne Fortune*, but no doubt can be entertained that
Baron was merely the adoptive father of the other piece.
Péchantré, who was the son of a surgeon at Toulouse,
had frequently been crowned at the Jeux Floraux, and
had recently come to Paris in the hope of gaining a
place by the side of Corneille and Racine.   He soon
afterwards submitted the tragedy in question to Baron,
who, desirous of posing before the world as a tragic
dramatist, resolved to pass himself off as its author.
With this object he unreservedly condemned it, and,
having impressed Péchantré with a belief that it had
no chance of even being accepted at the theatre,
intimated his willingness to give the small sum of
twenty pistoles for the privilege of appropriating the
" central idea."   Péchantré, a good easy man, little

versed in the ways of the world, and perhaps pressed by want, accepted the offer,—and the play was brought out with scarcely an alteration. Another version of the story is to the effect that the tragedy was partly written by a Languedocian, by name Dambelot, who died while at work upon it; that Péchantré brought it to Paris, that the players refused it, and that Baron, sensible of its merits, rewrote the fifth act — its weakest part — in order to make it presentable. However that may be, Péchantré, at the instance of Champmêlé, who objected to Baron enjoying undeserved honours, quickly asserted his claim to the tragedy, which was printed with his name on the title-page. If Baron had rewritten the fifth act, and if that act was printed and represented with the improvements he had effected in it, he was simply paid in his own coin.

The fame acquired by Baron as the author of *L'Homme à Bonne Fortune* and *La Coquette* excited a spirit of emulation in Dancourt, who quickly produced two of the best pieces to be found in his *théâtre*. The first, *La Désolation des Joueuses*, was suggested by the suppression of lansquenet, rendered necessary by the ruin to which several families had been reduced by that game. By the second, *Le Chevalier à la Mode*, Dancourt gained the highest place among the comic dramatists of the day. Resembling *L'Homme à Bonne Fortune* in conception, it goes far beyond it in adroitness of conduct, character, and liveliness. It is a well-drawn picture of the day, seasoned with searching ridicule of the parvenu financiers. In writing this comedy Dancourt had the assistance of Saintyon, but a perusal of the works of the latter will leave no doubt that the actor-dramatist supplied all that gave it permanent value. Neither auditor nor reader deems it overlong, although it is longer than any French comedy previously written. The *Chevalier* was played forty times in succession, in those days a sign of unusual success. The run was scarcely half over when Dancourt gracefully waived in favour of his collaborateur a further share of the receipts. "Je ne veux plus de part d'auteur," he wrote on the Register on the 23rd night, possibly as a sly hit at the comrade who, to say the least, had not been very ready to acknowledge obligations to professed authors.

Baron, annoyed to find his supremacy as dramatist-actor questioned, promptly entered the lists against the author of the *Chevalier à la Mode*. In his haste, however, to humble his rival, he not only selected a subject which had never been treated with good success on the French stage save in *Le Cocu Imaginaire* and *Le Jaloux Désabusé*, that of male jealousy, but appropriated with but few alterations the plot of *Don Garcie de Navarre. Le Jaloux*, as the new play was called, soon gave place to another novelty. Many authors had avoided the history of Regulus on account of the apparent impossibility of treating it in accordance with the unities. Pradon surmounted the difficulty by laying the scene in the Roman camp, with the walls of Carthage in the background. His *Régulus* (January 4) is a far from ineffective tragedy, especially in the scene where the Roman general, notwithstanding the passionate entreaties of the woman he loves, resolves, at the call of honour, to return to Carthage and die. Baron and Mdlle. Champmêlé had charge of the principal characters. Elated with his success, Pradon induced the players to revive his *Tamerlane*, which, however, did not please more now than at its first appearance. " Ah ! " said a peer in the green-room, noticing the poet come in with a shabby vest under a fine coat, " behold the mantle of Regulus over the waistcoat of Tamerlane."

In the mean time some changes were made in the company. Latuillerie, the clever and eminently presentable personator of young kings and peasants, died on the 13th February, and was buried with the usual rites at Saint Sulpice. There is no reason to believe that he wrote any of the comedies brought out in his name. His place was taken by Barthelemi Gourlin de Roselis, who appeared at Versailles on the 1st of

March as Mithridate, and in the Rue Mazarine on the
30th as Stilicon. The new-comer had a fine presence,
but his acting was without warmth. Sévigny, a provincial actor of repute, made his début on the 31st
March. His fate rested neither with the public nor
the company; the Dauphiness, favourably impressed
by a performance he had given at Versailles, issued
an order that he should be received. It is probable
that if she had not done so he would soon have gone
back to the country, for even in parts best suited to
him—second kings in tragedy and *rôles rompus* in
comedy—he exhibited many shortcomings. The two
débutants came forward one night in the same piece—
Polyeucte—and were " applauded by a large audience."
Polyeucte was played by Roselis, and Sévère, one of
Baron's best parts, by Sévigny. I have also to
chronicle for this year the début of a M. Fonpré.

Summer brought with it a new piece from the
genial pen of Lafontaine. *La Coupe Enchantée* (July
16) is founded upon Boccaccio and Ariosto, and is
pervaded by some of the graceful humour peculiar
to the author. It was brought out under the name
of Champmêlé, and is to be found in Champmêlé's
théâtre. Dancourt's *Maison de Campagne*, which followed, is a pleasant picture of one of those country
houses which, through being too often visited, bring
their owners to the verge of ruin. Here a prodigal

wife is pointedly contrasted with an economical husband, but the chief excellence of the little comedy consists in the dialogue.   Next came a new piece from the pen of no less a person than the late M. Molière.   *Les Amants Magnifiques*, originally played at Court eighteen years previously, was represented for the first time in Paris (October 15).   The company, I think, would have done better to let the piece remain on the shelf. Hastily written, it could not but disappoint an audience familiar with Molière's thought-out works, and the circumstances on which it relied to please were forgotten.   It was a play for the year 1670 rather than 1688, for the Court rather than the town, for an assembly of courtiers rather than the critical audience of the Rue Mazarine.

In the course of the winter no fewer than three unsuccessful tragedies were produced.   The first, *Annibal*, was written by M. de Riupérous, secretary to the Marquis de Créqui.   The repute of the author as a man of letters had hardly prepared the players for failure at his hands, although he was but twenty-four years of age.   The second son of a Calvinist advocate at Montauban, he distinguished himself while yet a boy by writing a tragedy and a treatise on medals, and the Intendant of the town, having induced him to embrace the doctrines of Rome, brought him to Paris in the hope of pushing his fortune.   His friend happened to be on good terms with Père Lachaise, who, delighted with the treatise on medals—a subject in which he himself took deep interest—gave Riupérous a canonry at Forcalquier. Before long, however, he laid aside his ecclesiastical habit, which never suited him, to accept a small state appointment—procured for him by another influential friend, the Marquis de Barbezieux, son of Louvois—and became secretary to the Marquis de Créqui. These duties occupied much of his time, but having a ready pen he wrote more than many men who devoted themselves exclusively to literature. "Monsieur de Riupérous," the Princesse de Conti said to him one day, "you have addressed verses to nearly all the ladies of the Court, but not a line to me." In less than an hour she received from him a well-turned sonnet in her praise. For such trifles, indeed, he had some talent; but the secret of the theatre was never his. *Annibal,* though supported by Baron and Champmêlé, proved a dire failure. The same must be said of Campistron's *Phocion* (December 16). The poet, overlooking the constitutional weakness of the play, ascribed his want of success to the pitiable manner in which one of the principal personages was represented — an allegation which must have embroiled him for a time with Champmêlé, Baron, Roselis, or Mdlle Raisin, all of whom figured in the cast. *Laodamie* (February 11)

met with a more favourable reception without deserving
it. The writer was Catherine Bernard, a native of
Rouen, where she made the acquaintance of Corneille.
In 1685, having abjured Protestantism, she came to
Paris and turned blue-stocking. Fontenelle, it is said,
gave her literary advice, and even had a share in
the works brought out in her name. Academies did
her honour, but it was only as a writer of romances
and fugitive verse that she gained distinction. Her
Laodamie satisfied no good judge of dramatic art, and
would now be forgotten by all save literary antiquaries
if it had not chanced to be the last original play
given at the historic theatre in the Rue Mazarine.

Yes, the Comédiens du Roi had had to shift their
quarters. For some time past, it seems, the scholars
of the Collége Mazarin, situated within a stone's throw
of the theatre, had been put to much inconvenience,
if not made victims of practical jokes, by the crowd
of bourgeois playgoers which daily assembled in the
Rue Mazarine. This inconvenience was felt particularly
at Easter, when, owing to the number of coaches which
brought up the wealthier section of the audience, the
fathers and mothers and friends of the pupils had to
go to the college by a circuitous route. The director
of the schools at length entered a formal protest
against the nuisance : the King required the players
to change their quarters, and three of the number

—Lagrange, Hubert, and Ducroisy—were appointed to select a building adapted or adaptable to theatrical purposes.   For some time the labours of the trio proved fruitless.   No sooner had they fixed upon a particular hôtel than insurmountable objections were raised to their taking it.   In more than one instance the King himself was opposed to them.   Eventually, however, their patience was adequately rewarded.   His majesty consenting, they purchased for 62,614 livres the Jeu de Paume de l'Étoile in the Rue des Fossés St. Germain des Prés, and on the 8th March 1688 the building passed into the possession of the Comédiens du Roi.   François d'Orbay, an architect of repute, speedily converted it into a handsome and a commodious playhouse, which, under the style and title of the Théâtre de la Comédie Française, was opened on the 18th of April 1689 with all the ceremonies befitting so important an event.

CHAPTER VI.

1689—1694.

ODDLY enough, the pietism of the Court under its new mistress was to be of direct service to dramatic literature. Madame de Maintenon had established at Saint Cyr a school in which well-born but impecunious girls might be educated. This education was in the main of a religious character, but as a means of purifying their tastes and strengthening their judgment the pupils were allowed to perform in strictly moral plays. By no one was this concession hailed with greater satisfaction than the preceptress, Madame de Brinon. Blessed with both the *cacoethes loquendi* and the *cacoethes scribendi*, she preached to and wrote comedies for the girls committed to her care. " I am disposed to think," said Madame de Maintenon after one of the performances, " that we might have something from Corneille and Racine—if there is not too much love in it." The ambitious preceptress swallowed the pill with as good a grace as she could command, and *Cinna* and *Andromaque* were played. In choosing the latter tragedy, perhaps, Madame de Brinon had her own interests in view.

Irreproachable as was the way in which the pupils
were trained, they would be daughters of Eve enough
to give the most fervid expression to all the tender
passages in the play, and it was probable that Madame
de Maintenon would deem it prudent to return to the
discarded pieces.   This hope was not realized, at least
for some time.   The pupils, it is true, acted *Andromaque*
with a degree of earnestness which inspired the King's
wife with the liveliest fears as to their future, but
instead of having Madame de Brinon's efforts played
again she requested Racine by letter to write for the
Maison de Saint Cyr "a dramatic poem, moral or
historic, from which love should be entirely excluded."

The illustrious poet, who continued to reside in
Paris, now playing the courtier, now discharging
his duties as historiographer royal, now writing a
pungent epigram at his enemies and aspiring dramatists, but more frequently than all engaged in religious
meditations and observances, was not a little troubled
by this letter.   He was about fifty years of age,
and might easily diminish the splendour of the reputation he had won at the Hôtel de Bourgogne.   " What
would his enemies say if, after having triumphed on the
secular theatre, he suffered a reverse on a theatre
consecrated to piety ? "   His first impulse was to excuse
himself ; and Boileau, often disposed to fall in with his
mood, advised him to do so.   But on further reflection

he determined to comply with the request, partly
in order to avoid giving any offence to one who, for
aught he knew to the contrary, was only the King's
mistress, and partly because he saw in the story of
Esther a subject at once worthy of his powers and suited
to the purpose in view. Boileau thereupon counselled
him not to excuse himself, and in a short time *Esther*
was completed. The poet's hand, it was clear, had not
lost its cunning. The tragedy is excellent in both form
and substance, and must ever hold a prominent place
among his works. He reverently adhered to the original
as far as the story is concerned, bore Herodotus in mind
to good purpose in delineating the character of Assuérus,
and introduced the chorus with a skill which might
have excited the envy of the Greek dramatists. It
must be specially observed that while restricting the
action to the palace he changes the decoration with each
act, not in the hope that such an infringement of the
rule as to unity of place would find imitators, but
simply to render the piece more acceptable to the young
players for whom it was created.

Doubtless to the chagrin of Madame de Brinon, a
staunch upholder of the proprieties, Racine was
requested by Madame de Maintenon to prepare the
pupils of Saint Cyr for their task—a dangerous undertaking for so impressionable a man, for most of them
were personally attractive. Esther was allotted to a

Mdlle. de Villeaune, Assuérus to a Mdlle. dé Lalie, Mardochée to a Mdlle. de Glapion, and Aman to a Mdlle. d'Abancourt. One pupil, the Madame de Caylus of after years, having testified an ardent desire to be included in the cast, Racine wrote for her the well-known prologue, which is spoken by Piety. It may be presumed that he fulfilled his duties *con amore;* the Esther resembled Mdlle. Champmêlé, and the Mardochée, to use his own words, " had a voice that went right to the heart." For the latter he seems to have entertained a warmer feeling than admiration. Rebuked by her preceptor for a temporary loss of memory, Mdlle. de Glapion burst into tears, and the sight of her grief affected him so deeply that after drying her eyes he found that his own were wet. It is satisfactory to relate that the poet underwent the ordeal unscathed. No scandal, well founded or otherwise, arose out of his presence at Saint Cyr.

Esther was played for the first time during the Carnival of 1689, the audience comprising the King, Madame de Maintenon, Louvois, and many others of the French Court. The success of the play was instant and decisive, partly on account of its poetical beauty, but chiefly, no doubt, because every one perceived in it an allegory flattering to the powers that were. The King was to be seen in Assuérus, the humbled Madame de Montespan in Vashti, the triumphant Madame de

Maintenon in Esther, and the relentless Louvois in
Aman. In regard to the third, it must be said, the
parallel was far from complete. Esther saved her
nation ; Madame de Maintenon, who had been brought
up as a Huguenot, allowed the God of her fathers to be
proscribed. This distinction was not suggested in the
play, but it is remarkable that only four years after
the revocation of the Edict of Nantes, and at a time
when a man who suggested that a King could be misled
was deemed guilty of " culpable temerity," Racine
should have caused such lines as

> On peut des plus grands rois surprendre la justice,

and

> Et le roi trop crédule a signé cet édit,

to be recited in the hearing of the authors of that
measure. If the King and his wife felt any resentment at these words it was carefully disguised. " His
majesty and all the Court," writes Madame de Sévigné,
who was present, " are charmed with *Esther*. Racine "
—and this seems to have echoed the general opinion
—" has surpassed himself. He now loves God as he
used to love his mistresses. He is for sacred as he
was for profane themes ; all is beautiful, all is great,
all is written with dignity." The performance over,
" the King, coming up to us, said, ' Madame, the Maréchal
de Bellefond tells me that you are pleased with the
play.' I replied with self-possession, ' Sire, I am

charmed ; what I feel is not to be expressed by words.'
The King said to me, 'Racine has much *esprit.*' I
replied, ' Sire, he has indeed ; but, in truth, these
young ladies have it also ; they enter into the subject
as if they had never done anything else.' He said,
' That is true ; ' and then his majesty went away, and
left me an object of envy." Not long afterwards the
King again came to Saint Cyr to see the play, bringing
with him no less a person than James II., who in the
previous December had abandoned the English throne,
and was now a guest of France at St. Germain.

The players were naturally anxious that *Esther*
should be brought out at their theatre, but Racine could
not be diverted from his resolution. Notwithstanding
its success at Saint Cyr, I doubt whether it would
have been well received at the Théâtre Français, seeing
that on being printed it evoked but little praise. La
Feuillade called the book a " requête civile contre
l'approbation publique." In default of anything better,
the first new piece brought out in the new house was
Démétrius, a tragedy by one Aubry, who had espoused
our old acquaintance Geneviève Béjart, and by mixing
with the players had been tempted to neglect the trade
to which he had been brought up—that of a paviour—
to write for the stage. On the 22nd August, after a
performance of the ever-popular *Venceslas*, came a trifle
called *Le Veau Perdu*, attributed in the registers to

Champmêlé, but really written by Lafontaine. Two *contes* by the latter, the *Gageure des Trois Commères* and *Le Villageois qui cherche son veau*, supplied the intrigue of the piece, which did not fail to please.

In *Le Concert Ridicule*, another one-act comedy of this year, we have the first example of the first systematic collaboration attempted on the French stage. Its authors were David Augustin de Brueys and Jean Palaprat, the Beaumont and Fletcher, *mutatis mutandis*, of seventeenth-century Paris. Both came from Provence, the former having been born at Aix in 1640, and the other at Toulouse about ten years afterwards. Brueys, who belonged to an old and estimable family (one of his ancestors, Pierre Brueys, had been ennobled by Louis XI.), began life as an advocate, but soon exchanged the study of jurisprudence for that of theology and *belles-lettres*. Educated a Protestant, he defended his religion with remarkable power and judgment, especially in a reply to the *Exposition de la Doctrine de l'Eglise*. Bossuet, quick to perceive the high qualities of his antagonist, determined that the Reformation should not have so doughty a champion. He attracted him to Paris, brought the whole influence of an unrivalled eloquence and learning to bear upon his mind, and finally won him over to the tenets of Rome. Brueys signalized his conversion in an *Examen des raisons qui ont donné lieu à la Séparation des Pro-*

testants, a copy of which he had the honour of present-
ing to Louis XIV. in person.   In this matter, it may
be assumed, he was not actuated by motives of ambition
or interest.   He declined to participate in the favours
lavished by the King upon the newly-converted.   " My
sincerity," he said to Bossuet, who wished to push his
fortunes at Court, " must not be open to question."
In 1683, a year after the publication of the *Examen*,
he thought of returning to Aix, but was requested by
the King to remain in Paris for the benefit of the many
Protestants to be found there.   " Formerly of their
persuasion," said his majesty, " you will know better
how to argue with them."   His wife dying, Brueys
determined to enter the ecclesiastical state, and a few
months before the proscription of the Huguenots he
received the tonsure at the hands of Bossuet.   Not
that he exactly responded to his austere friend's notions
of what an Abbé ought to be.   He united to a scrupulous regard for the duties of his calling an intense and
healthy enjoyment of life.   Rather above the middle
stature, dignified in manner, and short-sighted enough
to be under the necessity of always wearing close
spectacles, through which a pair of dark eyes gleamed
with an expression of rich but subdued humour, he
was constantly to be found at the theatre, in drawing-
rooms, and at lively little supper-parties.   Now and
then, too, we catch a glimpse of him at Versailles.   " I

hope your eyesight is improving, M. Brueys?" said
Louis XIV. to him one day.   " Sire," was the pleasant
reply, " my worthy nephew, Sidobre," the oculist, " tells
me that I am seeing a little better."   Before long, at
Jean Baptiste Raisin's table, the genial Abbé became
acquainted with Palaprat, who, after receiving a liberal
education, had gone to the bar at Toulouse, passed two
years in Italy, and soon afterwards, in 1671, settled
in Paris.   One fragment of autobiography in the young
lawyer's writings is not without interest.   " Every
Saturday night," he says, " I was in capital company
at the table of an Italian painter, Varro.   I there
met the players who appeared at the Palais Royal
alternately with Molière.   This great actor and a thousand times greater author lived in cordial agreement
with these Italians, because they were good actors and
excellent fellows.   There were always two or three of
the best of them at our suppers.   Molière also came
frequently, though not so frequently as we wished."
Like the great French fabulist, Palaprat combined a
lively imagination with the utmost simplicity of character, was at once " un bel esprit pour les saillies et un
enfant pour la naïveté."   Between this man and Brueys
a warm friendship sprang up ; they went to reside
together in the old Rue du Temple, and the lapse
of time seemed only to make them more inseparable.
French literature was to be a gainer by their meeting.

Each loved the theatre ; and at length, in order to win free admission to the Comédie—for neither of them had too much money—they proceeded to write *Le Concert Ridicule.* In substance a mere trifle, but treated in a pleasant spirit, it met with marked success—so marked, indeed, as to induce the delighted authors to determine upon the production of more ambitious work of the kind.

Two well-known names are missed from the bills at this period. The first was that of Ducroisy, who had joined Molière's country troupe nearly forty years before, and for whom the characters of Tartuffe and the philosopher in the *Bourgeois Gentilhomme* had been written. In April 1689 he quitted the Comédie with a pension of a thousand livres, which would have been well deserved if he had never played anything save countrymen and dotards. He died at Conflans-Saint Honorine, near Paris, about six years afterwards ; and the curé at that place, having learnt to esteem him, was so much affected by the event that he sent for another to perform the burial ceremony. The second player referred to was Dauvilliers, of the ugly face but silvery voice. Melancholy indeed were the circumstances in which he left the theatre. It seems that whenever he appeared at Court the Dauphiness derided his ugliness, often in so loud a tone as to reach his ears on the stage. She probably meant no harm, but the disparagement preyed so much on his mind that he lost his wits, as the anecdote which follows will sufficiently prove. The players one night represented Lachapelle's *Cléopatre*, Baron being Antoine and Dauvilliers Eros. The latter gave the former an unabated sword to fall upon, and the great actor would have killed himself in earnest if at the critical moment the weapon had not glanced against instead of striking his body. The company adopted the more generous—and probably the true—interpretation of Dauvillier's conduct; he was sent for the rest of his days to the Frères de la Charité at Charenton, and the Comédie lost an actor who in third-rate tragic characters and the elevated comedy had had but few superiors.

The year 1690 did not open under the most favourable auspices. *Adrien*, a "tragédie Chrétienne," by Campistron, had only eight representations. The author asks us to believe that his comparative failure was due to a cabal of "some rivals jealous of his fame;" its real cause was to be found in his own shortcomings. The players were soon consoled for their disappointment. Boursault submitted to them a piece in which the Fables of Æsop were treated in a dramatic form. The innovation was so great that some of the company became apprehensive as to the result. They nervously suggested the omission of the fifth scene in

the second act, and would have had their own way
had not the author persuaded the First Gentleman of
the Chamber that it ought to be retained. Boursault
himself did not confidently reckon upon success, as may
be seen from a letter he wrote at the time to his wife.
Nor did the public think much of the piece at the
outset. The author, they thought, had made too lavish
a use of the fables, which were in everybody's mouth.
Some hostility being manifested, Jean Baptiste Raisin,
who played Æsope, at once advanced. " Bear in mind,"
he said, " that this comedy is of an altogether novel
kind. The essence of Æsope's character would be
missed unless he recited his fables. If the piece
wearies you, Messieurs, say so at once, for I must tell
you that before the curtain falls I have eleven or twelve
more of the fables to recite." The parterre, after giving
him a round of applause, unanimously requested him to
go on ; and *Æsope*—which, let it be stated, is very
pleasantly written throughout—became the most profitable of its author's compositions.

Between the 20th April and the 3rd May the
theatre was closed on account of the death of the
Dauphiness, the lady to whom the King had confided
the management of the Comédie a few years previously,
and who had driven poor Dauvilliers out of his mind.
The first new piece presented after the reopening was
Audry's *Agathocle,* which failed so dismally that the

P 2

author thereafter gave up writing for the stage. Next
came a one-act comedy in prose called *La Folle Enchère*,
really written by Mdlle. Ulric, but often attributed to
Dancourt. The story is rendered amusing by a series
of disguises assumed by some of the characters in order
to induce a crabbed mother to consent to the marriage
of her son to a girl whom she holds in no particular
regard. The scene which gives the title to the piece is
eminently piquant. *Le Ballet Extravagant*, by Palaprat,
had good success, although given in the summer. Here
a music-mad mother has an opera played in her house,
and two sprightly youths take advantage of a ballet
introduced in it to carry off her two daughters. This
was followed by two remarkably poor trifles—the *L'Eté
des Coquettes*, by Dancourt, and *Les Bourgeois de Qualité*,
by Hauteroche. The latter piece—an imitation of *Les
Précieuses Ridicules* and *Le Bourgeois Gentilhomme*—was
the last written by the author, who, however, was to be
met with behind the scenes for seventeen years to come.

M.M. Brueys and Palaprat were more than usually
active at this period. It seems that one evening, while
at table with these eminent authors, Jean Baptiste
Raisin narrated a pleasant story. Some casks of wine
were being brought into Paris in a cart ; one of them
broke, and the carrier, after having endeavoured in all
good faith, but without success, to save the precious
liquor, proceeded to enjoy himself over what remained.

The more he drank the more he liked it, the consequence being that ere long he was scarcely master of himself. In telling this story, Palaprat says, Raisin proved an admirable actor, whether in illustrating the waggoner's distress at the mishap, his resolve to make the best of the circumstances, or the degrees by which he was overcome by the wine. " Such an incident," said Brueys, " would do well in a play." Palaprat thought not. " Je l'entreprendrai moi," remarked Brueys, adding, " si je l'avais résolu je mettrais les tours de Notre Dame sur le théâtre." In a few days he completed the plan of a little piece in which Raisin's story is made a means of discovering an abduction; Palaprat worked at it with him, and it was brought out at the Comédie under the title of *Le Secret Révélé.* Raisin's delineation of the inebriated waggoner was recognized on all hands as a work of art.

Le Secret Révélé withdrawn, the players put in rehearsal a five-act comedy by the same authors, by name *Le Grondeur.* Champmêlé did not think his comrades were well-advised in accepting the play. " What pleasure," he asked, " could a man who was incessantly grumbling or scolding afford ? " He was wrong; a character disagreeable in itself, provided it is not repulsive, may excite deep interest, especially when, as in this case, it is connected with excellent situations and dialogue. Brueys and Palaprat were

away in the south on urgent private affairs, and the
players, having received permission to make any
alterations they thought necessary, reduced the piece
to three acts.   During the rehearsals they brought
out a short comedy by Jacques Raisin, *Merlin Gascon*,
and a tragedy by Mdlle. Bernard, *Brutus*, in which
the illustrious Roman is made a comparatively
subordinate personage.   The authoress, at the instance
of her friend Madame de Pontchartrain, now laid down
her pen for ever as far as the theatre was concerned,
the more readily, perhaps, as her conversion to Roman
Catholicism had been rewarded by a comfortable
pension from the King.   Early in February 1691,
about six weeks after *Brutus* appeared, and before
Brueys and Palaprat returned to Paris, *Le Grondeur*
was produced.   In the cast were Mdlle. Raisin,
Guérin, and Mdlle. Beauval.   Condemned by the aris-
tocratic section of the audience—chiefly, I suspect,
on account of an injudicious prologue by Palaprat—
it was cordially received by the parterre, and instantly
became a part of the stock of the theatre.   On his
return, however, Brueys did not thank the players
for the changes they had made.   "Messieurs," he said,
in his Gascon manner, "you have mutilated my
comedy in seeking to improve it; I made it a pendulum,
you have made it a roasting jack (*tourne-broche*)."   Be
that as it may, he printed the piece as it was repre-

sented. "*Le Grondeur*," he said one night at a supper, " c'est une bonne pièce. Le premier acte est excellent; il est tout de moi. Le second, couci-couci; Palaprat y a travaillé. Le troisième ne vaut pas le diable; je l'avais abandonné à ce barbouiller." Palaprat—who, of course, was within earshot—replied in the same tone, " Cé coquin! il mé dépouille tout lé jour dé cette façon, et mon chien dé tendre pour lui m'empêche dé mé fâcher."

Nine days after the appearance of *Le Grondeur* we come to another clever play. This was Campistron's tragedy of *Tiridate*, in which the incestuous love of Amon for Thamar, a subject he would have done well to avoid, is treated as a matter of Parthian history and under other names. Baron and Mdlle. Champmêlé filled the principal characters, supported by Champmêlé, Raisin the elder, Lathorillière, Roselis, Sévigny, Mdlle. Raisin, and Mdlle. Poisson. Circumstances over which he certainly had no control compelled Campistron to leave the stage for a time. Louis XIV. was now engaged in another war—the war that was to break the spell of glory which had hitherto attended his arms. The men who surrounded the throne used to say that the whole business was due to a most trivial incident; the King had objected to the shape of a window at Trianon, and Louvois, " superintendent of buildings as well as minister," angrily

and significantly remarked that the King should soon
have matter of more importance to think of. However
that may be, war there certainly was—war on both
land and sea, war with England and Holland, with
Pope and Emperor, with Savoy and Spain. The contest with England was especially bitter, owing to the
practical support extended by France to the cause of
James, and to the avowed intention of William III.
to set limits to the ambition of the French monarch.
For a time France seemed to have the advantage;
worsted at La Hogue, she triumphed at Steinkirk
and Neerwinden, thanks in great measure to the
genius of Luxembourg. At Steinkirk the Duc de
Vendôme honourably distinguished himself. In the
heat of the fight, to his great surprise, he found
that Campistron had joined him. " Que faites-vous
ici ? " he asked. " Monseigneur," was the cool reply,
" voulez vous en aller "—a reply which diverted the
Prince not a little. Campistron remained with his
patron throughout his campaigns, finding time, however,
to finish a poor tragedy called *Aëtius*, which appeared
at the Français in the following year.

A misfortune second only to the withdrawal of
Racine was now to befall the theatre. In the autumn
of 1691, armed with what had proved two attractive
novelties,—*La Parisienne*, a sprightly one-act comedy
by Dancourt, and *Le Muet*, an equally sprightly

imitation by Brueys and Palaprat of Terence's *Eunuchus*,
—the players went to amuse the King at Fontainebleau,
where Baron formally applied for permission to leave
the troupe. This permission was soon afterwards given,
and the actor, with his wife, abandoned the stage on
the 21st October as the hero of Rotrou's *Venceslas.*
The event took all Paris by surprise, seeing that he
was only thirty-eight years of age, enjoyed more
popularity than ever, had yet some fine characters to
illustrate, and might set many powerful pens to work
by the slightest hint that he desired to appear in a
new play. Everybody was curious to know the cause
of his retirement. But on this point, strangely enough,
his lips were always closed, and to this day the mystery
has never been cleared up. It was alleged at the time
that he left the Comédie because the King would not
allow him to enjoy the authority possessed by the late
Dauphiness; but this is hardly to be reconciled with the
fact that, in addition to the regular pension, he received
one of 3000 livres from the Court. Indulgent as he
was to his favourite players, Louis XIV. would hardly
have tolerated such a display of peevishness. My own
impression is that the low estimation in which stage-art
was often held preyed deeply on the mind of one so
keenly conscious of his intellectual gifts, and that as
soon as he had amassed the means of living without the
aid of his profession he wished to become a man of

fashion. "Monsieur le Marquis," he once said to the
Marquis de Biron, "your people, your coachman and
your lackeys, have set upon mine ; I wish you to take
notice of it." "Mon pauvre Baron," replied the Marquis,
somewhat nettled at the implied equality, "how
comes it that you have any 'people' at all ?" Could
an actor the like of whom appeared only once in a
thousand years endure such rebuffs as these ? But
though he was lost to the stage—though some of the
greatest characters in the French drama lost the
advantage of his fine presence, his powerful sway over
the world of passion, his exquisite art, his eminently
natural tones and gestures—he was not to be entirely
lost to the theatre, and will not be entirely lost to us.
He had some plays in his desk for the Comédie, and
before reaching the eventful closing years of his life we
may catch some glimpses of him as, resplendent in long
periwig and brocaded coat, he gaily disported himself
in the drawing-rooms of Paris.

In the hope of filling in some degree the void thus
left among them, the players brought forward some
provincial actors of repute—Saint George Durocher,
Rosidor, Pierre Tronchon de Beaubourg, and Biet. All
failed with the exception of the third, who had married
one of the many daughters of Madame Beauval—a
circumstance which, I imagine, proved of some service
to him during the period of his début—and who was

received in the following year. Beaubourg, sad to relate, was somewhat knock-kneed, but a noble air and a handsome countenance went far to redeem the drawback. In point of intelligence and style he presented an unfavourable contrast to Baron. Delicate shades of meaning almost invariably escaped him; his manner was stiff, declamatory, hard. It was at first barely tolerated, but in course of time contrived to win popularity. The bulk of the public, it has been remarked, can be rather easily persuaded, in the absence of anything better, that what is set before them is excellent, and they forget nothing so easily as the talents which they have the most admired. I am not sure that Beaubourg was not regarded as a model; certain it is that for about a quarter of a century after his appearance French acting became less and less natural.

At the time of Beaubourg's début the company had in rehearsal a comedy called *Le Négligent.* The author, Charles Rivière Dufresny, had for many years been well known at Court and in Paris, partly as a man of varied talents, but still more, perhaps, on account of a striking resemblance he bore to Henri Quatre. "Had M. Dufresny passed through the streets in the dress of that esteemed monarch it is probable that many persons would have made the sign of the cross and fled." This resemblance is explained by the fact that he was

a great grandson of "la belle jardinière" of Anet, the
country girl who, as an old chronicler puts it, "eut
l'honneur" to please the genial Henri.   Dufresny began
life well : he became valet-de-chambre to Louis XIV.
and manager of the royal gardens, and finally received
the privilege of a manufacture of ices.   Nature had
endowed him with a fine sense of art and a quick
ear for music, and in the laying out and embellishment of gardens, as those at Mignaux and in the
Faubourg Saint Antoine showed, he was not to be
equalled even by Lenôtre.   But from the outset of his
career he persistently abused his gifts and opportunities.
He gave himself up almost unreservedly to pleasure, and
as a result was always in debt.   "There are two men,"
the King said, "whom I shall never make rich—Bon-
temps and Dufresny."   Now, disposing of his charges
and the privilege referred to for a mess of pottage, he
settled permanently in Paris, became a man about town,
and began to write for the stage.   In the art of construct-
ing a play he was not proficient, but many striking
characters and lively dialogues have to be placed to his
credit.   Curiously enough, this man, one of the most
licentious in Paris, manifested a peculiar regard for
decency in the selection and treatment of his subjects.
His defects and merits as a dramatist were foreshadowed
in *Le Négligent* (Feb. 27), in which he passes in review
a number of original figures rather than seeks to write

a comedy of the accepted pattern, and in which, giving way to a mania then not uncommon among authors, that of holding up their own profession to ridicule and contempt, he exhibits a poet doing a disreputable thing for the sake of half a dozen pistoles.

But few other novelties were seen at the Comédie this year. First comes *La Gazette de Hollande*, a comedy in one act, by Dancourt, with a groundwork similar to that of Boursault's *Mercure Galant*. The daughter of the correspondent of the *Gazette*, in order to elicit a declaration from her lover, inserts in the paper a notification that her father is ready to have her married,—and the trick succeeds. In the course of the piece a pleasant anecdote is glanced at. Not long previously a M. Delorme de Monchenay had brought out at the Italiens a rather satirical piece. The persons satirized went to the theatre in a body, and, mistaking the brother of the author for the author himself, caned him with right good will. M. Delorme took proceedings against the assailants, obtained compensation, and, in spite of the vigorous protests of his unfortunate brother, coolly pocketed the whole of the money. *La Gazette de Hollande* was followed by another one-act comedy from the same pen, *L'Opéra de Village*. Here, provoked by a new edict against the employment at the Comédie of singers and dancers, Dancourt indulged in some covert sarcasm at the expense of

Pécourt, the ballet-master. The first representation was marked by an untoward incident. One of the lines sung in the piece was " Les vignes et les prés seront sablés." The Marquis de Sablé, who, after dining freely, had taken a seat on the stage, imagined that this was pointed at him, and incontinently boxed the author's ears in sight of the audience. Dancourt was worldly wise enough not to return the blow, but it is difficult to say what might have happened if a similar thing had been done to Baron. He, I suspect, would have run the Marquis through on the spot, in hot defiance of the Bastille, Pignerol, or even the Place de Grève. Dancourt may have half forgotten his humiliation in fresh work; he retouched *L'Impromptu de Garnison,* by an anonymous author, and, in collaboration with Saintyon—who from and after this time was not seen at the theatre—wrote *Les Bourgeoises à la Mode.* It is sad to learn that the picture presented in the latter was one of real life. Two women abandon themselves to dissipation together, the fact that each is secretly loved by the husband of the other enabling them to find the requisite means. The hand of Dancourt may be perceived in every scene of this comedy, but he certainly should not have allowed it to be printed with only his name on the title-page. Saintyon appears to far greater advantage in the matter. He claimed his due share of the authorship, at the same time

modestly admitting that its success was due to what
M. Dancourt had done for it.

Meanwhile the players had again been casting many
wistful glances towards Racine. Naturally enough, the
success of Esther had revived in his mind the long-
repressed desire for literary fame, and at the end of
1690 he wrote for the girls at Saint Cyr another tragedy
of the same kind. I refer to *Athalie*, perhaps the most
serenely beautiful, though not the most forcible, of his
works. His enemies at Court were at once up in
arms. They assured Madame de Maintenon that the
performance of even a Scriptural play could not but
have a most pernicious effect upon immature minds.
Madame yielded to these representations so far as to
put an end to the spectacles at Saint Cyr altogether,
but she somewhat inconsistently brought the pupils to
Versailles on two occasions to represent Racine's last
tragedy. No stage was fitted up for the purpose,
and the young actresses, if we may so call them,
appeared in the simple costume which they wore in
the school. In spite of these drawbacks, *Athalie*
created a deep impression, and by way of testifying
his satisfaction with the play the King made the author
a *gentilhomme ordinaire*. In this case, however, the
Court did not give the law to the town. When the
tragedy was published it fell almost still-born from
the press. Surprising as it may be, fashion decreed

that a piece written for children should be read only
by children, and before long it became customary to
speak of *Athalie*—although nobody had read it—in
terms of mild contempt.

> Pour avoir fait pis qu'Esther
> Comment diable a-t-il pu faire ?

were the concluding lines of an epigram—erroneously
ascribed to Fontenelle—now directed against the
author. Indeed, the indifference his tragedy met
with was so great that Racine feared he had
really failed. " Reassure yourself," said Boileau ; " the
public will come to appreciate it at its proper value ;
it is your masterpiece." The Comédiens du Roi thought
so too ; but many years were to elapse before they had
the opportunity of convincing the public that such was
all but the case.

Molière's fellow-players were every year becoming
fewer and fewer. Lagrange, whose style as an actor
had been formed under the personal instruction of the
illustrious dramatist, died on the 1st March 1692 of
chagrin, caused by continuous ill-treatment of his
daughter by her husband. Even in old age this suave
and amiable man represented young lovers with much
of his former spirit and grace. He had time enough
to forswear his calling, and his body was buried at
Saint André des Arts. He left behind him no less than
a hundred thousand crowns, a proof of rare frugality.

His wife, *née* Raguenaud, was deeply affected by his death, although it had been written of her,

> Si n'ayant qu'un amant ou peut passer pour sage
> Elle est assez femme de bien
> Mais elle en aurait davantage
> Si l'on voulait l'aimer pour rien—

and in the following month she quitted the Comédie. Her pension, with the money left by her husband, enabled her to pass in more than comfort the rest of her life, which ended in 1727. "Marotte" was particularly clever as *ridicules*, and the playgoers long held her in affectionate remembrance.

Péchantré's second tragedy, *Jugurtha*, appeared at the end of the year, to be followed soon afterwards by Campistron's *Aëtius*. Neither was successful enough to be printed; but tradition has preserved one of the lines of the latter—

> Cegrand A ëtius, sous qui l'univers tremble.

Equally poor were a brace of little pieces—one *La Baguette*, by Dancourt, and the other *Le Sot Toujours Sot*, by Brueys and Palaprat. The genial Abbé—who, I fear, didn ot always practise what he preached, as the piece just named is stolen from Montfleuri's *Crispin Gentilhomme*—did himself greater justice in *L'Important*. "The younger Raisin," the author writes, "reflected deeply upon his art and the characters he had to represent. He had imagined to himself 'un sérieux

comique, une sotte gravité dans un fat, une manière de
grandeur affectée, artificielle pour ainsi dire, dans un
impertinent, qui à coup sûr aurait fait mourir de rire.'
One night when he was supping with us (the table was
nearly always the place of our conferences), he spoke to
us of the character, acted a thousand wonderful things
appropriate to it, and earnestly requested us to work
it out. The character pleased me beyond measure ; "
and *L'Important* was the result. The piece could
hardly have met the actor's expectations. The hero
—a coxcomb who makes people believe that he is a
man of influence at Court and in Paris, and the
hollowness of whose pretensions is at length made
apparent to the deceived—is, as has been well remarked,
rather a *chevalier de l'industrie* than what Raisin had
conceived. Nevertheless, *L'Important* proved popular,
thanks to the liveliness of the dialogue and more than
one dramatic situation.

The accomplished actor who originated the piece did
not live to see it played. On the 5th of September,
having incautiously taken a bath after a heavy supper,
he died of apoplexy, aged only thirty-seven. The
news, as may be supposed, excited more than passing
regret. " No actor," we are assured, " had played to
such perfection the parts he affected—*rôles à manteau*,
valets, coxcombs, drunkards, &c. He was a veritable
Proteus, not only in each of his characters, but in each

scene of those characters. In *rôles à manteau*, such as the Grondeur and Arnolphe, he had a severe and sullen air ; in the valets a hard and malicious physiognomy ; in the coxcombs a tender, gallant, and confident air." To this mobility he joined some wit, much humour, and a rare talent for telling a story, as those who were bidden to his charming little suppers were well aware. He had lived a merry life, but not without profoundly studying his art. Whether at Versailles, Anet, or at home, he was ever on the watch for anything that might assist him on the boards of the Comédie in the delineation of character. Some of the parts he had made his own were given to Guérin, others to Lathorillière. The former, we are told, gave satisfaction as Harpagon and the Grondeur, but without lessening the public regret for the loss of the " petit Molière." By his wife, Mdlle. Pitel de Longchamps, Raisin left two sons and two daughters, none of whom followed his profession.

In order to strengthen the company five provincial actors were submitted to the approval of the playgoers —a son of Devilliers, Poisson de Grandville, Lebrun, Quinault, Provost, Dumont de Lavoy, and Dufey. Of these only two were kept in the theatre. Quinault began as Harpagon in *L'Avare*, subsequently undertaking the onerous parts of Grichard in *Le Grondeur*, Mascarille in *L'Etourdi*, Sosie in *Amphitryon*, and Pasquin in *L'Homme à Bonne Fortune*. His face lent itself to a

great variety of comic expression, and as the only
fault to be found with his acting was that it occasionally
degenerated into buffoonery—a fault which the discipline
of the Comédie might at least keep within bounds—he
was admitted. The same good fortune fell to the lot
of Lavoy, though not until he had made a second début.
In *rôles à manteau* and valets he exhibited some cleverness. Dufey had three uncommon merits—patience,
industry, and a willingness to admit that nature had
not endowed him with more than humble talents. He
was well content to be a confidant, and a confidant
he became. In regard to the unsuccessful candidates,
Poisson de Grandville joined to good purpose a troupe
favoured by the King of Poland, and Devilliers, thanks
to the influence of his aunt, Mdlle. Raisin, enjoyed for
a short time a quarter of a share.

In the same year a remarkable actress appeared on
the scene. Marie Anne de Châteauneuf, calling herself
Duclos, came forward on the 28th October as Ariane.
Her parentage is involved in a little obscurity, one
writer stating that she was the issue of a marriage
between the daughter of M. and Madame Duclos, of
the old Théâtre du Marais, and a provincial actor
named Châteauneuf, and another that her father was
a captain of dragoons. The former statement is probably nearer the truth, not only on account of the fact
that her name was Châteauneuf, but by her want of

education. " Mdlle.," some one said to her in the wings,
" I will lay a wager that you do not know your creed."
" Not know my creed ? " she exclaimed ; " we shall see.
' Pater noster, qui—' " here she broke down : " prompt
me a little ; I almost forget the rest." Mdlle. Duclos,
who was born about 1664, had courted fame at the
opera, but to no purpose. Her strength lay in the
direction of declamatory tragedy, and not long after
her début at the Comédie Française she was elected
to double Mdlle. Champmêlé in the leading tragic
heroines. Nor was her success undeserved. She knew
how to touch the sensibilities of her audience, and the
impressive character in which she made her first bow
at the Comédie was long to be associated with her name.
In both acting and speaking, however, her style was
extremely affected—measured, stately, artificial. Perhaps this contributed to rather than diminished her
success, as the natural tone introduced by Molière and
Baron had temporarily gone out of fashion. What the
latter felt as he sat out a performance by Beaubourg
and Mdlle. Duclos has not been recorded, but may well
be imagined. The new actress, it must be added, was
not very popular with her colleagues, owing to an
ungovernable temper. The prospect of rehearsing with
her was one which inspired all of them with something
like terror. Even in the presence of the audience
she failed to maintain her self-control. If the parterre

gave way to unseasonable merriment she would inter-
rupt her performance to rebuke them; and on one
occasion, when Dancourt apologized to the audience
for her non-appearance as a youthful heroine, at the
same time indicating by a significant gesture the nature
of her indisposition, she wrathfully flew at and soundly
rated him before them all.

Racine, whose interest in the stage had been revived
by the appearance of a probable successor to Mdlle.
Champmêlé, went to the Comédie on the evening of
the 8th January 1694 to witness the first performance
of a new tragedy, *Adherbal Roi de Numidie*, by a Joseph
de Lagrange-Chancel. In this case, strange to say,
he was bent upon applauding the piece instead of
writing an epigram against it. For, as we shall
see, the Princesse de Conti took some interest in the
fate of *Adherbal*, and the satirist was temporarily
sunk in the courtier. Joseph de Lagrange, who only
a week previously had completed his eighteenth year,
seemed likely to eclipse the traditional glory of the
Admirable Crichton. Descended on his father's side
from a family which had been ennobled in return for
military services, he was educated in the first instance
at the Collége de Perigueux, his native place, and is
said to have lisped in numbers before he could read
or write. M. de Lagrange sen., having inherited the
post of a Conseiller au Parlement of Dijon, abandoned

arms, the profession to which he had been brought up,
for the law, but died before he could become an advocate. His widow then settled at Bourdeaux, and at
the age of eight Joseph was placed at the Jesuits'
College in that city to complete his education. Here,
in addition to surpassing all his schoolfellows, he
developed remarkable talents for poetry, throwing off
graceful verses on any subject which might be proposed
to him, and even correcting those of his masters. In
his tenth year he wrote a comedy on an adventure
which had just agitated the gossips of Bordeaux ; and
Madame de Lagrange, glowing with maternal pride,
had a theatre built in her house in order that it might
be played by the author and some of his schoolfellows.
The citizens invited to assist at the performance were
in ecstacies, and the piece might have had quite a
little run if Madame, yielding to the angry remonstrances of the persons who had been so irreverently
treated, had not shut up the theatre. More than duly
encouraged by his success, the boy proceeded to write
the tragedy of *Adherbal*, naming it in the first instance
Jugurtha. He did not, however, neglect his college
studies, as may be inferred from the fact that at the
age of fourteen he finished his classes, certainly a noteworthy feat. Then, rich in hope as to his future, the
mother brought him and *Jugurtha* to Paris, took lodgings
in the Temple, and proceeded to exercise in his behalf

the little influence she possessed. As luck would have it, a portion of the house they had selected was occupied by our old acquaintance Chapelle, now a member of the Academy. For so clever a youth he could not but feel some regard, and before long *Jugurtha* was read in his rooms to an audience composed of himself, the lively Abbé de Chaulieu, the younger Raisin, and, it need hardly be said, Madame de Lagrange. Raisin spoke of Joseph to the Princesse de Conti, who, anxious to become the known protectress of such a prodigy, invited him to her house, made him one of her pages, and sent *Jugurtha* to Racine for his opinion thereof. If it were really excellent, she said, she would try to get it played at the Comédie. Racine, to use his own words, " read the tragedy with pleasant astonishment." He would give the author all the advice he could. The poet kept his word, as Lagrange found to his advantage when, with the most deferential manner he could assume, he presented himself to the author of *Phèdre.* " I avow," he writes, " that the lessons he gave me in the form of advice were of more importance to me than all the works I have read, not even excepting the *Poetics* of Aristotle and the learned remarks of his last translator." For some time after this he might have been seen on the quays in search of old plays, especially those of Rotrou, of whose merits as a dramatist Racine had spoken in the highest terms. Eventually the tragedy was brought out at the Comédie, not under its original title, which had already been used, but as *Adherbal.* Racine, I fear, praised it to the Princesse de Conti because he shrewdly suspected that she would not like to hear it blamed. Lagrange, henceforward to be known as Lagrange-Chancel, was not to contribute to the French stage what may be termed a work of art. He delighted in ridiculously rapid transitions from one passion or emotion to another, gave us the shadows of characters rather than characters themselves, and was often weak and obscure in his versification. He devised some good situations, but generally spoilt their effect by awkward management and a tendency to quibble. In one sense he was too ingenious, most of his scenes being overcharged with incidents and language. He had been put forward as a possible successor to Corneille and Racine; as it was, he did not make even Campistron uneasy. His *Adherbal*, however, was favourably received, and Racine, we are told, "seemed to take extreme pleasure in all the applause" bestowed upon the play.

In spring another frequenter of the Hôtel de Conti, Longepierre, at one time secretary to the Duc de Berry, challenged the suffrages of the playgoer with a *Médée* written "in the style of Sophocles and Euripides." The announcement did not create much interest for its own sake, seeing that the author was

already known as a feeble translator from the Greek.
He was an excellent scholar in the narrower sense of
the word, but apparently unable to catch anything like
the spirit of his original.   Here is an epigram of the
time upon him—

> Longepierre le translateur,
> De l'antiquité zélateur,
> Ressemble à ces premiers Fidèles
> Qui combattaient jusqu'au trépas
> Pour des vérités immortelles
> Qu'eux-mêmes ne comprenaient pas.

Nevertheless, the production of his *Medée* occasioned
some commotion in Paris.   The controversy as to the
comparative merits of the ancients and moderns had
just been revived with extraordinary energy.   Perrault,
in order to flatter the vanity of the King, had published
a parallel in favour of the moderns; Boileau promptly
entered the lists on behalf of the ancients, and the battle
quickly spread over the whole of the literary world.
No educated man found it possible to observe neutrality
on the subject.   There was no evading the question,
"For the ancients or the moderns ?"   The combatants
on each side, as may be supposed, fell into some
ludicrous errors.   They all seemed to have at least one
object in common, and that was to prove how little they
knew what they were talking about.   Elaborate parallels
were drawn between men who in both aims and intellectual sympathies presented a direct contrast to each

other. The ancients held that in science as well as
poetry and eloquence their men were supreme ; Corneille
was declared by the moderns to be more than a match
for all the Greek dramatists together. Equally diverting
were the blunders made on the subject in England,
where the question was eagerly caught up. Sir William
Temple, for example, referred to the veriest fables as
facts, to Orpheus and Arion as historical personages, and
to the Copernican system as having led to "no change
in the conclusions of astronomy." Notwithstanding
Temple's ill-advised essay, the advantage in England
seemed to be with the ancients, though for no better
reason than that Dante and Shakspere, not to speak of
other modern luminaries, were just then unknown or
forgotten. The contest in France had a similar issue,
thanks to the equal ardour and good-sense with which
Boileau—assisted, I presume, by Racine—bore his part
in the controversy, but still more to the inadequate
comprehension by his opponents of their strength.
They, too, knew little or nothing of Shakspere and
Milton, Dante and Tasso, Camoens and Calderon. In
the midst of such a dispute, of course, a tragedy " dans
le goût de Sophocle et d'Euripide," no matter by whom
it was written, could not but cause some excitement.
The ancients were predisposed to condemn it as falling
below the standard aimed at ; and the moderns,
while ruthlessly deriding its deficiencies, resolved

to insist that it might be accepted as a fair sample
of what Sophocles or Euripides would have done if they
had had the good fortune to live in the age of Louis the
Great. *Médée* was not a work to withstand this double
ordeal, although Champmêlé represented the heroine.
The author, in his regard for the severe simplicity of
Greek tragedy, excluded anything in the shape of a
love-intrigue from the plot; but the consequent loss
of interest—a loss keenly felt by all sections of the
audience—was not atoned for by loftiness of conception, theatrical effectiveness, or force of diction. " If,"
writes M. Rousseau—

> " Si le style bucolique
>   L'a dénigré,
> Il veut par le dramatique
>   Etre tiré
> Du rang des auteurs abjects ;
>   Vive les Grecs."

The piece may have had a good *succès de circonstance*,
but as it was withdrawn after a few representations I
infer that Longepierre, perceiving he had failed, made
his pride as an author subordinate to his veneration for
the ancients.

Cervantes was certainly not one of the moderns with
whom the moderns were unacquainted. Don Quixote
enjoyed much consideration in Paris, although he had
never succeeded on the stage. Even when impersonated
by Molière he was pronounced dull. It became an

axiom, indeed, that Don Quixote and Sancho behind
the footlights were like fish out of water, and a further
proof of this was supplied by Dufresny's three-act
comedy *Sancho Pança* (January 27). Devilliers, Desmares and Sévigny were in the cast, but could not make
the piece popular. Its fate was sealed by one of the
unluckiest lines ever put in an actor's mouth. In the
third act the Duke has to say, " I am beginning to get
tired of this Sancho." " Et moi aussi !" shouted a
discontented auditor in the pit ; and the laughter
provoked by the jest was so loud and long that the
actors lowered the curtain without further ado. Scarcely
less unsuccessful, though for other reasons, was a five-
act comedy by Palaprat, *Hercule et Omphale*. Two
hours before the first performance an actress charged
with an important character fell ill, and on arriving
at the theatre the author found to his horror that her
place was to be taken by one to whom the task was
hopelessly unsuited. " It was as though the giant of
the Foire came forward as Brillon in *Le Grondeur*," he
used to say. The company, however, could not be
induced to defer the production, as Monseigneur and
the Prince de Conti had intimated their intention to
be present. Then one of the actors fell ill ; and the
comedy, after lingering some days, was consigned to
oblivion.

CHAPTER VII.

1694—1699.

THE next two novelties given at the theatre in the
Rue des Fossés St. Germain served to introduce a
dramatist who on all hands is allowed to have been
second only to Molière in French comedy—certainly
an enviable distinction.   Dufresny had lately thrown
off a one-act piece under the title of *Attendez-Moi sous*
l'Orme, a story of rural love intrigue, with divertissements of the now familiar kind.   Covetous of literary
fame, a wealthy friend of his, Jean François Regnard,
bought it for 300 livres—a sum much higher than
that which it would have realized in the ordinary
course of business—and had it produced at the Comédie
as his own.   Represented only eleven times at the
outset, it subsequently became a stock piece at the
theatre, and the supposed author did not scruple to
include it in a collection of his works.   That he had
largely added to its attractiveness there can be little
doubt, but even on this hypothesis his entire appropria-
tion of the piece is not to his honour.   In less than
seven weeks after the appearance of *Attendez-Moi sous*

l'Orme, however, he conclusively showed that he could succeed in the drama without assistance from Dufresny or anybody else. He wrote *La Sérénade*, a one-act comedy in prose, with a few divertissements (July 3). Conventional in plot and character, this trifle yet revealed a few of Molière's peculiar qualities in a high degree—gaiety, wit, ease, and intuitive dramatic skill.

Regnard might have found good materials for a romantic play in the records of his life. Eldest son of a prosperous grocer in Paris, he was born there in 1656 or 1657. In early manhood he lost his father, and, finding himself in possession of 40,000 livres, resolved to live for a time in Italy. He there became an inveterate gambler, but played with so much coolness and good fortune that on his return he was richer by at least 10,000 crowns. During a second visit to the land of song he met and fell in love with a married Provençale lady, "Elvire de Prade," then staying with her husband at Bologna. "To see her and to love her," he says, "was for me the same thing." Before long M. de Prade abruptly set out with his wife for Rome, ostensibly on urgent private business, but really because the young Frenchman, not dreaming who he was, had spoken in his presence of the passion with which she had inspired him. Regnard followed them in hot haste, though only to spend much time in a fruitless search for his inamorata. M. de Prade, taking up his quarters in an unfrequented part of the city, rarely allowed his wife to go out of doors, and it was to no purpose that the lover looked for her among the masks at popular revels. Eventually he had the felicity to cross her path, to address her in the language of the heart, and, without receiving positive encouragement, to see that he might hope. " More art," he complacently writes, " is needed to conceal love when it exists than to feign it when it does not, and the secret of that art was not hers." Madame's better resolutions appear to have soon given way, for a few months later, at Civita Vecchia, Regnard had the boldness to embark with her and M. de Prade on board an English ship bound for Toulon. Scarcely had they got out to sea when a Turkish pirate swooped upon them ; and after a short fight, in which the captain and most of his crew, as became their nationality, elected to be killed rather than surrender, the passengers were taken prisoners, landed at Algiers, and sold as slaves to one Achmet Talem.

For about two years the future dramatist had to do the hardest of menial work, but at the end of that period, having shown a remarkable turn for cookery, especially in the matter of *ragoûts*, he was promoted to his master's kitchen. In this capacity he was transferred to Constantinople, where Achmet Talem, " the

hardest man in all Barbary," found it expedient to set
up a commercial establishment. Regnard's burden was
lightened by two circumstances : Elvire had been sent
with him to the Bosphorus, and intelligence reached
them that M. de Prade had died in his captivity at
Algiers. Some accident gave Regnard an opportunity of
communicating with his family, who transmitted 12,000
livres to the French Consul at Constantinople to ransom
their unfortunate relative and his beloved Provençale.
By the time the money arrived, however, he had got
himself into an awkward position. Justly or unjustly,
he was accused of entering into an intrigue with a
Mahommedan girl, and was required by law to become
a convert to her religion or die. He promptly chose
the former course, but a slave in Achmet's seraglio,
inflamed by all the hate of a woman scorned, induced
her master to insist upon the immolation of his
accomplished cook. It was then that the French
Consul came forward with his offer to ransom the two
slaves. As might have been expected, Achmet's cupidity
proved stronger than his reverence for the laws drawn
up in the name of the Prophet. Regnard and Elvire
regained their liberty, and, imagining there was no
further obstacle to their happiness, repaired homewards
to be married. In Paris a terrible blow awaited at
least one of the lovers. Repurchased from Achmet
Talem by two priests, M. de Prade, the report of whose

death was wholly unfounded, reappeared in Paris; and
Elvire, perhaps struck with remorse for her virtual
infidelity towards him, resumed her position as his wife
with a determination never to speak to her companion
in slavery again.

Regnard, instead of abandoning himself to despair,
sought relief from his disappointment in the excitement
of foreign travel. He went to Flanders, Holland,
Denmark, and Sweden. Next, at the instance of the
Swedish King, to whom he had letters of recommendation, and accompanied by two friends, Defercourt and
Decorberon, he visited Lapland, then all but a *terra
incognita* to the rest of Europe. Having well explored
the country, the party penetrated to the Lake of Torno,
and, ascending Mount Metavara, within sight of the
Frozen Sea, carved on a rock the following lines :—

> Gallia nos genuit, vidit nos Africa, Gangem,
> Hausimus, Europamque oculis lustravimus omnem
> Casibus et variis acti terraque, marique ;
> Hic tandem stetimus, nobis ubi defuit orbis.
> De Fercourt, De Corberon, Regnard.
> Anno 1682 ; die 22 Augusti.

Earth had indeed failed them; they could get no
further north. Back to Stockholm they accordingly
turned, to be received there by the King with all the
honour due to travellers who had reached higher
latitudes than any of their predecessors. Regnard,
again left alone, passed into Poland, and was invited by

John Sobieski to Court. His majesty listened with evident interest to his guest's account of the Laplanders, sent every day to ascertain his wishes, and even entertained him at dinner. But these compliments, to use his own words, did not console him. He could not banish the image of Elvire from his mind. "Entraîné de son inquiétude," he extended his tour to Hungary and Turkey and Germany. In or about 1686, cured of his passion for travel, for gambling, but not for the bewitching Elvire, he reappeared in Paris, where startling news awaited him. M. de Prade had just died, and Elvire, still under the influence of remorse, was on the point of entering a convent. Regnard, as may be supposed, spared no pains to divert her from this grim resolution, but apparently without effect. Henceforward the fair Provençale has no place in his biography.

The discarded lover soon became a conspicuous figure in French society. Opulent, hospitable, handsome, of pleasing manners, and furnished by foreign travel and wide reading with a large store of anecdote and information, he necessarily found many friends. Prominent votaries of the muses and fashion gathered round him at his Parisian house, situated at the Montmartre end of the Rue Richelieu, and at a pretty little château which he built on the picturesque slopes of Grillon, near Dourdan, within a day's drive of the capital. In the *salon* of this country retreat, which he embellished with conspicuous

liberality and taste, was to be seen a curious relic of the
darkest period of his career—the chains he had worn
during his slavery at Algiers and Constantinople.
Presently, while his life seemed to be made up of an
unceasing round of pleasure, he began to aim at literary
distinction. In 1688 he wrote for the Théâtre Italien
a three-act comedy, *Le Divorce.* At first it did not
succeed; but Gherardi, who in the following year
selected it for his first appearance, gave it a long-endur-
ing vitality. By 1694 Regnard had added seven pieces
to the repertory of the same theatre, the best of all being
one entitled *La Coquette,* and had taken part with
Dufresny in at least four more. Of the circumstances
attending his first appearance as a dramatist at the
Théâtre Français I have already spoken at sufficient
length. Following in the footsteps of Molière, though
not in a servile spirit, he went very near his model in
genuine gaiety and dramatic skill, which form the
highest and most distinctive feature of his work. His
dialogues often show signs of hasty composition, but
this is not surprising in the case of a man whose social
popularity and hospitable generosity caused so many
demands to be made upon his time. As if those
demands were not more than enough for a man of even
his physical energy, which was considerable, he purchased a treasurership in the Bureau des Finances at
Paris, a lieutenancy of the Eaux des Forêts et des Chasses

of Dourdan and the surrounding country, and other
offices entailing some responsibility to the State.   None
of them, I should think, received a larger share of his.
attention than the first.   Delighted as he may have
been with Grillon, the lively capital was the home of
his choice, the atmosphere in which he had his true
being.   The Comédie Française had no more assiduous
frequenter than the author of the *Sérénade*.

In less than a month after the production of that
comedy another new dramatist came before the public
in the person of Jean Baptiste Rousseau, the author
of the epigrams on Longepierre and his *Médée*.   The
new-comer does not appear to great advantage as he
emerges into the light; he squinted, and it is said that
his face wore a sinister and even forbidding expression.
Nor can he be said to improve with better acquaintance.
He was the son of an honest shoemaker, who, with
ideas soaring above his humble craft, and proud of
some intelligence which the boy had displayed, had
him educated for the Church.   Jean Baptiste, however
had no taste for such a career, although, as we shall
see, he manifested a turn for literature of a devotional
order.   Then, at the instance of one of the shoemaker's
customers, M. François Arouet, the same whom we
have seen in the company of Corneille in the Rue
d'Argenteuil, Jean Baptiste was put into the office
of an attorney named Gentil.   Again were the hopes

of the shoemaker to be dashed; his son, instead of
attending to his duties, spent the day in reading
Catullus—that is, if he were not stalking about Paris
with the airs of a well-born youth—and in the evening
was to be found at the theatre. One day, the story
goes, he was requested to carry some law papers to
the office of a Conseiller au Parlement. Deeming the
office beneath his dignity, yet constrained to obey, he
resentfully sallied forth, appeared before the Conseiller
with a fashionable swagger, and said that as he was
to " pass that way " he had been "asked by his friend
M. Gentil" to deliver the packet. The Conseiller,
having to call upon M. Gentil soon afterwards, saw
the same young gentleman perched on a stool; explana-
tions followed, and in the result Jean Baptiste was
expelled from the office. He then became a man about
town, necessarily at the expense of his father, who could
refuse him nothing, and sought to make himself known
by writing more or less telling epigrams whenever he
had nothing to gain by keeping them to himself. An
excellent background for a one-act comedy soon obtruded itself upon his notice. Few institutions of recent
origin had been more cordially welcomed than the
café, now about five years old. Men of all classes
resorted to it, some to discuss the merits of a new
production in literature or art, some to talk in bated
breath of the politics of the day, some to do purely com-

mercial business. Every evening it boasted a good
company, and at no time was it so much crowded as an
hour or two before and after the production of a new
play at the Comédie Française. This must have been
particularly the case on the 2nd August, when a
performance of the *Cid* was followed by *Le Café*, a one-
act comedy in prose, by M. Jean Baptiste Rousseau.
The best known frequenters of such establishments are
here represented under fictitious names. In the hands
of the author of *Les Fâcheux* such a piece would have
been a long gallery of striking portraits ; but Rousseau,
so far from being a Molière, could not invent a good
plot, write a good dialogue, or sketch a good .character.
His father, shoemaker though he was, could hardly
have been blind to the faults of Jean Baptiste's first
essay in dramatic art.

Better success awaited Boursault's *Mots à la Mode*
(August 19), in which current affectations of speech are
amusingly satirized. Many of the words ridiculed, however, were to be sanctioned by usage. The next novelty
was Dancourt's *Vendanges*, with music by Grandval.
The plot is trite enough, but a lively dialogue saved the
piece. With the 29th November came a *Triomphe de
l'Hiver*, anonymously. I am tempted to think that
Devisé was the author, seeing that in the *Mercure Galant*
for December he inserted a gratuitous and violent
impeachment of the judgment of the pit.   Pradon

now came forward with a *Germanicus*, only, however, to experience fresh mortification. In the first two acts the characters were all men; at the commencement of the third two princesses and two confidants of the same sex met the astonished eyes of the audience. "Four women; are they respectable?" cried a spectator in a strong Gascon accent, and the fatal laughter set in. Racine's epigram on the tragedy was as follows :—

> Que je plains le destin du grand Germanicus!
> Quel fut le prix de ses rares vertus?
> Persécuté par le cruel Tibère,
> Empoisonné par le traître Pison,
> Il ne lui restait plus, pour dernière misère,
> Que d'être chanté par Pradon.

Germanicus was not printed.

While this tragedy was in rehearsal the Comédie suffered some appreciable losses. The clever but misguided wife of Molière took her leave of the scene on the 14th October, although her old power to please had not deserted her. It is true that she was more than fifty years of age, but time had neither made any havoc with her charming voice, seldom heard to better advantage than when she sang in Italian, nor decreased the brightness with which she had filled the characters created for her by her husband. Among these characters, it will be remembered, were the Princesse d'Élide, Célimène, Elmire, Psyché, Lucile, and Angélique. How she played the last, with Lagrange as

Cléante, may be seen from a description given in a little work published in 1681, *Les Entretiens Galants*. In second tragic parts, too, she also proved a valuable actress, and the chief comedy written by Baron, *L'Homme à Bonne Fortune*, owed much to her acting as Léonor. But if time had spared her talents it had at least cooled her head, and the remainder of her life, which ended on the 3rd November 1700, was probably clouded by remorse for her misconduct towards the man under whose fostering care she had grown from infancy to womanhood, whose affection she had repaid with something worse than ingratitude, whose death she had hastened, and whose fame now stood higher than that of any of the illustrious writers gathered round the throne of the Grand Monarque. Jacques Raisin withdrew into private life soon after the "pretty Armande," although he had not been at the Comédie half as long. Inferior as an actor to his brother, he played second tragic characters and lovers with considerable effect, and the comedies he wrote were not without merit, it is said. He died of pleurisy between 1697 and 1700, and was buried at St. Roch. Madame Poisson (Ducroisy's daughter), who had never played anything particularly well except Angélique in the *Triomphe des Dames*, also retired this year, but lived until 1756

Two dramatists who had not openly come forward

for about fourteen years were to resume their pens.
Devisé wrote a comedy under the title of *Les Dames
Vengées, ou le Dupe de Soi-méme,* and the Abbé Boyer
a tragedy in which Judith was the central figure. The
first was intended as a defence of the fair sex against
Boileau's satire, published a short time previously. The
story simply shows us how a libertine with a poor
opinion of women is brought to his senses, but as the
satire had occasioned no little commotion the comedy
achieved more popularity than it deserved, even when
it is allowed that the dialogue is often pointed and
bright. The Abbé Boyer's tragedy has a singular
history. For some time it created nothing less than a
furore. Both the Court and the town came in their
hundreds to see it. The players were at their wits' end
to accommodate the distinguished persons who nightly
presented themselves at the doors. "The seats on
the stage," says the author of the *Valise Trouvée,* "had
to be given up by the men to the women, whose
handkerchiefs were spread out on their knees to wipe
away the tears to be evoked by touching passages.
The usual occupants of the seats had to be content
with the wings. In the fourth act there was a scene
which proved particularly moving, and which for that
reason was called the 'scène des mouchoirs.' The pit,
where laughers are always to be found, made themselves
merry at the expense of these impressionable ladies

instead of weeping with them." Intoxicated with his
success, we are further told, the author frequently
went to the amphitheatre to receive compliments
which a Corneille and Racine might have coveted.
"Monsieur l'Abbé," said one, "this is a sublime and
pathetic piece." "You ought to be well satisfied,"
chimed in another, "with having given us so beautiful a
work; how appreciative the audience are!" "Ah!"
modestly replied the Gascon poet in the accent of his
country, "I shall give them more of the same kind;
I have the public with me now that I know what it
likes." Boileau, as may be supposed, was not carried
away by this current of admiration. "I reserve my
opinion," he said to M. Essain, brother of Madame
de la Sablière, "until the play appears on paper." In
an evil hour the Abbé submitted his work to this crucial
test. Easter having arrived, the theatre was closed
for the customary time, and in the interim *Judith* appeared in print. The charm which it had exercised over
the audience was at once dissolved. Ill-constructed and
badly written, this tragedy, which a few impulsive
admirers had ranked with *Polyeucte* and *Phèdre*, clearly
owed its success to the religious nature of the subject
and the acting of Mdlle. Champmêlé as Judith. In
the result, the public turned against the unfortunate
Abbé with something like fury. They were not
content with leaving the actors to play to empty

benches; the tragedy must be hissed. The theatre, as u~ual, was reopened at Quasimodo, and as soon as the curtain rose on *Judith* the players were saluted with a shower of hisses and derisive laughter. "Messieurs," said Mdlle. Champmêlé to the pit, "is it not rather surprising that you should so receive a piece which you have lately applauded?" "The hisses," replied a spectator, "were at Versailles, for the sermons of the Abbé Boileau." The conduct of the audience was unreasonable enough, but they persisted in their hostility to the piece until it was withdrawn. Racine, of course, did not fail to make an epigram upon it. At one of the representations, we are told, a financier was visibly affected. Boyer, who sat near him, complacently remarked, "Le beau vous touche?" Said the financier—

> Je pleure, hélas ! de ce pauvre Holopherne,
> Si méchamment mis à mort par Judith.

"Monsieur Essain," said Boileau to that person, passing him in the gallery at Versailles, " n'avez-vous point votre Boyer sur vous ?"

Dancourt was particularly active this year. Early in the summer he wrote an agreeable one-act comedy under the title of *Le Tuteur*. The *dénouement* is derived from Lafontaine's story *Le Cocu battu, content,* but the piquant nocturnal scene—imitated in at least two operas of the next century—is apparently original.

Near Paris is a place called Bézons, where a fair had been held from time immemorial at the beginning of every September. This fair, after having been neglected for some years, was now resorted to by the humbler classes of the community, and many pleasant adventures annually occurred there. Out of the materials thus provided Dancourt wrote his *Foire de Bézons* (August 13). The piece, as represented at the Comédie, presented a strong combination of attractions ; the incidents were lively, Gilliers and Montagne had provided it with music and ballets respectively, a good scene of the Fair was painted for it by a clever Italian artist, and two of the characters were charmingly played by daughters of the author. " The demoiselles Dancourt," says a contemporary, " proved particularly attractive. The younger," by name Mimi, " is only nine or ten years of age, but declaims very well. In the piece she is called Clonchette. She bears a strong resemblance to her mother," *née* Thérese Lenoir de Lathorillière, " whose part in the play is called Mariane. The elder," Marie Carton Dancourt, " ten or eleven years of age, has an exquisite face and the most beautiful hair in the world. Her dancing in the *espagnolette* delights everybody." The informal débuts, in fact, were so successful that the girls' parents resolved to prepare them for more onerous work on the stage. The *Foire de Bézons* had thirty-three representations, new scenes being added to

it as the run drew to an end.   Another one-act comedy
from ⁺he same pen, *Les Vendanges de Suréne*, remained
even longer on the bills, but was by no means so good.

Marie and Mimi Dancourt were not the only new
players brought forward at this time.   Etienne Baron
began a début in form after Easter, and was received
for second tragic characters and first parts in the *haut
comique*.   His acting is described as cold, but it is
possible that the ˙defect would not have been so
apparent if the name he bore had not brought him
into direct contrast with a greater player.   I also
perceive in the theatre a Mdlle. Clavel, received to
double Madame Raisin, but incurably nervous before
an audience, and a Madame Champvallon, who,
although her first essays were made in tragedy, could
play nothing well except *rôles chargés*.   Some losses,
too, have to be chronicled; Mdlle. Bélonde, who had
never realized the high promise of her youth, quitted
the theatre on the 1st of April; and Sévigny, persecuted by creditors, left Paris for the provinces.

More than one link between the halcyon days of
the French drama and the less fruitful present was
severed as the year wore on.   Lafontaine died in
the Rue Platrière on the 31st March, and, in compliance with his own request, was laid by the side
of Molière in that miserable little yard in the Rue
Montmartre.   He necessarily knew that it had been

set apart for the remains of felons and suicides and unchristened children, but this did not prevent him from resolving to be near his old friend in the grave. In *Le Veau Perdu*, produced about two years previously, his comparatively unimportant connexion with the theatre was brought to a close. Soon after the acceptance of that piece, believing that he had only a few hours to live, he sent for the curé of St. Eustache, who firmly refused to give him absolution unless he destroyed a five-act comedy which he had just finished for the Comédiens du Roi. Dramatic authorship had not been expressly stigmatized as a crime by the Church, but the curé took pride in being a little more bigoted and less inconsistent than his superiors. Lafontaine, deeming the condition too hard, referred the matter to the Doctors of the Sorbonne, especially as they had taken part with Anne of Austria when, about forty years previously, the curé of St. Germain l'Auxerrois held her to be guilty of mortal sin in favouring theatrical performances. In the opinion of that venerable body, however, a citizen was to be blamed for writing what a queen might listen to with impunity ; they promptly decided against the poet, and the manuscript of his unacted comedy was unwillingly put into the fire. Dramatic literature, it must be confessed, did not suffer a heavy loss by this new illustration of ecclesiastical intolerance.

Lafontaine had never possessed the secret of captivating an audience. His pieces are wanting in the essential qualities of good plays, and his delightful style was of a nature to be appreciated in the library rather than the theatre. Nevertheless, he had long believed that he was fitted to achieve success as a dramatist. His earliest known work, written at Château Thierry, his native place, soon after his marriage to Marie Héricart (who, by the way, was shrewish enough to pass for the original of Madame Honesta in *Belphégor*), and at a time when his peculiar genius, first aroused in him by admiration of Malherbe, had been nourished by a study of ancient and mediæval poetry, was a version of the *Eunuchus*. It was printed in 1654, but does not seem to have been represented in Paris. In all probability the players returned it to him as unsuited to their purposes. For about thirty years he did not again trouble himself with stage work. Indolent, careless of fame unless it came to him without much wooing, lifted above want by a little patrimony and the hospitality of friends, and discouraged, perhaps, by a rebuff such as I have suggested, the *bonhomme* now separated from his wife, to whom, however, he paid a friendly visit at Château Thierry every autumn, failed to muster more energy during that period than was necessary to produce the *Contes* and the first and second parts of the *Fables*. *Ragotin* broke his long silence in regard to the theatre, and it pleased the audience well enough to induce him to write the other pieces standing to his credit at the Comédie Française.   For the Palais Royal, while completing the third portion of his *Fables*, he invented two operas, *Astrée* and *Daphné*, neither of which succeeded. It appears that he did not rate his powers as a librettist very highly.   " Detestable ! " he frequently exclaimed in the theatre during the first act of *Astrée*.   " Monsieur," said a lady by his side, not recognizing him, " it is really not so bad as you say.   It is written by a man of fine wit—M. de Lafontaine."   " M. de Lafontaine," was the reply, " is an ass ; and as I am that person himself I ought to know."   Directly afterwards he went to the Café Procope, just opposite the theatre, and fell asleep. " How is this ? " asked a friend, coming in and waking him up; " ought you not to see the first performance of your opera ? "   " I have been," said the librettist with a yawn ; " but the first act was so dull that I came away when it closed.   I admire the patience of these Parisians ! "   As we have seen, this tendency to depreciate himself was allied to peculiar absent-mindedness, simplicity, candour, and warmth of heart, though some of the stories told of him on the first point are probably exaggerations.   Even the prospect of being denied a share of Court favour could not deter him from doing public homage to the disgraced Minister who had

befriended him in early life—an incident which led
the King to retard his admission to the Academy.
Notwithstanding the licentiousness of his conduct, he
seems to have been regarded with affectionate reverence
by his friends, and was never in want of a home in
the houses of the wealthiest of the number. For some
years he was the permanent guest of Madame de la
Sablière, who pleasantly remarked, after breaking up her
establishment, that she had "kept only her cat, her
dog, and Lafontaine." His proverbial laziness, perhaps,
was thrown into clearer relief by the industry of a man
of letters now on the point of seeking well-earned repose.
Since 1647, when *Les Engagements du Hasard* appeared,
Thomas Corneille had written thirty-seven plays, besides
contributions to the *Mercure*, a new edition of Vaugelas,
translations from Latin, and what not. He was now
old, feeble, and nearly blind ; and in the November of
this year, after writing a *Bradamanthe*, the subject of
which (taken, of course, from Ariosto) hardly suited
the anti-romanesque taste of the time, the brother of the
author of the *Cid* left Paris to spend the short remainder
of his life in the Andelys.

Bradamanthe was followed by another tragedy by
Longepierre, *Sésostris*. It failed ; and Racine, though
well aware that the author had praised *Andromaque* and
Phèdre with eloquence and judgment, wrote the following
epigram upon it :

Ce fameux conquérant, ce vaillant Sés stris,
Qui jadis en Egypte, au gré des Destinées,
Véquit de si longues années,
N'a vécu qu'un jour à Paris.

" M. Racine," said the author good-humouredly, " is
not quite correct ; *Sésostris* has had *two* representations."
However, he took his disappointment so much to heart
that nearly a quarter of a century passed before he
wrote another piece. *L'Aventurier*, a five-act comedy
in prose, by Devisé, did fall at the first representation ;
nor was a much happier fate in store for the piece which
followed. Regnard and Dufresny had sent to the
Théâtre Italien a comedy in three acts, *La Foire St.
Germain*, and Dancourt now brought out at the Français
a one-act piece under the same title. It was hissed ;
and the Italiens, overjoyed at the discomfiture of their
powerful rivals, held them up to public ridicule in a
couple of verses added to one of the songs in Regnard
and Dufresny's piece.

Polixène, the only new tragedy brought out at the
Français in the year 1696, was from a pen which
three years afterwards was justly pronounced inferior
only to those of Corneille and Racine. Antoine de
Lafosse, Sieur d'Aubigny, was the son of a Paris
goldsmith, and was born as far back as 1653. In
early life, thanks to the influence of his uncle, the
painter, he was appointed secretary to Foucher, French
envoy at Florence, and during his stay in that city

became a member of an important Academy. In
addition to various poems, he wrote at this time a short
but amusing treatise on the question whether black or
blue eyes are the more beautiful, a question which he
decides by awarding the advantage to those which
regard him favourably, be they of what colour they may.
He was now in Paris as secretary to the Marquis de
Créqui, and devoting his leisure to the composition
of tragedies in a long-discredited style. With the
dramatic policy of Racine he had little or no sympathy.
He loved to deal with a terrible event and its consequences, to excite admiration and terror rather than
the tenderer sensibilities. In Parisian society he was
known as a man of very engaging manners, modest
without affectation, and with a singularly abstracted
air. He one day left his house to dine with a M. du
Tillet, but his mind was so occupied with a passage
in the *Ilias* that he forgot the appointment, wandered
as far as Ivry, and did not remember the appointment
until he was nearly famished. His *Polixène*, in which
Mdlle. Champmêlé, Beaubourg, Etienne Baron, Roselis,
and Guérin appeared, revealed high qualities—breadth
of conception, clearness of characterization, and force of
language. The greatest blemish was an over-abundance
of incident, a fact which will astonish those who are
familiar only with his subsequent plays. Racine wrote
no epigram upon *Polixène*, a fact which, seeing that

he was unacquainted with Lafosse, is assuredly not without significance.

The last piece offered by Devisé to the Comédie Française, *Le Vieillard Couru*, was produced on the 24th March. In the character of Farfadet an old commissaire aux Saisies-réelles was put on the stage in his own name, an almost unprecedented circumstance. Devisé also projected at this time a *Divertissement pour Monseigneur*, but did not send it to the theatre. For the last four years of his life, which ended in 1710, the founder of the *Mercure Galant* was quite blind, but even in his affliction he retained the polished manners which he had acquired during his intercourse with the world. His *Vieillard Couru* was followed by Regnard's second piece at the Français, *Le Bourgeois de Falaise*, subsequently christened *Le Bal.* In this, as in other pieces of the time, a commonplace love intrigue is set off by a brisk dialogue and an entertaining valet. Both original and lively was the plot of *Le Moulin de Javelle*, a one-act comedy in prose (July 7). This mill was situated on the plain of Grenelle, near the bank of the Seine, and an adventure which occurred there forms the basis of the piece in question. *Le Moulin de Javelle* is to be found in Dancourt's works, but seems to have been only revised by that ever industrious author. In the registers of the Comédie for 1696 the following entry may be found: "On a accordé à M. Michault,.

de qui on a lu à l'assemblée une petite pièce intitulée
Le Moulin de Javelle, d'entrer à la Comédie *gratis*
pendant l'année, quoique la pièce," as he wrote it,
" n'ait pas été acceptée, afin de l'engager à travailler,
et qu'il puisse connaître le théâtre en voyant la
comédie." However this may be, two other one-act
comedies given this year—*Les Eaux de Bourbon* and
Les Vacances—are indisputably by Dancourt. Jean
Baptiste Rousseau seems to have undergone the course
of instruction recommended to M. Michault, for his
five-act comedy in prose, *Le Flatteur* (November 24)
was received with loud applause. What is alleged
to have been a faithful portrait of himself is presented
in a very dramatic setting, and the character is undoubtedly effective. Devilliers headed the cast, supported
by Guérin, Mdlle. Raisin, Mdlle. Beauval, Desmares, and
Lathorillière. In the pit, brimming over with parental
pride, was the shoemaker to whom the author owed his
being, his education, and the means of living as a man
of fashion. The performance over, we are told, the old
man went round to the stage-door, found his way to
the green-room, and, perceiving his son in the midst
of a group of beaux, bluntly gave expression to the
feelings which a proud father would naturally experience on such an occasion. But Jean Baptiste had a soul
above his humble extraction. " *He* my father," he said
to his companions in a contemptuous tone, " the fellow

must be mad!" and forthwith, no doubt, poor M.
Rousseau was shown the nearest way to the street.
Gaçon, "subaltern rhymester," probably knew something of Jean Baptiste's private character when he
wrote :

> Cher Rousseau, ta perte est certaine,
> Tes pièces désormais vont toutes échouer ;
> En jouant le Flatteur tu t'attires la haîne
> Du seul qui te pouvait louer—

and the prophecy was to be fulfilled.

The players, after wasting some valuable time over
Polymnestor, a tragedy by the Abbé Genest, turned their
attention to a comedy which is remarkable at once for
its intrinsic worth and for the circumstances in which
it was written.   I speak of Regnard's *Joueur*, represented
for the first time on the 19th December.   No one save
the creator of Tartuffe has set before us so striking a
character as that of the generous and high-spirited youth
who sacrifices to the dice-box most of what a man holds
dear—peace of mind, health, fortune, a promising future,
the portrait of a beloved mistress.   No doubt Regnard
was indebted to his own experience of the gaming-table
for some of the most graphic details of the picture,
but the picture in its entirety could not have been
executed by anything short of dramatic genius.   The
other characters, too, are drawn with singular skill.   It
is not easy to conceive a better specimen of the *coquette
ridicule* than the Comtesse, a livelier valet than Hector,

or a more engaging soubrette than Nérine. In all
respects, indeed, the work is one of the highest excellence ; and the scene in which Valère, stretched upon
a sofa, gloomily ponders over his losses, the valet
meanwhile reading to him with imperturbable *sangfroid* the discourse of Seneca on the vanity of riches,
stands alone. Nor were the audience lukewarm in
acknowledging the merits of the play. *Le Joueur*
became the talk of the town, and the man who had
worn chains at Algiers and Constantinople was recognized on nearly all hands as the first comic dramatist of
his time.

His triumph, however, was not without drawbacks.
Dufresny came out with a somewhat startling statement.
In the previous year he had written a play called *Le
Chevalier Joueur*, in which the baneful effects of gambling
had been set in the strongest light. The outline of
this play he had communicated to Regnard, who in the
Joueur had turned it to account with scarcely a single
alteration in outline. In fairness, therefore, the honours
bestowed upon Regnard should be shared by him with
his collaborateur at the Théâtre Italien. Nor, according
to Dufresny, could Regnard claim the credit of having
written the verse. In order to get *Le Joueur* out before
the other piece, he had called to his assistance the
poetaster Gaçon, carried him off to the little château
at Grillon, shut him up in a room overlooking the grounds,

gave him the *Joueur* in prose, and never allowed him to come out until he had declared upon his oath from the window that he had got through a certain number of lines. Apart from some comparatively unimportant details, therefore, Regnard was no more the author of the *Joueur* than the man in the moon, and, in addition to losing the credit of having written it, must stand convicted of an unscrupulous plagiarism.

How far these grave charges were justified we may soon ascertain. The players, with a keen eye to their own interests, brought out *Le Chevalier Joueur* with the least possible delay (February 27). Doubtless the resemblance between the two comedies was remarkably close. In each there was a gamester who sacrifices all to his dominant passion, a mistress who is predisposed to overlook his faults, a soubrette who discovers food for her wit in his madness. In some scenes, too, the language was to the same purport. It might be suggested that *Le Joueur* was written before the other play, and that to shield himself from an accusation of plagiarism Dufresny made such an accusation against Regnard. This idea, I think, is quite untenable ; it was obviously to the advantage of the needy Dufresny to continue on good terms with the opulent Regnard, and the history of *Attendez-moi sous l'Orme* is a proof that the latter was far from disinclined to pass off the work of another as his own. In my opinion, therefore, Regnard advisedly abused the confidence reposed in him by Dufresny to steal the plot of *Le Chevalier Joueur*—a breach of honour which, judged even by the then standard of morality, must be pronounced unsusceptible of palliation. But in admitting as much I do not allow that Dufresny's claim ought to be respected. He is no more entitled to share the credit of writing *Le Joueur* than the author of the *Troublesome Reign of King John* is entitled to share with Shakspere the credit of writing *King John*. *Le Chevalier Joueur* is similar to the *Joueur* in form and substance, but it emitted scarcely a gleam of the soul and spirit which distinguished the latter. Dufresny provided the statue; Regnard made it speak. And this was the judgment of the audience at the Théâtre Français. *Le Chevalier Joueur* would not do after the other play, and after a brief and inglorious existence was withdrawn.

Between *Le Joueur* and *Le Chevalier Joueur* there came yet another tragedy by Pradon—*Scipion l'Afriquain*. In the first instance it had been rejected, and might never have been heard of again if the author had not expressed his willingness to make the most sweeping alterations that might be required. It is to be regretted that the players did not adhere to their original intention. The stage could only be degraded by the production of a piece in which Hannibal becomes a mere vehicle of empty declamation, and Scipio, though introduced under circumstances of a nature to set off the elevation of his character, a coxcomb of a very ordinary stamp.

> Ses héros sont enfin si différents d'eux-mêmes
> Qu'un Quidam, les voyant plus masqués qu'en un bal,
> Dit que Pradon donnait au milieu de Carême
> Une pièce de Carnaval,

Gaçon asserts. In another epigram, suggested to Jean Baptiste Rousseau by a satire written at this time by Pradon against the critical Boileau, it is said—

> Hé ! croyez-moi, restez en paix ;
> En vain tenteriez-vous de ternir sa mémoire ;
> Vous n'avancerez rien pour votre propre gloire,
> Et le grand Scipion sera toujours mauvais.

M. Rousseau also found room for an epigram in the case of a comedy called *Le Lourdat*, by Debrie. This piece was condemned on the first night, although the author had filled the pit with men hired to applaud. Debrie, whom we shall not meet again, ascribed his failure to the warmth of the weather, just as he had ascribed the failure of another of his works, *Les Héraclides*, to the severity of the winter of 1695. Rousseau suggested that in each case the cause was the same—*le froid*.

By a rare stroke of good fortune for the Comédiens du Roi, who continued to make them the allowance decided upon in 1680, the Italian players were now to vanish from Paris. For at least twelve years the attractiveness of this troupe had been steadily declining.

Scaramouche, the actor so highly eulogized by Dangeau, died in 1685. He was more than eighty years of age, but is said to have retained much of his old mimetic power to the end. In order to counterbalance their loss, it would seem, his comrades began to give their pieces with a large admixture of French, if not in French altogether. The Comédie Française contended that this was an infringement of their privileges, and the King called upon Baron and Dominique to argue the point in his presence. "Sire," said Arlequin, when his turn came, "in what language shall I speak?" "In any language you like," replied the King. "In that case," said Arlequin, "I have nothing more to say; my cause is gained." Diverted by the trick, Louis declared that he would not go from his word, and the Italians triumphantly abandoned their mother tongue on the stage. Dominique did not live very long after this curious incident. "Arlequin," writes Dangeau on the 2d August 1688, "died to-day in Paris. Report says that he was worth 300,000 livres. He had been permitted to take the sacrament, having promised not to return to the theatre." Further weakened by his death, the company courted popularity by importing satirical portraits of influential personages into their plays, and by doing so completely cut the ground from beneath their feet. In the spring of 1697 they announced a novelty called *La Fausse Prude.* Madame

de Maintenon, learning that its satire was directed
against herself, induced the King to send them back
to their native country ; and the old Hôtel de Bourgogne, which may be called the cradle of the French
tragic drama, ceased for a time to be applied to theatrical
purposes.

But to return to the Comédie Française. In the
Abbé Bruey's *Empiriques* (June 4), *Le Malade Imaginaire* is more than once brought to mind. A hypocon-
driacal Baron declares that he will not consent to the
marriage of his daughter until he gets well. The
lover introduces his valet into the household as a
doctor, and the father, fed upon medicated soups and
wines of the finest quality, gaily concedes what is
required of him. In Dancourt's *Loterie* (July 10) we
have another *pièce de circonstance.* An Italian named
Fagnani, established for some years in Paris as a
" marchand curieux et procurateur," had just patron-
ized a lottery at a crown a chance, no blanks. It
was soon filled ; and great was the indignation of the
populace on discovering that nine-tenths of the lots
were mere bagatelles, and that by some unexplained
means every article of value had gone in one direction. In *La Loterie* Dancourt had the temerity to
hold up the impostor to public reprobation under the
name of Sbrigani, and as a man so far puffed up by
his ill-gotten money as for a time to refuse to allow

his daughter to marry a youth to whom her hand was promised. The latter, having stolen an interview with his mistress, finds it necessary to conceal himself in one of the lots, a china chest, just before it is sold, and is not a little dismayed to recognize in the winner of it an uncle from whom he had reason to keep his love-making a secret. *Le Charivari*, by the same author (September 19) owes its title to the divertissement rather then the intrigue, in which two lovers have to disguise themselves as loutish countrymen in order to win the daughters of a woman afflicted with an insane predilection for the bucolic. One of the characters, Thibaut, is of more than average excellence.

Regnard and Lagrange-Chancel were again before the public towards the close of the year, the former with *Le Distrait*, a five-act comedy in verse (December 2), the other with an *Oreste et Pylade*. In the former piece, it has been pointed out, the author does little more than dramatize a series of anecdotes strung together by La Bruyère in one of his *Caractères*, the Comte de Brancas. Now, a personage depending for effect upon sheer absence of mind is not, of course, very dramatic. It might be set with advantage in a one-act comedy, but can hardly bear the weight of five acts constructed with a view to its development. Evidently perceiving this, Regnard sought to make up for the want of interest by lively traits of character,

such as the extravagancies of a Dame Grognac, and
diverting minor incidents ; and he succeeded so well
that in the hands of a competent company the play
would give no inconsiderable pleasure. It seems that
this condition was not fulfilled at the outset ; the
Distrait, at all events, had only four representations.
Better success awaited Lagrange-Chancel's tragedy
(December 10). The omniscient fops of the day would
have it that Racine had sketched the plot and characters
of this tragedy at the request of the Princesse de Conti,
and that Lagrange-Chancel had merely written the
verse. Those who believed the report after seeing the
play must have been prepared to admit that Racine was
capable of standing in the way of a rising dramatist
under the pretence of serving him. So ill-contrived a
plot had never been developed in the theatre since the
days of Hardi. Important events sprang from ridiculously inadequate causes. If Racine really had a hand
in the work—certainly an improbable supposition—it
was to be found in the versification, which here and
there rose to eloquence, and in the characters of
Iphigénie and Oreste, which were drawn with some force.
Mdlle. Champmêlé, though no longer possessed of the
charms of youth, appeared as the heroine, and the
author not too modestly alleges that she " drew as many
tears in his tragedy as in the *Iphigénie* of M. Racine."

Early in the following year we find the Comédie

Française illuminated on account of the Peace of Ryswick, by which the war begun eight or nine years previously had been brought to a close. The players, to do them justice, were not unequal to the occasion. In front of their house, according to the *Mercure Galant*, there ran a balustrade decorated with trophies of arms. In the centre of it was a statue showing the Grand Monarque crowned by Victory and Peace. On lower pedestals were figures of Faith and Hope and Charity, "all seeming to look with pleasure upon the Prince whom they had made so perfect." Might, Prudence, Justice, and Temperance were also represented. On the pedestal which bore the statue of the King were these lines :

> Ludovicus Maximus
> Fide, Spe, et Charitate,
> Rex vere Christianissimus,
> Fortitudine Victor,
> Prudentia nodum solvit,
> Justitia dat pacem,
> Temperantia subsidia revocat.

For some days these and other decorations were brilliantly illuminated by countless lamps until two o'clock in the morning. Before midnight fireworks were let off amidst exhilarating music from the orchestra of the theatre, and the air resounded with acclamations.

Paris in general was drunk with joy. Illuminations met the eye at every turn. From the high summit of St. Germain l'Auxerrois the capital appeared like one blaze of light. Not that the terms of the Peace were exactly what a patriotic and discerning Frenchman would have wished. The advantage clearly rested on the side of England. Louis XIV. had had to relinquish most of his conquests, to abandon the Jacobites to their fate, and to recognize William of Orange as King of Great Britain and Ireland. He had waged a war without aggrandisement, but under existing conditions no better terms could be obtained. France at this time was in the deepest conceivable distress. Her corn and wine had more than once failed. The fresh imposts devised for the purpose of carrying on the war had reduced multitudes to the verge of starvation. "The strains of the *Te Deum* sung in the churches on account of the triumphs of the French arms were mingled with pitiful wails." Men and women and children died on the highways and in the streets. The military forces of the country were paralysed, and the King could do nothing but yield to the force of circumstances with the best grace he could assume. No wonder that the populace went into transports of delight on hearing of the peace. For once it mattered little to them how such a boon had been procured.

Perhaps no one felt more deeply for the impoverished people than a man who in many ways had shown himself to be strangely hard of nature. Historiographer to the King, Racine had bestowed his best attention

on public affairs, and the sufferings of his countrymen during the war could not but excite his compassion. He communicated his ideas on the subject
to Madame de Maintenon, who asked him to embody
them in writing. Might not the pen which had so often
moved the King in verse have a similar effect in prose?
Racine's self-esteem was so far flattered by the request
as to blind him to the dangers of compliance. He drew
up a plan by which the prevailing distress might be
materially alleviated. Louis, whose temper had been
visibly soured by his humiliations, chanced to find his
wife reading the paper. " M. Racine," he said after
looking at it, "must not imagine that because he is a
great poet he ought to be a minister of state." Racine
soon had cause to regret that he had meddled with
other than his own business. Not only was Madame
de Maintenon required to dispense with his attendance
at Court until further orders, but the King, meeting
him in the gallery at Versailles, passed him without
a sign of recognition. The poet felt his disgrace very
keenly, the more so because it must have become a source
of indecent mirth to the many enemies whom his success
at Court and chilling manners had raised against him.
His mortification aggravated a malady from which he had
long suffered, an abscess of the liver; and he returned
to the Faubourg St. Germain in a state of health which
justly gave rise to the gloomiest apprehensions.

News of a great dramatic success reached his ears soon afterwards. *Manlius Capitolinus*, unquestionably the best of the tragedies bearing Lafosse's name, appeared on the 18th January. By many estimable judges the play was deemed worthy of Corneille in his best days. In this they went too far; but I have no hesitation in affirming that few plays of the seventeenth century had come so near those of Corneille and Racine in depth of interest, artistic development, and beauty of detail. Not that these merits belong exclusively to Lafosse. His contemporaries supposed that he had merely borrowed the story from the conspiracy against Venice, as told by the Abbé de St. Réal. In point of fact he was considerably indebted to an English tragedy suggested by the same book—the ill-starred Otway's *Venice Preserved*, produced at Dorset Gardens, London, in 1682. *Manlius* was similar to that effusion of genius in its vividly conceived characters, its dramatic force, and its arrangement of scenes. In refinement of taste the copy is superior to the original, but a comparison of the two will prove that *Manlius* is really nothing more than a skilful adaptation of *Venice Preserved* to the French stage, with the scene of the story transferred to ancient Rome. It unfortunately remains to be added that Lafosse did not acknowledge his obligations to the English poet—a piece of disingenuousness for which even the ideas of that period afford no justification.

Mdlle. Champmêlé intended to play the Belvidera of *Manlius*, but was compelled by ill-health to transfer the part to another. Racine's erstwhile mistress now resided at Auteuil, in a house but a short distance from that formerly occupied by Molière. In the beginning of the spring it became evident that her end was at hand, and efforts were made to prevail upon her to reconcile herself to the Church by formally renouncing the stage. For some time these importunities proved of no avail. Proud of her art, she declared that, whatever the clergy might do with her remains, she would die as she had lived, an actress. Eventually her friends induced her to retract this determination, and the sacrament was administered to her with the usual solemnity. Not many hours afterwards, on the 15th May, the Parisians heard to their sorrow that Mdlle. Champmêlé, though only fifty-four years of age, had passed away. In her last hours, according to Racine, she was very contrite as to her transgressions, and viewed the approach of death with something like terror. Her body was interred at Saint Sulpice, in the presence of the flower of the Comédie Française. No less a mark of respect was due to her memory. For more than a quarter of a century her sympathetic and powerful impersonations of the heroines of French tragedy had placed her at the head of her profession ; and her style—just now out of fashion—had all the charms which a high regard for truth could impart. Her death must have been regretted by every thinking playgoer, especially as Mdlle. Duclos, her successor, did not catch her mantle, and as nothing now remained to interfere with the reign of inflated declamation on the stage.

For a year after her death the few tragedy writers of the time made no sign. As though to make amends for their unproductiveness, Dancourt worked with more than his usual assiduity. He gave the world two pleasant little comedies—*Les Curieux de Compiègne* and *Le Mari Retrouvé*. The former illustrated some adventures among the crowd which assembled in the neighbourhood of the place named to witness a mimic siege, arranged by the King for the military instruction of the Duc de Bourgogne. The incidents of *Le Mari Retrouvé* were derived from a *cause célèbre* of the day. In 1697 a Madame de la Pivardière was accused of having murdered her husband, who had mysteriously disappeared. Soon afterwards he reappeared in excellent health, but the magistrates of Châtillon-sur Indre, where he usually resided, treated him as an impostor until his identity was formally established by the Parliament. *Le Mari Retrouvé* was represented while the matter was *sub judice*, and may have done something to further the lady's cause. These *pièces de circonstance* remained on the bills much longer than

La Mort d'Othon (January 5), a tragedy by M. Belin, librarian to the Duchesse de Bouillon, and *Myrtil et Mélicerte*, heroic pastoral (January 10). The author of the latter was the son of Mdlle. Molière by her second marriage ; but, although his father was still at the Comédie, the piece would have been returned to him as worthless if Mdlle. Raisin had not induced Monseigneur to command its performance. M. Guérin jun. was both disliked and ridiculed behind the scenes ; he was a coxcomb of a particularly disagreeable type, and his extremely tall and thin figure, joined to a constrained manner, probably due to the fact that until a year or two previously he had been compelled by physical weakness to wear irons, made people say that he had " l'air d'un manche à balai habillé."

A well-graced actress made a formal début at the Comédie on the 30th January. This was Charlotte Antoinette Desmares, daughter of the clever representative there of peasants and other characters, and a niece, therefore, of Mdlle. Champmêlé. The new candidate's face was not unfamiliar to the audience, as for a few years she had been employed in the theatre to play child-parts. I do not meet with her name before the 23rd August 1690, when she appeared in an unsuccessful five-act comedy called *Le Cadet de Gascogne.* Had *Athalie* been represented she would probably have played Joas. It now became evident

that she had inherited in a large measure the fascin-
ations of her father's sister.   Inferior to Mdlle. Duclos,
perhaps, in parts demanding majesty of bearing and
impetuous sweep of passion, she undoubtedly surpassed
her in pathos and tenderness, whether as Queens or
Princesses.   In soubrettes, moreover, she displayed
qualities which Duclos could not pretend to possess—
archness, piquancy, the most subtle humour.   In her
portrait at the Comédie Française we see a personally
attractive woman, one whose lively and spirituelle face
had a distinct charm of its own.   The players received
her with acclamation ; and in the last character created
by Mdlle. Champmêlé, the Iphigénie of *Oreste et Pylade*,
she proved that her success was fully deserved.

During the début of Mdlle. Desmares more than one
altercation may have been heard behind the scenes.
The players, after bringing out an indifferent *Méléagre*
by Lagrange-Chancel, turned their attention to a tragedy
by the Abbé Brueys, *Gabinie*.   The character of Séréna,
Diocletian's wife, had been written expressly for Madame
Beauval, who, however, positively declined to accept it.
M. l'Abbé Brueys, she said, had allotted the chief part
in *L'Important* to M. Devilliers, although her kinsman
Beaubourg ardently wished to play it.   For this reason
she would not lend the advantage of her experience to
any play the Abbé might write.   But Mdlle. Beauval
was not the only actress in the world, however strong

her opinion to the contrary might be. The author, instead of withdrawing his tragedy in despair, as she probably anticipated, assigned Séréna to Mdlle. Duclos, who undertook it without hesitation. Brought out on the 14th March, *Gabinie* was rather well received, and the character refused by Mdlle. Beauval proved of marked service to its representative. In writing *Gabinie* the Abbé evidently desired to ascertain how far the vein of ore struck upon by Racine in *Esther* and *Athalie* might be worked with profit, and—perhaps in order to save time—he appropriated the plot of a Latin tragedy written nearly fifty years previously, under the title of *Susanne*, by a Père Jourdain. The name of Susanne not being deemed sufficiently " noble " for the theatre, the tragedy was christened after her father, little as he had to do with the story.

Gabinie, more fortunate than tragedies of higher claims, was not to be made the subject of an injurious epigram by Racine. Since his virtual expulsion from Court, it would appear, the health of the illustrious dramatist had been steadily giving way. Neither religion nor philosophy could reconcile him to the loss of the proud position he had enjoyed there for nearly thirty years. He found no consolation in his family, his books, or his work as an historian. Falling into a sort of lethargy, he ceased to take any pleasure in life, any interest in what was passing in the busy world

around him.   Nor had he reason to hope that the sun-
shine of royal favour would again light up his path.
It was in vain that he addressed to Madame de Maintenon a letter apologizing for the " presumption " which
resulted in his disgrace—" a singular instance how
genius can degrade itself when it has placed all its
felicity in the varying smiles of those we call the great "
—or that the uncrowned wife of the King now and
then dropped a word in his behalf.   One morning, as
the story goes, she met him in the gardens of Versailles,
and, drawing aside into an unfrequented grove, assured
him that all would yet be well.   " Never, Madam,"
said the dispirited poet.   " Have you any doubts as to
either my goodwill or my influence ? " she asked.   " I
am aware of both," he replied ; " but I have an aunt
who thinks of me in quite a different way ; every day
that pious woman implores God to bestow humiliation
and occasions for penitence upon me, and she has more
influence than you."   At this point the rumbling of
coach-wheels over the gravelled path was heard.   " It
is the King ! " cried Madame ; " quick ; hide yourself ! "
And in a moment he had disappeared in a thicket.
Returning to his house in the Rue du Marais St.
Germain, he was seized with a rather violent fever, and
the internal malady already spoken of assumed alarming
proportions.   In extreme pain, but cheered to the last
by the presence and sympathy of Boileau, the staunchest

of friends, he died on the morning of the 21st April, aged fifty-nine years and four months.

In him, as every student of literature knows, there passed away the last of the few great poets who shed lustre upon the Louis Quatorze era. He had given a new charm to existence; and. his successor at the Academy, the erudite Valincourt, bore eloquent testimony within its walls to the pure intellectual pleasure afforded by his work. "His natural gifts as a poet," said the orator, "were seconded by an excellent education. In boyhood, captivated by the beauties of ancient poetry, he would bury himself in the woods near Port Royal to study Homer, Sophocles, and Euripides, whose language became as familiar to him as his own. Before long, putting into practice what he had learnt from these great masters, he produced his first great work at an age when it is still a merit to have only read the works of others. Pierre Corneille was then in possession of the stage. The admiration he excited went to the verge of idolatry. Racine, instead of seeking to imitate a man who was deemed on all hands to be inimitable, opened out a path for himself. Contrary to the practice of Corneille, he entered, so to speak, into the spectator's heart, of which he made himself the master. He painted human nature on a less ambitious scale than his predecessor, perhaps, but with greater truth and sensibility. In the result, the impartial public, without ceasing to admire the majesty of Corneille, began to appreciate the graces of Racine; and the French stage, rising to the height of its glory, had no longer reason to envy the achievements of the theatre at Athens. But when, abandoning the profane Muses, he devoted his pen to objects more worthy of his genius, what miracles he still contrived to produce! *Esther* and *Athalie* are equal, if not superior, to *Andromaque* and *Phèdre.* I need hardly speak of the inexpressible charms of his conversation, of the brilliant imagination which made the simplest things attractive in his mouth. And who could believe that a man born with so rare a command of poetry would be a fine orator as well? It would not have been credited in Rome or Athens, but the French Academy is constantly furnishing illustrious examples of such a combination. You do not forget the force and grace with which he spoke at your meetings, especially in descanting upon the merits of the great dramatist whom he followed. To do his own merits justice I should have to borrow the flowers he scattered over the tomb of Corneille on that occasion."

Louis XIV. spoke with respect of the man whom he had hurried to the grave. "Despréaux," he said to the satirist at their next meeting, "you and I have suffered an appreciable loss in the death of Racine." "Sire," replied Boileau, "we have indeed; but I have the consolation of knowing that my friend died as became a

true Christian, and, afraid though he had always been of
death, with unfaltering courage." In a Latin epitaph,
too, he tells us that the poet passed away with a "firm
hope and confidence in God." Nor are the depth and
sincerity of his faith open to question. It was chiefly
from a mistaken sense of religious duty that at the early
age of thirty-eight, before his genius had reached its
maturity, he deliberately abandoned what to him must
have been the most fascinating of pursuits. But the
elevating influences which then came upon him could
not soften the repelling traits in his character. Except
as regards his domestic life, which from the time of his
marriage presented no opportunities for scandal, he was
very much the same Racine as of yore. In the records
of his latter years we still find him supercilious, vain,
envious, waspish, and incapable of gratitude to those
who had done him service. Inconsistently counten-
ancing by his presence an art for which he deemed it
sinful to work, he delighted in making bitter epigrams
upon a new play unless the author was known to
ladies at Court, and the homage done to him in print
by Longepierre could not prevent him from holding up
Sésostris to the laughter of the world. Before long,
principally by reason of his excessive self-consciousness,
he became an object of almost general dislike, Boileau
being the only man whose friendship for him remained
unbroken to the end. Even that friendship, it appears,

was occasionally exposed to a severe strain. In a discussion at the Académie des Inscriptions, as we learn from *Bolœana*, the tragic poet, finding that his old instructor in the art of versification had put forward an untenable proposition, fell upon him with a " rudeness amounting to insult." Boileau resented this rudeness with some heat. " I admit," he said, " that I was in error ; but I would prefer to be wrong if I could not prove myself right in a less offensive way." By what must be regarded as a significant omission, the poet's eulogist at the Academy said nothing of his personal character except that he was a " zealous and faithful friend," and the return he made for the kindness extended to him by the Port Royalists and Molière goes with other incidents to show that even this tribute was ill-deserved. In many relations of private life, it must be said, Racine revealed a singular coldness of heart. Yet, by a contradiction of which literary history affords but few examples, he would be deemed exactly the reverse of this if we studied him only through the medium of his works. Here, in diction of peculiar beauty and grace, we find a warm sensibility allied to a keen sympathy with all that is most worthy of human admiration. He seems to have possessed the very spirit of pathos and tenderness. It would be a great deal too much to suppose that the power he thus exercised over his audience was simply the result of profound study in books and the world of the language of passion.

Si vis me flere dolendum est
Primum ipsi tibi ;

and his work could hardly have had the qualities just glanced at if they had not existed in himself. Consequently, looking at him from all points of view, we are tempted to think that he was composed of two different natures—a duality marked enough to incarnate an unceasing oscillation in action between the extremely great and the extremely little. In *Le Chevalier Double*, a story founded upon Norwegian legend, a knight is represented as being under the sway by turns of two influences, one baleful, the other ennobling. It is only by assuming such a twofold individuality in Racine that we can understand how the author of *Andromaque* and *Iphigénie* could have been one of the most callous of men when the pen was out of his hands.

CHAPTER VIII.

1698.

The Comédie Française, as the organization begun nine years previously now came to be termed, will repay much closer study than it has hitherto received. No other work of Louis XIV. is equally symbolical of the principles by which the whole of his domestic policy was shaped. It indicated his faith in centralization, his conviction that literature and art stood in need of practical encouragement from the Court, his determination to cripple every existing means of reawakening the long dormant spirit of freedom among his people. Notwithstanding a widespread prejudice against any new form in which this system of government might reveal itself—a prejudice born of the misery his prodigality and lust of military glory had already entailed—the theatre so established immediately took root in Parisian soil, and the pernicious nature of the theories it embodied should not blind us to the fact that its success was in many respects a matter of congratulation. From its earliest years, in truth, this one home in the capital of the drama proper, this little

republic in the midst of an absolute monarchy, presented
a remarkable exception to the rule that subsidies from
the State are injurious to the interests they are intended
to serve.   Independent to some extent of public caprice,
with the assurance of a not inadequate provision for
their old age, the original members of the Comédie,
instead of abandoning themselves to a life of comparative ease, as might have been expected, took
advantage of the slight assistance they received to
aim at the highest accepted standard of theatrical
excellence, and in doing so, it would seem, displayed
the energy of a company working under the healthier
conditions of free-trade.   They enlisted the best avail-
able dramatic talent of the time in their service, did
much to establish the claims of acting to a place among
the fine arts, and generally strengthened the hold which
the theatre had obtained upon the affections of nearly
all classes.   For the memory of the illustrious dramatist-
player in whose mind the idea of the Comédie is said to
have been first conceived, and whose troupe, it is hardly
necessary to point out, contained the germ of that in
question—a circumstance rather agreeably recorded in
the custom of calling the royal theatre the Maison de
Molière—they cherished more than a reverence of the
lip ; and this feeling, joined to a natural pride in the
distinction they enjoyed as Comédiens du Roi, united
them by a bond strong enough to resist the pressure

of petty rivalries and dissensions. Nor can they be
accused of having become a servile instrument of the
despotism by which they were befriended. From the
scanty annals of their doings it may be seen that they
were animated by the spirit of the nation at large
rather than that of the Court, even to the extent of
indirectly drawing attention to glaring abuses of power.
In going so far, perhaps, they were emboldened by the
example of the trio of dramatists whose works formed
the backbone of their repertory.   Buckle, in the course
of his cogent argument against State protection in
literature, does not, it is true, exempt that trio from
the strictures he passes upon the Louis XIV. writers in
the mass.   "In no age," he tells us, "have literary
men been rewarded with such profuseness as in that
reign ; and in no age have they been so mean-spirited,
so servile, so utterly unfit to fulfil their great vocation
as the apostles of knowledge and the missionaries of
truth.   The history of the most celebrated authors of
that time proves that, notwithstanding their acquirements and the power of their minds, they were unable
to resist· the surrounding corruption.   To gain the
favour of the King they sacrificed that independent
spirit which should have been dearer to them than life :
they gave away the inheritance of genius ; they sold
their birthright for a mess of pottage."   If the historian had thought fit to read the works of the "most

celebrated authors of that time "—*i.e.*, the masterpieces
of the French drama—he would hardly have committed
himself to so unqualified a statement. He might have
discovered that the influence of royal patronage did not
prevent Corneille from testifying a robust sympathy
with his overburdened countrymen, or Molière from
questioning the doctrine of the right divine of kings to
govern wrong, or Racine, courtier though he was,
from denouncing the proscription of the Huguenots
in the presence of the author of that measure. In
other words, they often had the courage of their
opinions, and the players were not to be deterred
from expressing popular sentiments on the stage when,
as in the case of *Phraate*, the informal censorship established by Louis XIV. had chanced to overlook such
passages. Enough, perhaps, has been said to account
for the triumph of this remarkable troupe over the
sort of hostility arrayed against them at the outset
of their career. No error of judgment could visibly
diminish the strength they derived from their zeal,
their liberality, their talents, their *esprit de corps*, their
self-respecting attitude towards the powers that were.
Generally, too, their practice became a law to their
successors, the consequence being that the Comédie
Française acquired the stability to weather a political
and social storm by which institutions of greater
antiquity and magnitude were swept away. In all

these circumstances, perhaps, a rather close description
of a "first evening" at the old Comédie Française, with
the conditions under which it was given, will not be
unacceptable ; and accordingly, at the risk of seeming
to repeat myself needlessly upon one or two points,
I ask the reader to accompany me in an imaginary
visit to the theatre on such an occasion in the winter
of 1697-8.

Between three and four o'clock, or about an hour
before the time fixed for the performance, we start
from the eastern end of the Rue St. Honoré, a quarter
particularly favoured by the few Englishmen to be met
with in Paris, and make for the Faubourg St. Germain
by way of the Pont Neuf.   It is not too much to say
—and the little crowds assembled round the street
posts on which playbills are hung may help to bear
out the statement—that the species of entertainment we
are about to share in has a wider popularity here than
any other.   The Comédie Française is a haunt of the
old and the young, the rich and the poor, the learned
and the unlearned, the busy and the idle.   And the
taste thus shown has not been a thing of recent growth.
Indirectly fostered, perhaps, by the Roman occupants
of Gaul, who erected many stately amphitheatres in
the country, it found its first recorded expression in
the Carlovingian *urbanae cantilenae*, and was still more
strongly shown in the later Middle Ages by the

U 2

tensons written for the jongleurs, the plays designed
to promote religious knowledge and fervour among the
masses, and the merry productions of the Clercs de la
Basoche and the Enfants sans Souci.   By the time of
the Renascence, therefore, the ground was well prepared
for the cultivation of the regular drama, which found
acceptance in Paris from the moment it was transferred
from the platforms of the colleges to the boards of the
Hôtel de Bourgogne.   For nearly half a century it
continued to gain in public favour, though none of the
dramatists who sprang up during that period had the
power to animate tragedy with genuine passion, to lift
comedy above the level of extravagant farce, or to give
to either the charm of orderly and artistic development.
Hardi's sorriest patchwork, like the insipid pastorals
derived from *Astrée*, could be relied upon to fill the
house again and again.   It must not be supposed, however, that the audience were incapable of appreciating
higher excellence.   Intense enthusiasm was aroused
by the plays in which Pierre Corneille created a new
tragedy for France.   His name became great in the
mouths of all save a knot of overshadowed and envious
rivals.   He found himself in a position to deride
the efforts made and countenanced by the powerful
Richelieu to convince the world that in the author of
the *Cid* and *Horace* it had set up a false idol.   He
might be as little able to deal with the passions of the

heart or draw womanly women as to give sustained force
to the whole of his verse; but it was also felt that on
his deliberately chosen ground, the portraiture of moral
heroism, of the triumph of mind over matter, he had
the strength that comes of fervid imagination, elevated
thought, energy of reasoning, grasp of character,
lucidity of arrangement, and at times overwhelming
force of · expression.   In the lighter drama, too, he
found encouragement to adhere to innovations associated
with his name—the substitution of order for confusion,
of probability for burlesque, of portraits for caricatures,
and of genuine pleasantry for rather depressing jest.
By-and-by, as a result of his success in this way, the
comedy of yore was displaced by one reflective of
character and manners; the favour extended to Scarron's
pieces, which in substance belonged to the former
group, being wholly attributable to the remarkable
briskness of their dialogue.   In the space of a few years
Molière carried the new school to a point little short
of perfection.   Endowed with a combination of qualities
separately rare, he gave us vivid and fascinating tran-
scripts of Louis Quatorze society, at the same time showing that he could illustrate human nature in its eternal
as well as fleeting aspects, in its essence as well as in its
more superficial manifestations.   Nor did the public for
which he wrote fail to perceive his genius.   From and
after the production of *L'Ecole des Maris* he was hailed as

the first of writers in his own walk of literature ; and if
the province of comedy did not extend beyond the representation of real life, with an elevating moral implied,
the author of *Don Juan* and *Le Bourgeois Gentilhomme*,
though disposed to throw the leading traits in his
personages into too clear a relief, would have to be
deemed worthy of that splendid distinction.   Hardly
less proud a triumph fell to the lot of the tender Racine
when, acting upon suggestions indirectly held out in
Le Misanthrope, he so far deviated from the practice of
Corneille as to blend the beautiful with the true, to
occupy himself with delineations of the tenderer passions,
to create specimens of pure and gentle womanhood in
some of his heroines, and to write with almost unvarying
grace, refinement, and harmony.   For work of this kind
he wanted little that profound sensibility or command
of language could give ; Parisian opinion placed him at
least on a level with Corneille, and it became evident
that any tragedy without a love element or the charm
of noble versification would thenceforward be at a
disadvantage.   I need hardly stop to point out the
inference that must be drawn from the estimation in
which the three great French dramatists of the century
were held by the mass of their contemporaries.   In some
cases the public fell into curious errors of judgment, but
it is evident from the foregoing record that to their
delight in playgoing they united no inconsiderable

degree of intelligence, taste, and discernment.   For the
rest, Racine left the drama in a very different state
from that in which Corneille found it.   Its wide popularity ; the unique gifts employed in its service ; the
prominence assigned to it in the diversions of the Court
since the closing days of Richelieu ; and also, perhaps,
the importance it derived from the persecution of the
Cid and the controversies aroused by *Don Juan* and
Tartuffe, have contributed to make it the chief department of letters.   Nearly all the poets of the time give
it their best energies.   Doubtless they suffer grievously
by comparison with Corneille and Molière and Racine ;
but it is also true that by winning the applause of the
town they experience a gratification far higher than any
other kind of literary triumph can afford, that no work
of the mind is so likely to commend them to the notice
of the pension-giving King as a good tragedy or comedy,
and that their earnings from the theatre, exclusive of
the sum paid by the bookseller for the privilege of printing a successful piece, will exceed what may be gained by
even a noble epic.   In its turn, the general taste for the
theatre has seemed to increase with, as it is largely
refined by, the literature it assists to produce.   The
Comédie Française is really independent of the little
subvention it receives from the State.   New plays are
in constant demand ; an old one, with or without the
interest arising from a début, seldom fails, familiar as

it may be, to attract an ample and well-disposed audience.

After crossing the Pont Neuf, which presents the appearance of a fair, we halt for a moment or two to see the hoary towers of the Louvre and the Palais de Justice in the radiance of a cloudless sunset—certainly a picturesque effect—and then strike into the street where the Petits Augustins have taken up their quarters. During the remainder of our walk, by your leave, I will endeavour to describe, if only in the way of warning, a distinctive aspect which the drama here has assumed. Deeply imbued with the spirit of the Renascence, or at least with an almost superstitious reverence for the works of antiquity, France, like Italy, but unlike England and Spain, has become a disciple of the classical school, though not without making a few important deviations from its theory and practice. In tragedy it is deemed necessary to observe the utmost precision of form, to write in alexandrines with an alternation of masculine and feminine rhymes, to preserve the unities inviolate, and, avoiding anything in the nature of comedy, however refined, to aim at a general stateliness of incident, thought, and language. Introduced by some of the Ronsardists, this mixed system acquired sufficient credit by the time of Henri Quatre to hold out against a long series of efforts to overthrow it, then gathered fresh vitality from the artificial tastes diffused by the *précieuses*, and eventually, having found more or less ardent advocates in four men separately able to set a fashion in literature—Corneille, Louis XIV., Boileau, and Racine—was accepted on all hands as a perfection of wisdom. Now, no very profound argument is required to show that the yoke thus forced upon the dramatist is both unnecessary and mischievous. Insisted upon in every case, regularity of form is to him a matter of intrinsic importance, even to the extent of being allowed to visibly interfere with the fulfilment of what constitutes the *raison d'être* of his piece. In comparison with his clearly rhymed alexandrines, particularly after the alternation of the masculine and feminine has obtruded itself upon our notice, blank verse is an unconstrained mode of speech, if not simplicity itself. Next comes his custom of restricting the action of a piece to one consecutive chain of events, to the space of one day, and virtually to one place. Interpreting the first of the unity laws in the strictest sense—namely, that every part should bear an organic relation to the whole—he misses the relief and additional strength to be drawn from collateral interest. He crowds into twenty-four hours a series of incidents which in the nature of things would extend over weeks, months, or years. By holding to the unity of place he obliges himself to appeal to the ear rather than the eye—in other words, to make his heroes and heroines

explain themselves to confidants, to bring on messengers
to acquaint us with what we ought to see, and generally
to subordinate action, the life-blood of the drama, to
mere description.   In support of the second and third
rules, however, it is contended that they are essential
to dramatic illusion.   Such a plea argues a curious
deficiency of perception, to say nothing of its inconsistency with the use of affectedly rhymed alexandrines.
Is it not within the province of the imagination to
annihilate time and distance?   Moreover, the application of the second rule is somewhat illogical, for if
that rule had any validity the duration of the action
should not exceed the time occupied in the performance.
Possibly you sympathize with the objection to a change
of scenery in the presence of an audience, but the solu-
tion of this difficulty lies in effecting such changes
behind the curtain at the end of an act.   And it is not
only on the ground of expediency that the unities of
time and place are upheld.   Had they not been adhered
to by the Greek dramatists with the sanction of Aristotle? the Frenchman asks.   It is a matter of slight
importance whether practices repugnant to common
sense have been approved by luminaries of the past or
not, but I should be glad to remind you that the
question so put cannot be answered in the affirmative
without considerable qualification.   In Athens, as you
know, the second and third unities were maintained

purely for the sake of convenience. One or the other
was set at nought in at least five plays—the *Agamemnon,* the *Supplices,* the *Eumenides,* the *Trachiniæ,* and the
Ajax. Aristotle, while agreeing with the unity of action
in the largest meaning of the phrase, has nothing to say
of the unity of place, and in regard to the unity of
time is content to record without comment a usage not
uncommon on the Greek stage. He may have perceived
what experience has taught us, that the " Aristotelian
precepts," as the learned world in Paris unlearnedly
call them, are incompatible with a full development of
the resources of the drama. Barely less pernicious than
the observance of these precepts is the presumed need
of stateliness in principle and detail; in every serious
piece the story has some connexion with a palace, the
dialogue is for the most part conducted in long and
grandiloquent speeches, no gleam of pleasantry is
permitted to any of the characters, references to ordinary
things are sedulously excluded, and extremely fine
thoughts, such as the description in *Iphigénie* of the
Greek host at rest on that fatefully calm night,

Tout dort, et l'armée et les vents et Neptune,

are assigned to mere serfs. In brief, French tragedy, as
a result of its submission to the laws I have enumerated,
is deficient in verisimilitude, interest, breadth, variety,
relief, colour, and picturesqueness. It may even be

condemned as essentially unreal, laboured, thin, monotonous, declamatory, cold.   It bears about the same
analogy to the "romantic" drama that sculpture bears
to vivid painting.   Heaven-sent gifts have been brought
to its aid, but never under the conditions needed to
produce their due effect.   Had Shakspere followed the
Ronsardist system—and this consideration furnishes
the strongest argument against it—his work would
have been less in bulk, poor in what constitutes its
chief attractions, and probably without a *Macbeth* or
a *Romeo and Juliet* at all.   Both Corneille and Racine
were endowed with high creative power, and it is
melancholy to think that a large portion of their lives
should have been spent in rhyming verses, accomplishing
idle *tours de force*, and generally impairing the value of
their bequest to posterity.   I should also remark that
the monotony arising from their method of treatment
is deepened by a virtual restriction in the choice of
subject-matter.   Nine-tenths of the serious plays now
written are founded upon the history or legends of
antiquity.   Here, as in their severe and elaborate
etiquette, they supply additional testimony to the
influence of the King, whose classical proclivities are
strong enough to make him deface the fairest examples
of Gothic architecture around us, and who, for reasons
not far to seek, is inclined to discourage any tendency
to bring latter-day personages on the stage.   I think

an earthquake under his feet would not startle him so
much as a proposal among his players to represent a
piece relating to the fall of our Charles I.   Even in
dealing with Greek themes, however, the French tragic
poets do not catch the essential spirit of their model,
though they persistently strive at the ideal rather than
the real, at serene beauty rather than expression, at
the conventional rather than the true.   The heights
to which they rise "are not lost in a sphere peopled
by the myths of a national religion; Orestes and
Iphigenia have not brought with them the cries of
the stern goddesses and the flame on the altar of
Aramis; their passions, like their speech, are cadenced
by a modern measure," and in other respects are illustrated by thoroughly modern means.   Fortunately, none
of the rules laid down for tragedy are stringently
applied to the outpourings of the rival Muse.   Molière,
for instance, looked in the first place to the exigencies
of his story, often substituted prose for verse in work
far above the level of farce, did not scruple to encroach
a little upon the venerated unities, and generally
displayed a strong sympathy with nature at the expense
of spurious dignity.   It is to be regretted that on two
of these points he did not go further; the *Misanthrope*
itself might have been more effective in prose, and
the total absence of restrictions as to action and
time and place would have enabled him to delineate

his deathless characters with more fulness than he
usually attains. Be that as it may, the precedents he
established are not lost upon his successors, and the
comparative freedom thus gained is doing much to
keep comedy where he placed it—at the head of the
literature of France. Nevertheless, classical tragedy
continues to exert a sort of fascination over the play-
going world. I doubt whether any of the men and
women who are outstripping us on the way to the
theatre would readily tolerate it in a different shape.
Besides being associated with their earliest impressions,
it appeals to their leaning to extremes by its unrelieved
solemnity, to their admiration of mere cleverness by
its elaborate artifice, to their proverbial love of the
language they speak by its general beauty of diction.
In their belief it is the largest manifestation of the art
practised by Æschylus, Sophocles, and Euripides. To
you, on the contrary, it will probably seem destitute
of the first qualities demanded in the drama. Its most
typical example is not so much an acting play as a
succession of majestic and impassioned conversations,
the effect of the whole being distinctly cold. But do
not always view it by contrast with what has been
achieved elsewhere. Rather approach it in a truly
catholic mood, and, banishing for a time your recollec-
tions of Shakspere and Calderon, judge it by no other
standards than those it seeks to reach. For only by

doing so can you hope to adequately appreciate the beauties in which it abounds, and which, whatever we may think of its errors of principle, are of a kind and degree to make it one of the intellectual treasures of the world.

Soon after passing the home of the Petits Augustins we find ourselves in the Rue des Fossés St. Germain, at the entrance to the Comédie. Lively indeed is the scene presented to us between these two lines of quaintly overhanging houses in the fast-waning light of day : imposing coaches and sedan chairs arriving in rapid succession; gallants airily springing from horseback to pay deference to the fair ; a host of the bourgeoisie pressing hard against the walls of the theatre; incautious stragglers frantically trying to avoid being run over ; itinerant musicians and singers jostling against link-boys, mendicants, and sellers of cheap fruit and confectionery;—in short, a crowd composed of all classes of the Grand Monarque's subjects, from the ducal courtier downwards, but collectively animated just now by one thought and purpose, that of "assisting" at the performance to be given by the royal players this evening. Naturally enough, such assemblages are often attended with breaches of the peace, and the Lieutenant of Police has found it necessary to lay down a variety of regulations for the preservation of order. No one here is at liberty

to carry firearms, to draw a sword, or do any violence
to his neighbour in the inevitable struggle for the
best places.   Pages and lackeys are forbidden to carry
weapons at all.   Some of the disturbances, I fear, are
due to the fact that the Comédie stands between two
cabarets, the Cormier and the Alliance, though your
Frenchman rarely drinks anything stronger than the
wine of his own country.   Built of free-stone, the
frontage of the theatre, as might be expected, is of
simple classical design, with an incongruous iron balcony
extending from side to side over the doors, of which
there are four.   Above the balcony, beginning at the
top, we find the arms of France, a figure of Minerva
in half relief, and a black marble tablet bearing this
inscription in big gold letters—

HÔTEL DES COMÉDIENS
DU ROY
ENTRETENUS PAR SA MAJESTÉ
MDCLXXXVIII.

In reference to the last line, by the way, be on your
guard against a mistake to which it often gives rise ;
the players obtained possession of the building in 1688,
but did not act in it until the following spring.   It
was then nearly a century old, having been erected
as a tennis-house by Louis Andran, a master of that
game, at the instance of Henri Quatre, who often
came over from the Louvre to handle a racket with

him—certainly an interesting association.   The ground
so taken up once formed part of the Pré aux Clercs,
which from the time of Philippe Auguste has been a
favourite haunt of university students (hence its name),
and also of the Parisians in general.   Behind the
houses to our left, with its square tower faintly
discernible in the deepening gloom, is the church of
St. Germain des Prés, the chosen burial-place of
Merovingian kings.   Few quarters of the city, indeed,
are richer in interest than that in which the Comédie
Française stands, and I should be tempted to say more
on this head if the ringing of a bell in the theatre did
not warn us that the porters there are about to do
their office.   Fixed in 1609 at 2 o'clock, the hour of
performance, owing chiefly to a prevailing tendency
among the *beau monde* to dine later and later, has by
degrees been put off to five o'clock; and we are now
within twenty minutes of that time.   Curiously enough,
the bills still announce "qu'on commence à deux
heures," and many Pourceaugnacs unversed in the
fictions of Paris are consequently put to inconvenience.
"Monsieur," was the pert answer of Mdlle. Poisson
to a remonstrance from one of the victims, "the
ordinance of King Henri Quatre—rest his soul!—has
to be respected.   My comrades are ready to begin at
two o'clock, but they have to wait until an audience
assembles."   On this occasion, it might be suggested,

they have "waited," and are keeping us waiting, a little longer than is necessary. By the dim glare of torches and links, supplemented by that of the lanterns placed over the doorways of houses by the police to light up the streets, but merely with the effect of making darkness more visible, we see what the deep and sullen roar now filling the air might lead us to expect—a crowd large enough to fill the theatre to its utmost capacity.

Eventually, amidst a loud clanging of bolts and bars, the doors are thrown open ; a forward movement among the people surrounding us makes itself felt, and we seem to be borne upon a resistless tide into the interior of the theatre. Impressive as was the scene in the street, it is surpassed, I think, by that presented to us in front of the dark green curtain. Disposed in the form of a parallelogram, with its sides tastefully ornamented, and having over the proscenium a painting by Bon Boullogne of allegorical figures proper to the drama, the *salle* is divided into five parts—to quote the official list, into "amphithéâtre, loges, loges hautes, loges du troisième rang, et parterre." It is illuminated by oil lamps and groups of candles, which are attended to at stated intervals by persons employed for the purpose. Each of these snuffers is enjoined to work "avec propreté," so as to prevent any "mauvaise odeur." By no means good, the light thus afforded

enables one to recognize well-known faces at some
distance, and we are not long in discovering that the
audience now settled down in their places—this forest
of periwigged and gesticulating heads—is of a peculiarly
representative character.   Especially striking is the
appearance of the amphitheatre and boxes, in the former
of which, for the sake of having the most comprehensive
view of the house, we are now taking seats.   Here are
Court personages of various degrees—men and women
who will go down to the latest posterity in the letters
of Sévigné, the memoirs of Saint Simon, and other
mirrors of the time—gorgeous things in laced and
embroidered coats, with diamond-hilted swords and
muffs suspended by ribbons from the neck, or in bodices
of very formal pattern, tightly laced, and surmounting
enormous skirts.   It is in vain to hope that the King
will join this brilliant throng; when his majesty desires
to be edified or amused by a play, as he not unfrequently
does, the Comédie Française goes to Versailles.   The
next tier, the *loges hautes*, is occupied by well-to-do
bourgeoisie; higher still, in the *loges du troisième rang*,
or what we should call the gallery, a gathering of the
same class, but probably with less money to spare,
sit in front of the lackeys—a noisy set—of the fine
ladies and gentlemen below.   The pit, which extends
right down to the stage, is filled with men of letters,
artists, doctors, lawyers, abbés, professors, students

and other Parisians of various ages, sorts, and conditions.
For this has ever been the most popular part of the
theatre, not only as being the cheapest, since many of
the persons in it could well afford to take more expen-
sive places, but because it serves the purpose of a public
rendezvous. Nevertheless, presumably with the object
of making the tiers more attractive, the players allow
it to remain in a comfortless state; it is unprovided
with seats of any kind, and the gradient in the flooring
is so slight that comparatively few of the " groundlings "
have a good view of the performance. Near the stage,
in a rather narrow enclosure, is what has been called the
banc formidable—a long form to accommodate tried
dramatists and newsletter-writers, all of whom enter
free. Among these guests of the players are Thomas
Corneille, Brueys, Campistron, Palaprat, Pradon, Boursault, Genest, Dufresny, Boyer, and Devisé, the last of
whom, with his nose almost touching the paper, is
taking notes for a little article in the *Mercure Galant*.
For the most illustrious of living authors, however, we
must again turn to the boxes. Faultlessly dressed, the
icy Racine and joyous Regnard are engaged there in
a keen encounter of wits, the literary Mentor of the
age, Boileau, bending forward to catch what they say.
And the author of the new tragedy ? In company with
two or three friends, he has ensconced himself in that
grated box on the third tier, hard by the proscenium.

I am not surprised to see him directing wistful and anxious glances at the surging mass in the parterre. For there is the jury by whom his work is to be tried, the supreme arbiters of its fate as an acting play. He knows that in the event of a conflict of opinions as to its merits their verdict would be final, even if all the rest of the audience were arrayed against them. He also knows that it is easier to miss than win their suffrages. Euripides' *Orestes*, as the story goes, fell at its first representation in Athens because Hegelochus moved the spectators to merriment by managing his respiration so clumsily as to make one word sound like another. Incidents less amusing than this have ruined the effect of a tragedy at the Théâtre Français. Assuming greater freedom than the occupants of the amphitheatre and boxes, where a severe decorum is usually maintained, the parterre seizes with avidity upon anything in the piece or the acting which appeals to their inborn sense of the ridiculous, and we may be sure that if laughter once sets in they will insist upon treating the remainder of the performance as mere farce. Sometimes they are brought to this condition of mind by an audible joke amongst themselves at the expense of a poor production, serious or otherwise. Not long ago, towards the end of a tragedy which few could understand, one of the personages had to say in effect that he would throw a little light upon the motives of their proceedings.

"Ma foi, it is time somebody did!" cried a shrill voice in the pit, and the mirth aroused by the joke was so great that the players had to abandon their task. Moreover, this dread army of critics are extremely difficult to please. Intimately acquainted with the masterpieces of Corneille and Molière and Racine—so intimately, in fact, that many of them know by heart such passages as the Cid's account of his victory over the Moors, the chief scenes between Alceste and Célimène, and the description in *Phèdre* of the death of Hippolyte—they have formed to themselves a lofty ideal of what (from their point of view) constitutes dramatic excellence. I am inclined to believe that the majority of them are alive to violations of good taste, to shallowness of thought, and to incorrectness of versification itself. Generally, it is certain, they are intolerant of blunders in either construction or detail, and are apt, despite an official prohibition of the practice, to indicate disappointment by hissing with tremendous energy.

> Vous sifflez d'une manière
> A désespérer les gens ;
> Ou ressuscitez Molière
> Ou soyez plus indulgents,

pleaded one of their victims. Altogether, the poet in the grated box has no slight ordeal to pass through to-night. Let him take courage, however. If he has not mistaken his vocation, and has avoided the pitfalls—the numerous pitfalls—in the way of the dramatist, the public will applaud him with over-abounding generosity. It will not be long before he is placed upon his trial. Lamps and candles at the foot of the stage are lighted by unseen hands; the music of the six violins in the orchestra dies away; three heavy knocks behind the scene announce that the players are ready to begin, and then, with the din of several thousand voices abruptly changing into profound silence, the curtain goes up.

In one respect, you will observe, the players have no very keen sense of the fitness of things. Here, as at the London theatres, a swarm of fops occupy cane chairs or forms at each side of the stage, in full view of the audience in the *salle*. Evidently under the impression that their presence enhances the attractiveness of the piece, these *gens du bel air*, stretching themselves out with a fashionable affectation of languor, reset their periwigs and cravats, illustrate the nice conduct of a clouded cane, fondle the jewelled hilts of their swords, take snuff in a style possible only to the man of quality, and fall to chattering among themselves in tones not always under a whisper. Every sprig of the aristocracy thinks it necessary

> A faire, aux nouveautés dont il est idolâtre,
> Figure du savant sur les bancs du théâtre ;
> Y décider en chef, et faire du fracas
> A tous les beaux endroits qui méritent des *Ah !*

In the Mysteries, as I have said, the actors not engaged
in a scene would stand round those who were. But
there is reason to believe that the custom of admitting
spectators to the stage was of late origin. D'Aubignac's
Pratique du Théâtre, brought out in 1657, has no reference to anything of the kind; Tallemant des Réaux,
writing a year or two afterwards, speaks of it in effect
as one recently established. By 1661, when *Les Fâcheux*
appeared, it had come to be grossly abused. Note what
Molière says at the outset of that play :—

> J'étais sur le théâtre en humeur d'écouter
> La pièce, qu'à plusieurs j'avais ouï vanter ;
> Les acteurs commençaient, chacun prêtait silence,
> Lorsque, d'un air bruyant et plein d'extravagance,
> Un homme à grands canons est entré brusquement
> En criant : Holà ! ho ! un siége promptement ;
> Et de son grand fracas surprenant l'assemblée
> Dans le plus bel endroit de la pièce troublée . . .
> Tandis que là-dessus je haussais les épaules,
> Les acteurs ont voulu continuer leurs rôles ;
> Mais l'homme pour l'asseoir a fait nouveau fracas,
> Et, traversant encor le théâtre à grands pas,
> Bien que dans les côtés il pût être à son aise,
> Au milier du devant il a planté sa chaise,
> Et de son large dos morguant les spectateurs,
> Aux trois quarts du parterre a caché les acteurs.

In course of time, too, the nuisance became more and
more intolerable. The *homme à grands canons* was not
content with coming late, creating a disturbance, and
hiding the actors from the people in front of the house.
He would occasionally " chaff " the piece, cross the stage

in mid-performance to chat with an acquaintance, and otherwise manifest a sturdy contempt for the laws of decency. At the first representation of Dancourt's *Vendanges*, we may remember, the drunken Marquis de Sablé, imagining that he was glanced at in one of the lines, cuffed the author in the sight of the whole audience. Eventually the long-suffering players appealed to the authorities for protection, with the result that visitors behind the scenes were required to arrive punctually, preserve silence, and keep inside a barrier thenceforward placed round their seats. Of these regulations, however, only the last is strictly obeyed; the buzz of talk at the wings frequently reaches our ears, and it is no un-common thing to see some water-fly come on while the piece is in progress.

> On attendait Auguste; on vit paraître un fat.

Why such a custom is permitted we are at a loss to understand. It interferes with movement on the stage ; it makes a change of background almost impossible; it tends to throw ridicule upon anything like gravity or earnestness of action; it is inimical to the illusion which the unities of time and place are supposed to assist. Dramatists, players, the public at large,—all of them have a direct interest in its suppression. To us, moreover, it has the further disadvantage of aiding to make French tragedy a series of noble dialogues instead

of a picture of human events.   Nor is there reason to
hope that it will soon be honoured in the breach.   By a
strange want of spirit, the great mass of playgoers, whose
word is law, quietly submit to the annoyance inflicted
upon them; the members of the Comédie, fearing that
the expulsion of the intruders would be followed by a
dangerous riot in the theatre, are reluctant to move in
the matter, and the dramatist can do nothing but
complain of the obstacles so unnecessarily put in his
way.   Money considerations, I think, can have had
little to do with the attitude of the players in this
matter.   Banished from the stage, their unwelcome
visitors would appear in other parts of the house, for the
simple reason that it is the fashion to see a new play.
This, however, was not the opinion of a *marquis ridicule*
in Regnard's *Coquette*, performed by the Italians seven
years ago.   "Do you really think," he is asked, "that
the pittites pay to see you pose your wig, take your
snuff, and disport yourself on a form?   Why don't
you go into the boxes?"   "In the boxes?" is the reply;
"*I?* Monsieur, I kiss your hands.   I do not hear from the
boxes; I like to be seen from head to foot; and, mordi!
I give my crown only to stroll about and be near the
actresses during the *entractes*.   The stage," he complacently adds, "is never empty while I am upon it."
In this last view the marquises on the boards of the
Comédie Française are confirmed by the amiable Chap-

puzeau, who, ever ready to look upon all as for the best in the best possible of worlds, maintains that their presence there is a " rich ornament " to the theatre.

You will note a whimsical contrast between the dress of these Louis Quatorze exquisites and the scenery before which they are assembled. For that scenery is intended to show us a vestibule in republican Rome, and has been prepared with some respect for archæological accuracy. It presents an imposing combination of massive-looking columns, seemingly paved ground, and groups of real statuary. In France, you must know, the regular drama has not always been acted with such aids to the imagination of the spectator, although they were freely employed in the religious plays contrived by the mediæval laity. It was long the custom at the Hôtel de Bourgogne to perform both tragedy and comedy without anything in the shape of pictorial accessories—to be more precise, in a semicircle of tapestry or other hangings, through which the exits and entrances were made. Paintings of no higher value than those executed for the Mysteries would have evoked a storm of merriment, and the players, finding that the audience were to be charmed by ornate versification alone, had no inducement to spend the little money at their disposal in procuring better work of its kind. Towards the end of Hardi's career, however, a reaction against this state of things

became manifest.   Most of the pastorals given at *fétes*
in the châteaux of the nobles were provided with
pretty and tasteful decorations.   Scholars, perhaps,
pointed to what must have been accomplished by the
scene painters of Athens, particularly in *Prometheus*
and *Iphigenia*, and by the showmen of the Eternal City
in the decline of her greatness.   Last, but not least, it
could be seen that in this walk of art France was far
behind other civilized nations.   Italy may be said to
have redeemed the promise held out about a century
previously in the magnificence with which Leo X.
caused Rucellai's *Rosamunda* to be produced at
Florence ; England was no longer under the necessity
of acquainting an audience with the physical character
of a scene by means of an inscription in chalk on a
board at the side of a bare stage ; Spain, thanks in
some part to the inventive cleverness of Lope de Rueda,
had revived the chief theatrical appliances known to the
ancient world.   In the end, about thirty years after the
introduction of the classical drama at the Hôtel de
Bourgogne, people began to ask whether the stage was
to be always like a platform for recitation.   Surely it
was not unreasonable to look for some attempt at
historical illustration in the theatres of Paris ?   The
players met the demand with commendable promptitude.
For each new tragedy and comedy they provided a
rather appropriate background, with wings to match.

Still greater advances were made in performances at
private theatres as time went on. In the hope of
weakening the impression created by the *Cid* and
Horace under far less favourable conditions—a hope
completely shattered by the result—Richelieu gave
Mirame the advantage of an elaborate and brilliant
setting. Mazarin, never parsimonious where the gratification of his tastes was in question, enabled Torelli to
exercise all his rare talents for stage embellishment in
pieces which, like *Andromède*, might help to pave the
way for the introduction of the opera into France. *La
Toison d'Or*, in common with other graceful freaks of
fancy, was represented on an even more imposing scale
at the Château de Neubourg, the owner thereof, the
Marquis de Sourdéac, having effected an appreciable
improvement in the theatrical machinery previously in
use. Magnificent in all things, Louis XIV. employed
such men as Vigarini (a second Torelli) to decorate
the comedy-ballets produced at Court in the earlier
years of his reign, and it is probable that Italy itself
had not witnessed so perfect a *mise-en-scène* as those of
Molière's *Princesse d'Elide*, *Mélicerte*, and *Psyché*. In
the mean time, as may be supposed, the players had not
been unmindful of the little wonders just enumerated.
Fettered by commercial considerations, they yet came
to bestow an independent value and interest upon their
scenery. Especially was this the case with the company

at the Marais, who, comparatively unheeded by the greater dramatists, sought to disguise the feebleness of their repertory by aiming at spectacular excellence, and were successful enough to obtain a virtual monopoly of the *pièce à machines.* For the latest developments of the art so cultivated we shall have to visit the theatre constructed by Richelieu for the sake of *Mirame* —the Palais Royal. Hallowed by its associations with the memory of Molière, this costly building is now the home of French opera, each example of which has the advantage of a succession of diversified and picturesque backgrounds. At the Comédie Française, owing to the general adoption by its dramatists of the place-unity, the scene-painter finds less scope for the display of his talents. He is seldom called upon to depict more than the interior of an ancient palace and a Parisian street or *salon.* But within these limits he manifests both skill and taste. In addition to bearing traces of archæological study, the canvas we are facing is commendable in point of drawing, perspective, and colour.

Fixing our attention upon the players, who have just warmed to their work, we find new matter for inquiry and reflection. To begin with, their costume has little of the comparative accuracy which characterizes the scenery. If this element of theatrical effect was not entirely ignored in the Mysteries, as would seem to be

the fact, it can hardly be said to have entered into
the representation of the regular drama. From the
time of Jodelle it was the practice on the stage to
dress ancient personages in the latest French fashion
Horace and Auguste, for instance, appeared in perukes
à trois marteaux, that of the latter being surmounted
by a laurel wreath. Mondori had the courage to
discard anything like a headdress where it was out of
character, but the sight of his closely cropped hair was
so horrifying to the ladies of the Hôtel Rambouillet
that no other actor would follow his example. Even
at the best period of the Golden Age, when a knowledge of classical antiquity became widely diffused,
these grotesque anachronisms, despite a little raillery
at their expense in Sorel's *Maison des Jeux* and the
Roman Comique, continued to flourish with unabated
vigour. Racine, perhaps aware that they served to
make the French tone of his tragedies unnecessarily
apparent, then exerted his influence with the Troupe
Royale in favour of historical dresses, of which it
was not difficult to procure models. How far the re-
form he contemplated has progressed a glance at the
figures moving about the stage will show. It is clear
that all the actresses of the Comédie have resolutely
set their faces against the suggested change. In
common with her sisters in art, Mdlle. Duclos, who
has to represent a Roman matron, is arrayed after the

manner of her fair auditors in the boxes—namely, in
an enormous hoop, tightly-laced bodice, and powdered
coiffure. On the other hand, the actors, headed by
Beaubourg, have adopted a sort of compromise between
the ancient and modern. They wear *calcei* over silk
stockings, helmets with large red feathers over elaborate
periwigs, and swords suspended by shoulder-belts over
something like Roman tunics. It is difficult to maintain any gravity before so heterogeneous a combination as this, but at the same time we see that
France is becoming alive to the absurdity of the custom
still retained by her actresses—a point which no other
nation has reached—and that Racine's dream is likely
to be realized before many years have passed away.
Unfortunately, it is not only in regard to costume that
the players invite adverse criticism. Their style of
declamation is sufficiently artificial to remind us of the
melopœa attributed to the Greek stage. It is formal,
measured, sing-song, grandiose. In adopting this style,
which dates from the origin of the drama proper in
Paris, the Comédie have not erred for the want
of knowing better. Molière, unconsciously following
the example of Shakspere, delighted to ridicule the
mechanical and inflated recitation of his contemporaries.
Mascarille is greatly astonished when Cathos asks him
to which troupe he intends to give his piece. " A
pretty question to ask ! " he replies ; " why, to the

great Comédiens," those of the Hôtel de Bourgogne,
"of course. It is only they who are able to do justice
to such things. The others," those led by Molière,
"are ignoramuses who recite as they speak off the
stage ; they know not how to roar their verses and
bring down the house." In his *Impromptu de Ver-*
sailles the dramatist returns to the charge. "What !"
he asks, "do you call that reciting ? You are joking.
It must be said with emphasis. Listen to me." And
therewith he gives an imitation of the stagy Montfleuri. "Note me well. Mouth the last line. That
is the way to bring down the house." Probably
wincing under the laughter evoked by the satirist,
Floridor showed a tendency to speak his lines instead
of intoning them, and Mdlle. Champmêlé, with whom
he was associated in after years, must be credited with
equal discernment. Baron, strengthened by the precepts
he had received from Molière, went much further than
either. He reconciled the demands of theatrical effect
with those of natural truth. His utterance was distinguished by a noble and unaffected simplicity.
Believing the observance of metre to be mischievous
in the highest degree, he uniformly recited verse as
elevated prose, and there can be no doubt that he
succeeded in depriving the alexandrine of its peculiar
monotony. Most of his comrades seem to have made
him their lawgiver in this respect, but the influence

he had over them did not last beyond his premature
retirement.   Beaubourg and Mdlle. Duclos created
a reaction in favour of the old school of elocution,
which, despite the continued presence of Marie
Champmêlé on the scene, soon regained its former
ascendancy.   It has become a rule with the Comédiens
du Roi to observe syllabic quantities, to clearly indicate the rhyme, and to roll forth their speeches with
elaborate emphasis.   In point of illustrative action,
too, an equal degree of artificiality becomes apparent.
Gait, attitude, the use of the arms, facial expression,—
all are governed by arbitrary laws, are executed with
mechanical precision, and are of a more or less stagy
character.   Except in the days of Baron, who assumed
a greater freedom and variety of gesticulation, this
method has always existed in the theatres, and the
devices he laid aside are still preserved with pious
care.   Looked at as a whole, therefore, French tragic
acting is wanting in the charm of ease, fidelity to
nature, and the semblance of spontaneity.   It is as
formal and constrained as the drama on which it lives.
But its defects are not without alloy.   Every word is
distinctly articulated, the portraiture of strong passion
seldom falls to the level of rant, and we are frequently
reminded of the value of self-contained repose.   "In
Paris," you may see, "a great tragedian employs
much less action than his English brethren.   Motion-

less, with his arms gracefully disposed, he occupies the
whole stage, and in this statuelike posture gives vent
to feelings that fill the breasts of his audience with
astonishment, terror, or pity." I need not say that
such feats denote a combination of imaginative power,
sympathy, and technical skill. Moreover, a tone of
refinement and good taste pervades the performance
throughout. The members of the Comédie Française,
with one or two exceptions, belong to the educated
class. Some have sprung from the higher bourgeoisie;
others might boast of gentle birth. Nor will this
appear surprising if the social status of the player is
borne in mind. Formerly held in unthinking contempt,
though never branded in the statute-book as a *fieffé
coquin* (rogue and vagabond), he is now allowed to have
a valid claim to the title of artist. His profession has
been publicly declared by Richelieu to be worthy of
respect, and by Louis XIV., who may have thought
the Cardinal's phrase rather vague, to be not incompatible with the quality of a gentleman. By the elevation
of the theatre to the dignity of an institution of State,
of course, it has been still further honoured. Many
years must elapse before the stigma cast upon it can be
wholly removed, but enough has already been done in
that way to make it adopted by men who in different
circumstances would have become lawyers, doctors, or
abbés. And his majesty's players are the flower of the

calling thus reinforced. Their achievements may be taken to indicate the high-water mark of histrionic capability in France. It is in the hope of winning a place at the Comédie that the young provincial actor endures privation and disappointment; it is from the ranks of clever provincial actors that vacancies there are usually filled. Brought to Paris, the selected aspirant goes through a period of trial before the public (*début*), and then, if the authorities are not dissatisfied with his work, finds himself in possession of the prize he has so long sighed for in vain.

Let us now give our attention to the character and fortunes of the new piece. You may accept it as a typical example of French tragedy in the reign of Louis XIV. Its plot has been suggested by the Spanish conspiracy against Venice; but the author, aware that the *cognoscenti* of Paris, headed by the King, hold modern history to be incompatible with the dignity of Melpomene, places his scene in the Rome of about four centuries before the Christian era, the preserver of the Capitol being one of his leading personages. In handling such a theme, of course, a dramatist ought to entirely discard the unities of place and time. No elaborate State conspiracy could be hatched and developed in the palace of its intended victim—under the very noses, as it were, of his friends and dependents—and all within the space of a revolution of the sun. In

effect, however, this is what the poet in the grated box
asks us to believe probable.   His scene never changes ;
the incidents he sets out extend only from one dawn to
the next.   In observing the laws of art, as the Académie
sensibly remarked of Corneille in their otherwise shallow
criticism upon the *Cid,* he disregards the laws of nature.
In short, like all of his fellow-writers for the theatre, he
has unreservedly adopted the principles of the classical
school.   He has obviously devoted much thought to
considerations of form ; he brings on no character without a direct and palpable relation to the story ; he
uniformly observes an alternation of masculine and
feminine rhymes in his alexandrines; he strains at
uniform stateliness by making long speeches a rule
instead of the exception, by avoiding any touch of
humour, and by putting poetry into the mouths of
plebeians as well as patricians.   Ideal beauty, undisturbed by an admixture of more realism than a play
must necessarily possess, is to him the end and purpose
of the serious drama.   For all these reasons, then,
his work is not exempt from the description I have
given of French tragedy as a whole.   It has little or
no probability, variety, relief, picturesqueness, colour,
or animation.   But do not allow its stiffness and frigidity
to wholly alienate it from your sympathies.   You will
gain much by listening to it in a broad and independent
spirit.   Its plot is managed with sufficient skill to

deepen our interest in the climax with each successive scene ; its characters are firmly drawn and effectively grouped ; its versification is the offspring of an imaginative, cultivated, and well-stored mind. If our poet is not a Corneille and Racine rolled into one, as has been suggested, he may be said to unite their excellences in a minor degree ; Roman patriotism and energy are painted with sonorous eloquence, and the sorrows of the heroine, another Belvidera, betoken a rare command of pathos and tenderness. In this view, it would seem, I am at one with the audience at large. How closely they watch the players ; how eagerly they follow the march of the story ; how deep is the silence they maintain except when a roar of applause is wrung from them by some burst of passion, some impressive image, some ingenious combination ! Nor is their evident enjoyment qualified by a sense of the disadvantages inseparable from the theory on which the play is written. For the classical system they feel an extreme veneration, partly because their acquaintance with the romantic drama is at best slight (as yet, by the way, Shakspere is unknown here even by name), but chiefly on account of the influence exercised over them by the conventional. Moreover, the presence of spectators on the stage and the glaring anachronisms in the costume of the players do not prevent a sort of theatrical illusion from being created. It might

have been thought that a people like the French, ever
prompt to perceive the ridiculous side of things, would
laugh outright at what we are now witnessing—
a trio of antique Roman conspirators, each with a
periwig on his head and a baldrick over his tunic, proceeding to discuss their plans " in profound secrecy "—
within a few feet of many visible Parisian dandies.
In point of fact, neither of these anomalies, though
set in high relief by the attempt at archæological
accuracy in the scenery, arouses so much as a titter ;
both have become parts of the convention of the stage,
and under the spell of the poetry and the acting they
are often lost sight of altogether. Disastrous hilarity
would follow a stupid line or a *contretemps* among the
players, but there is nothing of the kind to mar the
effect of the tragedy, which, represented with all the
power at the command of the Comédie, is making
triumphant progress. Pleasant visions fill the mind of
the poet in the grated box as his success becomes more
and more certain—visions of a performance of the piece
at Court, of compliments paid to him by royalty, of his
name being put on the State pension list, of players
coming to him with his share of the receipts, a free
admission to the Comédie for life, and solicitous inquiries
as to any new tragedy he might have ready for production. It is not unlikely that the most high-flown of
his expectations will be realized. The curtain falls

upon an unforeseen and well-contrived catastrophe ; loud acclamations, emphasized in the parterre by the waving of hats and handkerchiefs, split our ears for several minutes ; the whole audience, particularly the men of letters, begin to discuss the quality of the play with an interest keen enough in some instances to make them heedless of the importunities of comely damsels who are going over the house to sell lemonade, " liqueurs qui chauffent l'estomac," and other mysterious decoctions—and a world of pleasant excitement prevails.

No, we are not to remain in the *salle* while the afterpiece is being got ready. Bearing a letter of introduction to the players from the newly-arrived British ambassador in Paris, my high-natured lord of Portland, we are conducted through a door at the side of the stage to the green-room—a spacious apartment immediately behind the scenes, with carefully polished flooring, elaborate stamped velvet furniture, and some portraits and busts of past and present lights of the theatre. Here, mingled with the actors and actresses who a few minutes ago were at their work, and who have not yet thrown off their curious amalgam of ancient and modern costume, are the laced and scented haunters of the wings, the poets of the *banc formidable*, a sprinkling from the amphitheatre and boxes, and gossips anxious to know how the new tragedy has been received. None of the visitors come but in full dress, and the

consequent wealth of colour, together with the eager
conversation going on all round, inclines us to doubt
whether we have not been suddenly transported by
enchantment into a brilliant *salon*. It is not merely at
first representations that such gatherings are to be
witnessed within these walls. Night after night, in the
interval between the two pieces of which the programme
is composed, the *foyer des artistes* is a resort of the wit
and fashion of the town. Everybody brings with him
an anecdote, a bon-mot, a piece of scandal, a more or
less pointed criticism, or a scrap of news from beyond
the frontiers. For a time all social distinctions seem to
be forgotten ; the peer meets the artist and the man of
letters on a footing of perfect equality. "For myself,"
writes one actor, "I must acknowledge that to the
reunions in our green-room—to the discussions on matters
of literature and art, to the brilliant remarks made by
the combatants, and last, but not least, to the exquisite
taste and good breeding which preside over the whole
intercourse—I am indebted for the elements of my
professional success." "In this *foyer*," says another,
"there is much that can help to form the taste and
mature the judgment of a young player—intellectual
energy and .elegance of manners. Besides that, the
actresses feel themselves in a measure forced to adopt
the tone of high rank, and to observe, above all, a strict
regard for decorum." Regard for decorum, indeed, is a

rule of conduct with the most feather-brained of the *gens
du bel air*.   His gallantry is never coarse, and an actress
joins the little crowd in this room without fear of
experiencing any rudeness at his hands.   In this we
have another proof of the social influence of the King,
who carries respect for women to the point of raising his
hat to his chamber-maids on passing them in the palace
—we have Saint Simon's authority for the statement—
and who would not fail to take part with a daughter of
Molière if an indignity were put upon her by even the
proudest of the nobles.   As for the assemblage on the
present occasion, it can hardly be inferior in brillancy
and interest to any the room has yet contained.   It
includes a large number of men distinguished by rank,
wealth, or genius, their elaborate and diversely-coloured
dress being set off in some instances by a profusion of
gems.   Flushed with excitement, but outwardly calm
and diffident, the author of the tragedy is the centre of
one group ; a second has formed round Mdlle. Champmêlé, Beaubourg, and other players.   In a corner, with
the old self-satisfied look and manner in no wise abated,
Baron is airily talking to the Duc d'Aumont, probably
of the halcyon days at the Palais Royal; M. l'Abbé
Brueys, with his merry little eyes gleaming through
close-fitting spectacles, is telling a Gascon story in true
Gascon style to a lover of such things ; Pradon,
manifestly on the brink of the grave, indulges in a

sarcasm at the expense of the literary hero of the
night; Regnard, ever in the best of spirits, invites a
titled wit to pass a few days with him at Grillon; the
editor of the *Mercure Galant*, barely able to recognize
anybody, so poor-sighted is he, moves about in the
hope of catching some of the pleasantries in which the
conversation abounds. Racine, perhaps to avoid the
embarrassment of meeting his former mistress, has
remained away; but Boileau, now " growing old and a
little deaf," comes in with a seigneur of literary tastes,
to whom he is laying down the law on a question
of style. Near him, in the place of honour upon
the walls, is a half-length portrait of the man he
so well understood, appreciated, and loved—Molière.
It represents the dramatist-player sitting with careless
grace at the side of a table, with his head resting upon
his left hand, and with an expression of profound
humour lighting up his large, dark, eloquent eyes. He
seems to be mentally elaborating the first conception
of a *Bourgeois Gentilhomme*, a *Monsieur de Pourceaugnac*,
or a *Malade Imaginaire*. But this is not all; the face
has a nameless something which suggests his tenderness,
his power of observation, his nobility of nature, his
immense force of intellect and character. Glancing at
the picture, Boileau cannot resist the temptation to
speak of his life-long friend, and there are tears in the
voice of the adamantine critic as he proceeds. " In point

of style," he adds, " the Golden Age has had only three great writers—Corneille, Molière, and myself." His companion mentions Racine. " Doubtless a remarkable man," is the reply; " I taught him to write difficult verse. Molière is unapproachable in all he did. Regnard comes next as a comic dramatist, though at a very long distance. I have heard him called mediocre; there is no mediocrity in his gaiety." But let me present you to Mdlle. Champmêlé, who is advancing towards us. In the vale of years, yet retaining much of the beauty and grace which brought Racine to her feet, she returns our low bows with an elaborate curtsy, bids us welcome to the Comédie, and evinces some curiosity as to the achievements of Betterton and Mrs. Barry. May she hope that we will do his majesty's players the honour of occupying seats on the stage during the afterpiece ? For the sake of consistency we ought not to take advantage of a custom we have unreservedly condemned, but it might seem a little ungracious to decline what is intended as a high compliment, and I more than suspect that you would like me to accept the invitation. In the end, with many of the fine gentlemen of the green-room, who laugh loudly, comb their periwigs, and complacently survey themselves in hand mirrors, we find ourselves in one of the enclosures at the side of the stage, on which some actors in costume are thinly scattered.

Everything being ready for the performance, the

fiddlers in the orchestra bring their labours to a close, a liveried servant solemnly knocks three times on the floor with a sort of club, the signal for the curtain to be drawn up is given, and in an instant we are confronting those countless faces in the *salle*. In the rear of the stage, with the light of a row of lamps and candles well upon it, is a canvas representing the depths of a forest; a peasant and his wife, moving almost within reach of the spectators at the wings, pit their tongues at each other in a very comic quarrel, and before the scene is half over a general ripple of mirth has set in. Yes, the piece is the second of Molière's assaults upon the doctors of his day, *Le Médecin Malgré Lui*. For more than one reason I am glad that it has been chosen to follow the new tragedy. It is the best of a few plays in which the spirit of mediæval farce survives in a latter-day form. Molière, who combined wide reading with catholicity of taste, did not share in the all but universal contempt induced by the Renascence for the literature of what are called the Dark Ages. He took the story of *Le Médecin Malgré Lui* from a fabliau of the twelfth century, *Le Vilain Mire*, the only known copy of which is in the royal library. In its turn, *Le Vilain Mire*, like many other productions of the Trouvères, had its origin in one of the Oriental tables brought to France by returning Crusaders. "In this tale," as a writer not unknown

to fame puts it, " the hero, having been cudgelled into
a leech of deep skill, is commanded by the King, on
pain of perishing under the bastinado, to cure at once
all the sick of the capital. The mock doctor dexterously
extricates himself from his dilemma. He assembles his
patients in a great hall, at one end of which is lighted
a mighty fire. 'My friends,' he says, 'it is true that
I can cure all your complaints. But an indispensable
ingredient in my panacea is the ashes of a man who
has been burnt alive. No doubt the patient who feels
himself most deplorably indisposed will sacrifice himself
for the sake of the others. You, sir,' addressing a
gouty patient, 'seem to be the greatest invalid present?'
'I?' replies Gout; 'appearances are deceitful; I was
never better in my life than at this moment.' 'Then
what business have you among the sick? Get you
gone. You,' to a paralytic patient, 'have, I presume,
no objection to become the scapegoat?' 'Every objection p-p-possible,' stuttered Palsy; and he is turned out
to hobble after Gout. The doctor gets rid of all his
patients in the same manner without any loss of reputation, for as they leave the hall they are interrogated
severally by the King, to whom, under apprehension of
being sent back to be calcined, they all report themselves
perfectly cured." Molière, advisedly or otherwise, did
not introduce this incident into his drama, which, however, is sufficiently rich in matter to make us regardless

of the omission.   And in working out the story he was perceptibly influenced by the leading characteristics of the farce to which the fabliaux gave rise.   One of those characteristics was a free use of the stick ; in *Le Médecin Malgré Lui,* as in other Molièrean pieces, the stick plays a prominent part.   But the dramatist does not fail to set upon his continuation of the old farce the impress of his unique individuality.   *Le Médecin Malgré Lui* reveals his distinctive humour, his distinctive pointedness of satire, his no less distinctive power of clothing the broadly farcical with the attributes of true comedy.   Of the higher qualities laid under contribution in his graver work he is debarred by the nature of the subject from offering an illustration.   In the structural arrangement, too, he strengthens himself by an assertion of all the freedom conceded to the comic dramatists in regard to time and place.   Not only does the story extend over more than twenty-four hours, but the background, despite the inconvenience caused by an audience at the wings, is repeatedly changed.   Unfortunately, the unity of action, though barely less irksome than its companion rules, is practically respected ; and the tendency shown in French literature from a very early period to substitute types for human beings—a tendency which the stock-character pieces of the Italians did nothing to check—is deepened by the consequent deficiency in the means of throwing

side lights on the personages.   Both tragedy and comedy
in general are open to this reproach, the characters in
the drama being divided by the players into kings,
queens, princes, princesses, noble fathers, coxcombs,
ingénues, crabbed or indulgent parents, well-graced
lovers, soubrettes, *rôles à manteau,* countrymen, financiers, etcetera.   Sometimes, as in the case of Crispin,
the same figure appears in different pieces under the
same name.   But the short-comings of *Le Médecin
Malgré Lui* are less apparent in the performance than
in the reading.   The acting is marked by a genial
sympathy with the spirit of the work, a high degree
of technical skill, a naturalness of movement and speech
in odd contrast with the style cultivated in tragedy,
and last, though not least, a distinct feeling for general
besides individual excellence.   Dressed after the fashion
of the Molièrean doctors, in a high pointed hat and
grotesquely formal garb, the representative of the
médecin malgré lui is extremely diverting, whether in
the solemn pedantry of his air, the unintelligible Latin
which makes his ill-educated listeners think that he is
a very learned man, his immortal saying on finding that
he has mistaken the relative positions of the heart and
the liver (*nous avons changé tout cela*), his discovery
that as dead men tell no tales his new trade has peculiar advantages, or in the terrible threat to his wife—
" the anger of a doctor is more to be feared than you

can think ! " As for the audience, they seem beside themselves with mirth, however familiar they may be with the incidents and wit of the piece. One roar of laughter has scarcely subsided when another is raised. Suddenly the *dénouement* is sprung upon us ; the players, ranging themselves in a line before the footlights hand in hand, make a stately bow to all parts of the house, and the curtain again falls.

Presently, with the smell of extinguished lamps and candles qualified by the perfume from the dresses of the coxcombs surrounding us, we pass out at the stage door, turn into the Rue des Fossés St. Germain, and make our way through the dispersing crowd of play-goers and a line of those ponderous coaches to an overhanging house opposite the façade of the Comédie, the Café Procope, so called from the name of its proprietor, by birth a Sicilian, but with much of the enterprise and perseverance of our own race. Introduced into Paris by a Turkish ambassador about thirty years ago, the use of coffee, probably to the disgust of Madame de Sévigné, who once predicted that, like Racine's plays, it would soon go out of fashion, has become quite common of late, and establishments for the sale of the beverage are neither few nor far between. Of these, there can be no doubt, the Café Procope, which has existed since 1689, is, as it deserves to be, the most successful. Passing through the door, where three or four sous are exacted from each of us for admission, we enter a room of unusually large size, fairly well lighted, decorated in good taste, amply provided with chairs and tables, and numbering among the company assembled in it—what a clatter all their tongues make!—some men distinguished by talent or rank or wealth. For this café is to Paris what Will's coffee-house is to London. Every evening, especially when there has been something new at the theatre, men of letters and artists meet here for the feast of reason and the flow of soul. In the Covent Garden haunt, as Ned Ward's *London Spy* will put it, "beaux and wits are conceited if they have but the honour to dip a finger and thumb into Mr. Dryden's snuff-box." M. Despréaux Boileau, who has come over from the Comédie to regale himself with a dish of tea, is an object of equal veneration to the patrons of the Procope. Now he is begged by Campistron and others to become arbiter in a critical dispute; anon a few young actors gather round him to learn how a particular part was played by his friend Molière. In the obviously high spirits of the latter group we have a proof that the new tragedy has triumphed. Had its fate been different they would not laugh quite so cheerily. For the income of a Comédien du Roi is scarcely large enough to permit him to view a single failure with equanimity. In the aggregate, it is true, the receipts for a year amount to

about 250,000 livres (francs), the prices of admission,
which are doubled on the first six representations
of a novelty, being fifteen sous for the parterre, one
livre for the third tier boxes, one livre ten sous for the
loges hautes, and three livres for the boxes, the amphitheatre, and seats on the stage. Probably this total
would be more by 50,000 livres if the trifling subsidy
from the State were not frequently reduced, if fine
gentlemen whom it is inexpedient to dun did not come
to the theatre on credit, and if the doors were not closed
for a fortnight at Easter, on festival days, and at times
of public mourning. On the other hand, the outlay of
the players is relatively high. In addition to paying
the ordinary expenses of a theatre, which are greater
here than in London, they have to allow each retired
sociétaire a pension of 1000 livres, contribute to various
public charities, and share in the cost of cleansing and
lighting the streets. From next March twelvemonth
this load of taxation will be largely increased by an
order requiring them to set apart a sixth of their
receipts for the benefit of the poor, and the prices of
admission will then be raised respectively to eighteen
sous, one livre four sous, one livre sixteen sous, and
three livres twelve sous. As it is, the expenditure
amounts to about 100,000 livres a year, and a profit of
150,000 livres is accordingly left for the twenty-seven
persons who form the company. In accordance with the

King's regulations, this profit is divided into twenty-
three parts, eighteen of the players taking one each,
six a half part each, and three a quarter part each.
What is done with the remainder I do not know.
In round numbers, therefore, a full part comes to
6500 livres (about £260) per year—a sum which,
good as it may be for the time, does not represent a
golden shower. It is only a *sociétaire* who receives as
much, and the promotion of a *pensionnaire* to that rank,
like the leadership in a particular *emploi*, is determined
less by merit than seniority. One item in the expenditure of the players calls for special notice. Continuing the
arrangement entered into with Quinault at the Hôtel de
Bourgogne in 1653, they give the author of a five-act
tragedy or comedy a ninth of the gross takings until
the audience on two consecutive nights, or three times
separately, yields less than 500 livres, when it
becomes the property of the theatre. Pieces in three
acts are paid for on the same principle, but on a lower
scale. *Levers du rideau*, if I am not mistaken, are
bought outright. Under the remuneration-by-results
system, which in some cases, of course, may operate
unfairly, a successful play of orthodox dimensions will
bring its author between 2000 and 3000 livres, in
addition to any profit he may reap by printing it.
Neither the *Cid* nor *Horace* could have put more than
half this amount into Corneille's pocket. In another

respect does the dramatist of to-day find himself in a
position different from that of his predecessors.   Not
only is literature honoured at Court, but his power over
public opinion, like that of the book-writer, has been
practically recognized by the despotic government under
which he lives.   The theatres in Paris are under the
control of the First Gentleman of the Chamber, and no
sentence can be uttered in them until it has received
the sanction of an informally-established censorship.
Social abuses are still as open to attack as they were in
the days of Molière, but anything that may serve to
discredit the existing political system or the heads of
the Court is carefully weeded out.   It is only by a
culpable oversight that such lines as these,

> Esclave d'une femme indigne de ta foi,
> Jamais la vérité n'a percé jusqu'a toi !

could be permitted to remain in a tragedy represented
in the reign of Madame de Maintenon.   In the talk of
the men of letters around us, too, we may detect a new
sense of the dignity of their profession ; they are free
from the once common folly of affecting to write merely
for their own amusement—an affectation which led the
lackey poet Gaillard in 1634 to reproach Corneille for
"selling his plays"—and are gradually profiting by
their increased emoluments to dispense with the rewards
of fulsome dedications to the great.   In no other literary haunt, perhaps, is the change on the latter point

equally apparent.   Hacks from the Grub-street of Paris are seldom to be met with here.   Signor Procope's café has become the resort of the better class of writers, a sort of *académie au petit pied.*

Issuing from this snug sanctuary of genius into the cold night air, and taking care, especially at dark corners, to be on our guard against an attempt in the tortuous and uneven and dimly-lighted streets to relieve us of our purses, we start homewards by way of the riverside, the Port Royal, and the Rue St. Thomas du Louvre.   Yet another subject in connexion with the theatre presents itself for consideration as we go along, —a subject I would willingly avoid, since to speak of it with candour and independence is to speak ill of a body of men engaged in the noblest of causes.   Probably you will agree with me in thinking that our evening's amusement can bear the morning's reflection.   Nothing in the two plays we have witnessed is unfit for the ears and eyes of a daughter, a wife, or a sister.   And this remark may be justly applied to the French drama as a whole.   From the outset it has been above the accepted moral standards of the time.   It is largely free from indelicacy of incident and language.   Tragedy, ever striving at ideal beauty, instinctively avoids such contamination ; comedy, in which greater freedom might be assumed, is content to rely upon wholesome illustrations of character and manners.   A theory sometimes adopted in England, that the peculiar obscenity of the Restoration drama there is due to Parisian influence, is absolutely without foundation.   No writer for the Comédie Française would advisedly appeal to the baser passions of his audience.   In the contrary case, perhaps, he would find it impossible to get his piece represented. The royal players, who in rectitude of conduct do not fall below the level of the class to which they belong, the educated and reputable bourgeoisie, would certainly refuse to appear in such abominations as the *Country Wife* and the *Plain Dealer*.   I must also point out that they hold religion in at least outward respect ; the theatre, as we already know, is closed during the *quinzaine de Pâques* and on the festival days, and infringements of the Third Commandment, with expressions open to an irreverent interpretation, are expunged from what is said on the stage ("O God !" for example, would be changed to "O Heaven !").   Altogether, the work of the French theatre is conducted in a commendable spirit, and I am within the limits of the truth in asserting that it secures the maximum of invigorating pleasure at a minimum of the harm which, like painting and sculpture, it might cause in unscrupulous hands.   Nevertheless, this work continues to encounter a bitter and uncompromising foe in the Roman Catholic Church.   Nearly the whole of the clergy are united in an attempt to abolish the institution which for six or seven centuries after the

Carlovingian era was employed as a handmaid to religion, but which, as they can clearly see, has become a great popular educator in something more than a religious sense, and is doing much to strike away the fetters they impose upon the human mind. Discreetly concealing their real motives in the matter, they vaguely contend that dramatic performances are pernicious in both principle and practice, if not the most formidable means devised by the spirit of evil to keep souls out of Heaven.

In most plays, whether they be grave or gay, the tender passion, of course, is a conspicuous ingredient. Bossuet, who in his *Maximes et Reflexions* has been at pains to state the case against the stage with the utmost care, argues that the representation of even honourable love is harmful. " For," he says, " marriage presupposes concupiscence, an evil we are bound by the rules of faith to resist." If anything, tragedy is viewed with less abhorrence than comedy, probably because comedy is better adapted to the purpose of satire. " Posterity," continues Bossuet, speaking of Molière, " may possibly hear of the end of this poet-comedian, who, while acting in his *Malade Imaginaire* or his *Médecin par Force*, received the last stroke of the illness from which he died a few hours later, passing from the pleasantries of the theatre, among which he drew almost his last breath, to the tribunal of Him who has said, ' Woe unto ye who

laugh now, for ye shall mourn and weep!'" In plainer
language, laughter of any sort is as sinful as it appeared
to St. Basil, and comedy must therefore be deemed an
indefensible means of recreation.   Again, the periodical
assemblage of many persons in one place is held to be
fruitful of immorality, and the denunciations levelled by
the early Christian Church at the degrading exhibitions
in the Roman amphitheatre are applied to the unsullied
poetry of Corneille, Molière, and Racine.   By way of
giving effect to the hostility thus explained, it has
long been decreed that players shall not receive the
Communion or be buried with any of the usual rites
unless they have solemnly sworn before a priest to give
up the stage.   Bossuet, doubtless with some of the fierce
joy he felt in the cruelties perpetrated to enforce the revocation of the Edict of Nantes, tells us that sacraments are
" constantly denied " to those who have resorted to and
not renounced this particular means of livelihood.   During the present reign, too, the clergy, aware of the
reluctance of Louis XIV. to set his authority above that
of the Church, have prosecuted their aims with additional energy.   Besides consigning the remains of
Molière, the Shakspere of France, to an unconsecrated
grave, they have now decreed that players shall not be
married unless they have sworn to leave the stage
forthwith.   Consequently, a player enamoured of his
profession is under a direct inducement to lead an ill-

ordered life or perjure himself, and it is satisfactory to find that of these courses he usually prefers the latter. But this determined persecution of the drama, while serving to keep many off the boards, has little or no influence upon the minds of the great mass of the people. In the first place, few of them are blind to the shallowness of the arguments put forward to justify it. Elevating or amusing without impurity, the drama acted in Paris would not be censured by the fathers of the Church if they were to rise from the dead, and to acknowledge any validity in the plea respecting regular assemblages of the public in one place would be to show a reason for closing markets, fairs, and the house of prayer itself. In their relations with the theatre, moreover, the clergy fall into inconsistencies by no means favourable to the object they have in view. Prelates at Court, the austere Bossuet not excepted, attend dramatic performances at the bidding of their royal master, thereby giving the sanction of their presence to an amusement which they declare to be essentially opposed to the highest interests of mankind. Ecclesiastics incur no reproach by going to the theatre, by writing plays for representation, and by mixing freely with a class stigmatized in the laws of the Church as public malefactors. Religious charities, as there is ample evidence to prove, are ready to accept and even ask for money earned in what preachers call the House of Satan. "Les

Pères Cordeliers," runs one of many such letters addressed to the Comédiens du Roi, "vous supplient très-humblement d'avoir la bonté de les mettre au nombre des pauvres religieux à qui vous faites la charité, et ils redoubleront envers le Seigneur leurs prières pour la prosperité de votre chère compagnie." It is curious to think that if a member of this "chère compagnie" were to die suddenly he would be buried like a dog by the recipients of his open-handedness. Dancourt, meeting that incorrigible rake, Archbishop Harlai, at Court, asked him whether the generosity of the players ought not to save them from excommunication. "Monsieur," was the reply, "we have ears to hear you, hands to receive your offerings, but not the tongues to reply to you." In the opinion of the clergy, to be brief, the theatre is a wicked institution *à capite ad calcem*, but may be turned to their profit as long as it holds out against their attacks—a contradiction which Frenchmen have become a little too keen-sighted to ignore. Lastly, the Church in France has lost much of the authority it possessed down to a comparatively recent time. Its doctrines and fulminations are held in daily increasing disrespect. Infidelity, particularly of the kind just revealed in the pages of Bayle, has taken deep root in the country. "Religious belief," writes the Princess Palatine to the Electress Sophia of Hanover, "is so thoroughly extinct in France that one seldom meets a

young man who does not wish to pass himself off
as an atheist," or rather as a deist.   Looking into the
future, I find that the historian of the seventeenth
century sees the chief causes of this decline of the
power of the clergy in their attempts to fetter the
human mind in an inquiring age, their hostility to
education worthy of the name, their extravagant pretensions, their bitter crusade against the Huguenots,
their not infrequent profligacy.   But the list is far
from being complete unless it includes the indignity
they put upon the remains of Molière—an incident
which may be said to have outraged the moral sense
of the whole nation—and their indefensible attitude
towards what has always been, and will long continue
to be, the most favoured of public amusements.

CHRONOLOGY

OF

THE FRENCH STAGE.

789—1699.

CHRONOLOGY OF THE FRENCH STAGE.

789—1699.

EIGHTH CENTURY.

Histrions recite dialogues relating to acts of the saints.
Charles the Great suppresses the company.

NINTH CENTURY.

Dialogues like those of the Histrions written by Thiébaut de Vernon.

TENTH CENTURY.

Sacred *tableaux vivants* exhibited in the churches.
Liturgical dramas in Latin prose performed before the altar.
Fêtes des Foux.
Appearance of the wandering minstrels.

ELEVENTH AND TWELFTH CENTURIES.

Minstrelsy gives rise to a revival of poetry.
Appearance of the Trouvères and the Troubadours.
Evolution by the former of the Mystery from the Liturgical play.
Invention of *fabliaux, tensons,* and *romans,* in all of which a strong dramatic
    element is perceptible.
Minstrels become the interpreters of the new poetry to the people, as also
    do some of the poets themselves.

THIRTEENTH CENTURY.

Robin et Marion and *Le Jeu de la Feuillée,* by Adam de la Halle, contain
    the germs of farce and comic opera respectively.
Self-degradation of the minstrels.
Decline of poetry.
The Mystery usurps the place of the Latin prose play in the churches.
It divides itself into Mysteries and Miracles.

FOURTEENTH CENTURY.

The sacred drama emancipates itself from direct ecclesiastical influence,
    returns to the market-place, and becomes an independent institution.
Scenery first used.
Historical Mysteries produced.

The Confrères de la Passion authorized by Charles VI. to perform Mysteries in the Hôpital de la Trinité.
Establishment there of the first theatre in Paris.
The Clercs de la Basoche begin to perform in the hall of the Palais de Justice.
Evolution by them of the Moralité and the Farce from the allegorical poems and the *fabliaux* of the Trouvères respectively.
The Enfants sans Souci invent a political and satirical sort of farce, the Sotie.
They play at the Hôpital de la Trinité.
Establishment of a censorship.
The Basochians sent to prison.
Production of *Maistre Pierre Pathelin.*
The Basochians forbidden to act; are again imprisoned.

Louis XII. concedes full liberty to the Basochians and the Enfants sans Souci.
Pope Julius II. satirized in a piece by Pierre Gringoire, *La Mère Sotte.*
Jean Serre on the stage.
Marot an Enfant sans Souci.
François I. renews the privileges of the Confrères de la Passion.
Contests between the Parlement and the Basochians.
The censorship abolished.
Marguérite de Valois a play-writer.
First effects on the French stage of the Renascence.
Hecuba and *Electra* translated by Lazare de Baïf for the Collége de Coquerel.
The Confrères establish themselves at the Hôtel de Bourgogne.
Prohibition of Mysteries and Miracles.
Change in the attitude of the Church towards the stage; players denied Communion or Christian burial.
Plutus translated by Ronsard, *Hecuba* by Bouchetel, and *Iphigenia* by Sibilet.

THE REGULAR DRAMA IN FRANCE.

1552.

Cléopatre Captive, tragedy, *Eugène*, comedy, and *Didon se Sacrifiant*, tragedy, by Jodelle.

1554.

Médée, by Jean de la Péruse.

1555.

Death of Jean de la Péruse.

1556.

Agamemnon, by Toutain.

1558.

Le Monarque, comedy, by Habert.
Les Femmes Sallées, farce, anonymous.
La Trésorière, comedy, by Jacques Grévin.

1559.

Sophonisbe, tragedy in prose, by Mellin de St. Gelais.

1560.

La Mort de César, by Jacques Grévin.
Les Esbahis, comedy, by Grévin.
La Soltane, tragedy, by Gabriel Bounyn.

1561.

Agamemnon, tragedy, by François le Duchat.
Tragedy, " à huit personnages, traictant de l'amour d'un serviteur envers sa
 maîtresse, et de tout ce qui en advint," by Jean Brétog.

1562.

Les Corrivaux, comedy in prose, by Jean de la Taille.
Daïre and *Alexandre,* tragedies, by Jacques de la Taille, who died the same
 year.

1563.

Achille, tragedy, by Nicholas Filleul.
Philanire, tragedy, by Claude Rouillet.

1564.

La Reconnue, comedy, by Rémi-Belleau.

1566.

Lucrèce, tragedy, and *Les Ombres,* pastoral, by Filleul.

1567.

Le Brave, ou Taillebras, by Jean Antoine de Baïf.
Jepthé, ou le Vœu, tragedy, by Florent Chrétien.

1568.

Saul le Furieux, tragedy, by Jean de la Taille.
Porcie, tragedy, by Robert Garnier.

1570.

Death of Jacques Grévin.

1571.

Panthée, tragedy, by Jules de Guersens.
La Famine, ou les Gabaonites, tragedy, by Jean de la Taille.

1573.

Les Morts Vivants, farce, anonymous.
Jodelle died.
Hippolyte, tragedy, by Garnier.
Alexandre, tragedy, by Bondaroi.

1574.

Cornélie, tragedy, by Garnier.
Adonis, tragedy, by Guillaume le Breton.

1575.

Le Muet Insensé, comedy, by Pierre le Loyer.

VOL. II.   A A

1576.

Lucelle, comedy, by Louis Lejars.
Didon, tragedy, by Guillaume de Lagrange.

1577.

Death of Rémi-Belleau.
The Gelosi, a band of Venetian players, come to France.
Abraham et Agar, tragi-comedy, by Duvivier.

1578.

Les Delicieuses Amours de Marc Antoine et de Cléopatre, by Guillaume Belliard.
Marc Antoine, tragedy, by Garnier.
Le Laquais, La Veuve, Les Esprits, Le Morfondu, Les Jaloux, and *Les Escoliers*, comedies in prose, by Pierre de Larivey.

1580.

Holopherne, tragedy, by Adrien d'Amboise.
Antigone, tragedy, by Garnier.
Les Contents, comedy in prose, by Odet de Tournebu.
Clytemnestre, ou l'Adultère, tragedy, by Pierre Matthieu
Histoire Tragique de la Pucelle de Dom-Remi, aultrement d'Orléans, by Fronton du Duc.

1581.

Death of Tournebu.
Le Jeune Cyrus, tragedy, and *La Joyeuse*, comedy, by Nicolas de Montreux.

1582.

Bradamanthe, the first tragi-comedy, introducing the first confidant, by Garnier.
The Clercs de la Basoche cease to act.
Régulus, tragedy, by Jean de Beaubreuil.
Meléagre, tragedy, by Pierre de Boussy.

1583.

The Enfants sans Souci disbanded.
Les Juives, tragedy, by Garnier.
Death of Jules de Guersens.
Tragédie de l'Histoire Tragique d'Esther, by Pierre Matthieu.
Sophonisbe, tragedy, by Claude Mermet.
Thyeste, tragedy, by Roland Brisset.

1584.

La Peste de la Peste, tragedy, by Dumonin.
Baptiste, tragedy, by Brisset.
Les Contents, tragedy, by Tournebu.
Les Napolitaines, comedy, by François d'Amboise.

1585.

Athlète Pastourelle, ou Fable Bocagère, by Montreux.

1586.

Acoubar, ou la Loyauté Trahie, tragedy, by Jacques Duhamel.

1587.

Vashti and *Aman*, tragedies, by Matthieu.

1588.

The Hôtel de Bourgogne let by the Confrères de la Passion to a company of provincial actors for the representation of tragedy and comedy ; Valeran Lecomte appears there ; tapestry used in place of painted scenery.

1589.

Death of Jean de Baïf.
Hercule Furieux, Agamemnon, and *Octavie,* tragedies, by Brisset.

1590.

Death of Garnier.

1592.

La Diéromène, ou le Repentir d'Amour, pastoral, by Brisset.

1593.

La Fable de Diane, by Montreux.

1594.

Isabelle and *Cléopatre,* tragedies, by Montreux.
La Françiade, tragedy, and *Les Déguisés,* comedy in eight-syllable verse, by Jean Godard.

1596.

La Machabée, Tragédie du Martyre des Sept Frères, et de Solomone leur Mère, by Jean Dugravier.
Dioclétian and *Horace,* tragedies, by Daigaliers.
Radégonde, Duchesse de Bourgogne, tragedy, and *Beauté et Amour,* pastoral, by Dusouhait.
Sophonisbe, tragedy, by Antoine de Montchrétien.
Farce joyeuse et profitable à un chacun, contenant la ruse, méchanceté, et obstination d'aucunes femmes, anonymous.
L'Arimène, pastoral, by Montreux.

1597.

Cammate, tragedy, by Jean Hays.
Polixène, tragi-comedy, and *Hypsicratée, ou la Magnanimité,* tragedy, by Jean Béhourt.
Thobie, tragi-comedy, by Jacques Ouyn.
Clorinde, ou le Sort des Amants, pastoral, by Pierrard Poullet.
Esau, ou le Chasseur, " en forme de tragédie," by Jean Béhourt.
Pyrrhe, tragedy, by Jean Hendon.

1599.

Clorinde, tragedy, by Aimard Deveins.
Octavie, Femme de l'Empereur Néron, tragedy, anonymous.
Les Lacènes, tragedy, by Montchrétien.
Saint Clouaud, tragedy, by Hendon.
Riot at the Hôtel de Bourgogne.
Establishment of the Théâtre du Marais in the Rue de la Poterie, by Laporte.

Appearance there of Marie Vernier, the first French actress, Matthieu Lefèvre, Lecomte, Dame Gigogne, and Docteur Boniface.

1600.

Ulysse, tragedy, by Jacques de Champ-Repus.
Tragédie de la Divine et Heureuse Victoire des Machabées sur le Roi Antiochus, by Jean Duvirey.
Sichem, Ravisseur, tragedy, by Duhamel.
L'Adamantine, ou Le Désespoir, tragedy, by Jean Depanney.
Priam, Roi de Troye, tragedy, by François Bertrand.
Les Amours de Dalcméon et de Flore, tragedy, by Etienne Bellone.
David, ou l'Adultère, tragedy, by Montchrétien.

1601.

Italian players in Paris.
Three stock characters—Le Docteur Boniface, Perine, and Dame Gigogne—appear at the Hôtel de Bourgogne.
Les Chastes et Loyales Amours de Théagène et Chariclée, by Alexandre Hardi.
Sophonisbe, tragedy, by Montreux.
Achab, tragedy, by Roland Marcé.

1602.

La Chasteté Repentie, pastoral, by Lavalletrye.
Aman, ou la Vanité, tragedy, by Montchrétien.

1603.

Didon se Sacrifiant, tragedy, by Hardi.
Hector, tragedy, and *Bergerie*, pastoral, in prose, by Montchrétien.

1604.

Scédase, ou l'Hospitalité Violée, Panthée, and *Méléagre*, tragedies, by Hardi.
Lucelle, tragi-comedy, by Duhamel.

1605.

La Rodomontade and *La Mort de Roger*, tragedies, by Charles Bauter.
L'Ecossaise, ou le Désastre, tragedy, by Montchrétien.
Procris, ou la Jalousie Infortunée, tragi-comedy, by Hardi.
Alceste, ou la Fidelité, tragedy, by Hardi.

1606.

Dina, ou le Ravissement; Josué, ou le Sac de Jéricho; and *Debora, ou la Delivrance*, tragedies, by Pierre de Nancel.
Ariadne Ravie, tragi-comedy, by Hardi.
Alphée, ou la Justice d'Amour, pastoral, by Hardi.

1607.

La Mort d'Achille and *Coriolan*, tragedies, by Hardi.
Polixène, Gaston de Foix, and *Meronée*, tragedies, by Claude Billard de Courgenay.

1608.

Death of Jean de la Taille.
Tyr et Sidon, tragedy, by Jean de Schélandre.

Amon et Thamar, and *Alboin, ou la Vengeance,* tragedies, by Nicolas Chrétien.
Panthée, ou l'Amour Conjugal, tragedy, by Dorouvière.
Panthée, and *Saul,* tragedies, by Courgenay.

1609.

L'Ethiopique, ou Les Chastes Amours de Théagène et de Chariclée, tragi-comedy, by Octave Genetay.
Cornélie, and *Arsacome, ou l'Amitié des Scythes,* tragi-comedies, by Hardi.
Alboin, tragedy, *Genèvre,* tragi-comedy, and *Henri le Grand,* tragedy, by Courgenay.

1610.

Théocris, pastoral, by Pierre Trotterel.
Mariamne, tragedy, and *Alcée, ou l'Infidélité,* pastoral, by Hardi.
Phalante, tragedy, anonymous.
The Trois Farceurs, Gaultier-Garguille, Gros-Guillaume, and Turlupin, joined the troupe at the Hôtel de Bourgogne some time before this : so, too, did Bruscambille.

1611.

Le Ravissement de Proserpine par Pluton, tragi-comedy, by Hardi.
Le Fidèle, La Constance, and *Les Tromperies,* comedies, in prose (probably not represented), by Larivey.
Tragédie de Jeanne d'Arques, anonymous.

1612.

Les Corrivaux, comedy, by Pierre Trotterel.
La Force du Sang, comedy, by Hardi.
La Gigantomachie, ou le Combat des Dieux avec les Géants, by Hardi.
L'Ambition Romain, tragedy, by François Bernier.

1613.

Baptiste, ou la Calomnie, tragedy, translated from Buchanan, by Brinon.
Les Amantes, ou la Grand Pastorelle, by Nicolas Chrétien.
Félismène, and *Dorise,* tragi-comedies, by Hardi.

1614.

L'Ephésienne, tragi-comedy, by Brinon.
Œdipe, tragedy, by Nicolas de St. Marthe.
Corine, ou le Silence, pastoral, by Hardi.
Œdipe, Turne, Hercule, and *Clotilde,* tragedies, by Jean Provost.

1615.

Timoclée, ou la Juste Vengeance, tragedy, and *Elmire, ou l'Heureuse Bigamie* and *La Belle Egyptienne,* tragi-comedies, by Hardi.
Sainte Agnès, tragedy, by Trotterel.

1616.

Lucrèce, ou l'Adultère Puni, tragedy, by Hardi.
Death of Adrien d'Amboise.
La Comédie des Proverbes, three-act comedy in prose, by Montluc.

1617.

By this time the players at the Hôtel de Bourgogne have become known as Comédiens Ordinaires du Roi ; also as the Troupe Royale.

La Persanne, ou la Délivrance d'Andromède, and *La Fatale, ou la Conquête du Sanglier de Calydon,* tragedies, by Jean de Gallardon. *Les Urnes Vivantes, ou les Amours de Phelidon et de Polibelle,* tragi-pastoral, by the same.

Farce Plaisante et Récréative, played by Gros-Guillaume, Turlupin, and others.

La Perfidie d'Aman, Mignon et Favori d'Assuérus, tragedy in three acts, anonymous.

Pirame et Thisbé, tragedy, by Théophile Viaud.

1618.

Alcméon, tragedy, and *L'Amour Victorieux ou Vangé,* pastoral, in ten-syllable verse, by Hardi.

Cyrus Triomphant, ou la Fureur d'Astyage, Roi de Mède, tragedy, by Pierre Mainfray.

L'Amour Médecin, comedy, by Pierre de St. Marthe.

Le Martyre de Saint Vincent, and *Le Martyre de Ste. Catherine,* tragedies, by Gallardon.

Les Bergeries, ou Arthénice, pastoral, by the Marquis de Racan.

1619.

La Mort de Daire, tragedy, by Hardi.

Gillette, comedy, in eight syllable verse, by Trotterel.

Farce de Tabarin.

1620.

Théâtre du Marais transferred to a tennis-court in the old Rue du Temple.

Iris, pastoral, by Bourron.

La Rhodienne, ou la Cruauté de Soliman, tragedy, by Mainfray.

Les Ramoneurs, prose comedy, anonymous.

Chriséïde et Armand, tragedy, by Jean Mairet.

La Mort d'Alexandre, tragedy, by Hardi.

1621.

Aristoclée, ou le Mariage Infortuné, and *Frégonde, ou le Chaste Amour,* tragi-comedies, by Hardi.

Death of Montchrétien and Pierre Matthieu.

La Silvie, tragi-comedy-pastoral, by Mairet.

1622.

Gésippe, ou les Deux Amis, tragi-comedy, by Hardi.

Le Trebuchement de Phaëton, tragedy, anonymous.

La Mort de Roger, tragedy, anonymous.

La Mort de Bradamanthe, tragedy, anonymous.

1623.

Phraate, ou le Triomphe des Vrais Amants, tragi-comedy, and *Le Triomphe d'Amour,* pastoral, by Hardi.

Adiator, tragedy, anonymous.

Andromède Delivrée, interlude in three acts, anonymous.

Athamas Foudroyé par Jupiter, interlude in three acts, anonymous.
La Folie de Silène, pastoral, anonymous.

1624.

Parithée, tragi-comedy, by Trotterel.

1625.

L'Amaranthe, pastoral, by Gombaud.
La Silvanire, ou la Morte Vive, tragi-comedy-pastoral, by Mairet.

1626.

Rhodes Subjuguée, Béral Victorieux sur les Génevois, Achille Victorieux,
    and *Tomyre Victorieuse*, tragedies, by Borée. *La Justice d'Amour,*
    pastoral, by the same.
Death of Théophile Viaud.

1627.

Les Galanteries du Duc d'Ossone, comedy, by Mairet.

1628.

Agimée, ou l'Amour Extravagant, tragi-comedy, anonymous.
La Climène, tragi-comedy-pastoral, by C. de Lacroix.
L'Hypocondriaque, ou le Mort Amoureux, tragi-comedy, by Jean Rotrou.
La Virginie, tragi-comedy, by Mairet.
L'Inn ocence Découverte, tragi-comedy, by Jean Auvray.
L a Bague de l'Oubli, comedy, by Rotrou.

1629.

Bellerose appears at the Hôtel de Bourgogne.
Les Folies de Cardénio, tragedy, by Pichou.
Célinde, "poëme-héroïque" in prose, by Baro.
Ligdamon et Lidias, ou la Ressemblance, tragi-comedy, by Georges de Scudéri.
Les Avantures de Rosiléon, tragi-comedy-pastoral, by Pichou.
La Fillis de Scire, pastoral, by Simon Ducros.
L'Esprit Fort, comedy, by Jean Claveret.
Sophonisbe, tragedy, by Mairet.
Mélite, ou les Fausses Lettres, comedy, by PIERRE CORNEILLE.

1630.

Philine, ou l'Amour Contraire, pastoral, by Morelle.
Les Amours d'Astrée et de Celadon, tragi-comedy-pastoral, by Rayssiguier.
Mondori becomes chief actor at the Théâtre du Marais.
Jodelet and Gandolin appear there.
Cléonice, ou l'Amour Téméraire, tragi-comedy-pastoral, by P. B.
L'Infidèle Confidente, tragi-comedy, by Pichou.
Marc Antoine et Cléopatre, tragedy, by Mairet.
Cléagénor et Doristée, tragi-comedy, by Rotrou.
Argénis et Poliarque, ou Théocrine, tragi-comedy, by Duryer.
L'Amphitrite, by Monléon.
La Belinde, tragi-comedy, by Rampale.
La Madonte, tragi-comedy, by Auvray.
L'Inconstance d'Hylas, pastoral, by Maréchal.
Les Avantures Amoureuses d'Omphale, tragi-comedy, by Grandchamp.
La Fillis de Scire, comedy-pastoral, by Pichou.

Le Grand et Dernier Soliman, ou la Mort de Mustapha, tragedy, by Mairet.
Ladiane, comedy, by Rotrou.

1631.

L'Argénis (continuation), by Duryer.
Les Travaux d'Ulysse, tragi-comedy, by Durval.
L'Indienne Amoureuse, ou L'Heureux Naufrage, tragi-comedy, by Durocher.
L'Aminte du Tasse, tragi-comedy-pastoral, by Rayssiguier.
Pichou assassinated.
La Clorise, pastoral, by Baro.
La Dorinde, tragi-comedy, by Auvray.
Les Occasions Perdues, tragi-comedy, by Rotrou.
Le Trompeur Puni, ou Histoire Septentrionale, tragi-comedy, by Scudéri.
L'Heureuse Constance, tragi-comedy, by Rotrou.

1632.

Hardi dead.
La Dorimène, tragi-comedy, by Lecomte.
Les Menechmes, comedy, by Rotrou.
Les Passions Egarées, ou le Roman du Temps, tragi-comedy, by Banchereau.
Les Avantures de Policandre et de Basilie, tragedy, by Vieuget.
Le Ravissement de Florise, ou l'Heureux Evénement des Oracles, tragi-comedy,
    by Cormeil.
Attempt to establish a theatre in the Rue Michel-le-Comte.
Lisandre et Caliste, tragi-comedy, by Duryer.
Hercule Mourant, tragedy, by Rotrou.
Clitandre, tragi-comedy, by Corneille.
Le Vassal Généreux, tragi-comedy, by Scudéri.

1633.

Montfleuri appears at the Hôtel de Bourgogne.
Les Amours Infortunées de Léandre et d'Héron, tragi-comedy, by Laselve.
La Fidèle Tromperie, tragi-comedy, by Gougenot.
La Sœur Valeureuse, ou l'Aveugle Amante, tragi-comedy, by Maréchal.
La Celimène, comedy, by Rotrou.
Pirandre et Lisimène, ou l'Heureuse Tromperie, by Boisrobert.
La Comédie des Comédiens, tragi-comedy, by Gougenot.
In addition to Bellerose, Montfleuri, and the Three Farceurs, the company
    at the Hôtel de Bourgogne now consists of Alizon, Le Capitan
    Matamore, Boniface, Mdlle. Valliot, Mdlle. Beaupré, Mdlle. Beau-
    château, Madame Bellerose, Madame Gaultier, and Madame Lafleur.
Le Thyeste, tragedy, by Monléon.
La Bourgeoise, ou la Promenade de St. Cloud, tragi-comedy, by Rayssiguier.
L'Heureux Naufrage, tragi-comedy, by Rotrou.
La Veuve, ou le Traître Puni, comedy, by Corneille.
La Melise, ou les Princes Reconnus, pastoral comique, by Durocher.

1634.

Bruscambille dead.
La Céliane, tragi-comedy, by Rotrou.
L'Impuissance, tragi-comedy-pastoral, by Veronneau.
La Galérie du Palais, ou l'Amie Rivale, comedy, by Corneille.
La Belle Alphrède, comedy, by Rotrou.
Alcimédon, tragi-comedy, by Duryer.

La Pélerine Amoureuse, tragi-comedy, by Rotrou.
Death of Loyer.
La Comédie des Comédiens, by Scudéri.
L'Amour Caché par l'Amour, tragi-comedy-pastoral, anonymous.
La Suivante, comedy, by Corneille.
Deaths of the Trois Farceurs.
Six members of the company at the Marais—Jodelet, La France, Judot,
  Le Noir, L'Epi, and Mdlle. Le Noir—ordered by the King to go
  over to the Hôtel de Bourgogne.
Guillot-Gorju appears there.

1635.

Richelieu forms the brigade of the Cinq Auteurs to assist him in the com-
  position of plays.
Hippolyte, tragedy, by Pinélière.
Orante, tragi-comedy, by Scudéri.
La Place Royale, ou l'Amoureux Extravagant, comedy, by Corneille.
Agarite, tragi-comedy, by Durval.
Le Fils Supposé, comedy, by Scudéri.
Le Filandre, comedy, by Rotrou.
Les Tuileries, by the Cinq Auteurs.
Le Roland Furieux, by Mairet.
Les Vendanges de Surêne, comedy, by Duryer.
Le Jaloux sans Sujet, tragi-comedy, by Charles Beys.
Agésilan de Colchos, tragi-comedy, by Rotrou.
Disagreement between Corneille and Richelieu.
Les Tuileries, tragi-comedy, by Rayssiguier.
Le Prince Déguisé, tragi-comedy, by Scudéri.
La Cléopatre, tragedy, by Benserade.
L'Innocente Infidélité, tragi-comedy, by Rotrou.
L'Hôpital des Foux, tragi-comedy, by Beys.
Cléomédon, tragedy, by Duryer.
Medée, tragedy, by Corneille.
La Mort de Mithridate, tragedy, by Calprenède.
L'Illusion Comique, comedy, by Corneille.

1636.

Iphis et Iante, tragedy, by Benserade.
Clorinde, tragedy, by Rotrou.
Le Torrismon du Tasse, tragedy, by Alibrai.
Le Railleur, ou la Satire du Temps, comedy, by Maréchal.
Aspasie, comedy, by Desmarets.
L'Athénaïs, tragi-comedy, by Mairet.
Mariamne, tragedy, by Tristan.
La Mort de César, tragedy, by Scudéri.
Amélie, tragi-comedy, by Rotrou.
Bradamanthe, tragi-comedy, by Calprenède.
Didon, tragedy, by Scudéri.
Les Sosies, comedy, by Rotrou.
La Mort d'Achille et la Dispute de ses Armes, tragedy, by Benserade.
L'Amant Libéral, comedy, by Bouscal and Beys.
L'Amant Libéral, comedy, by Scudéri.
Les Deux Pucelles, comedy, by Rotrou.

Celine, ou les Frères Rivaux, tragi-comedy, by Beys.
Le Cid, tragedy, by Corneille.

1637.

Laure Persécutée, tragi-comedy, by Rotrou.
La Mort de Brute et de Porcie, ou la Vengeance de la Mort de César, tragedy, by Guérin de Bouscal.
Jeanne d'Angleterre, tragedy, by Calprenède.
L'Illustre Corsaire, tragi-comedy, by Mairet.
Eurymédon, ou l'Illustre Pirate, tragi-comedy, by Desfontaines.
Mondori stricken with apoplexy.
Panthée, tragedy, by Tristan.
Le Véritable Capitan Matamore, ou le Fanfaron, comedy, by Maréchal.
Les Trahisons d'Arbiran, tragi-comedy, by Douville.
Le Clarionte, ou le Sacrifice Sanglant, tragi-comedy, by Calprenède.
Le Soliman, tragi-comedy, by Alibrai.
Orphise, ou la Beauté Persecutée, tragi-comedy, by Desfontaines.
Lucrèce, tragedy, by Duryer.
La Suite et le Mariage du Cid, tragi-comedy, and *L'Avocat Dupé*, comedy, by Chevreau.
La Vraie Suite du Cid, tragi-comedy, by Desfontaines.
La Sidonie, tragi-comedy, by Mairet.
Gustaphe, ou l'Heureuse Ambition, tragi-comedy, by Benserade.
La Lucrèce Romaine, tragedy, by Chevreau.
Alison, comedy, by Discret.

1638.

Le Docteur Amoureux, comedy, by Levert.
L'Aveugle de Smyrne, tragi-comedy, by the Cinq Auteurs.
Panthée, tragedy, by Durval.
Antigone, tragedy, by Rotrou.
Coriolan, tragedy, by Chevreau.
Hermogène, tragi-comedy, by Desfontaines.
L'Aminte, pastoral, anonymous.
Les Rivaux Amis, tragi-comedy, by Boisrobert.
Les Noces de Vaugirard, ou les Naïvetés Champêtres, pastoral, anonymous.
Les Visionnaires, comedy, by Richelieu and Desmarets.
Les Captifs, ou les Esclaves, comedy, by Rotrou.
Le Véritable Coriolan, tragedy, by Chappoton.
Les Deux Amis, ou Gésipe et Tite, tragi-comedy, by Chevreau.
Clarigène, tragi-comedy, by Duryer.
La Mort de Pompée, tragedy, by Chaulmer.
Lizidor, ou la Cour Bergère, tragi-comedy, by Maréchal.
Le Galimathias, tragi-comedy, by Beaulieu.
Hercule Furieux, tragedy, by Nouvellon.
L'Amour Tyrannique, tragi-comedy, by Scudéri.
Don Quixote de la Manche, comedy, by Bouscal.
Le Comte d'Essex, tragedy, by Calprenède.

1639.

Horace, tragedy, by Corneille.
Le Ravissement de Proserpine, tragedy, by Claveret.
La Quixaire, tragi-comedy, by Gillet de la Tessonnerie.

La Mort des Enfants d'Hérode, ou la Suite de Mariamne, tragedy, by
    Calprenède.
Erigone, tragi-comedy in prose, by Desmarets.
Saint Eustache, tragedy, by Baro.
Don Quixote de la Manche (2nd part), comedy, by Bouscal.
Alcionée, tragedy, by Duryer.
Crisante, tragedy, by Rotrou.
Scipion, tragi-comedy, by Desmarets.
Le Manzolée, tragi-comedy, by Maréchal.
Roxane, tragedy, by Desmarets.
La Chute de Phaëton, tragedy, by Tristran de Vozelle.
Le Jugement de Paris et le Ravissement d'Helène, tragi-comedy, by Saillebrai.
Marie Stuart, Reine d'Ecosse, tragedy, by Regnault.
Mirame, tragi-comedy, by Richelieu and Desmarets.
Saul, tragedy, by Duryer.
Policrite et la Mort du Grand Promédon, ou l'Exil de Nerée, tragi-comedy,
    by Tessonnerie.
Edouard, tragi-comedy, by Calprenède.
L'Innocent Malheureux, ou la Mort de Crispe, tragedy, by Grenaille.
Cléomène, tragedy, by Bouscal.
L'Inceste Supposé, by Lacaze.
Cinna, tragedy, by Corneille.

1640.

Eudoxe, tragi-comedy, by Scudéri.
La Clarimonde, tragi-comedy, by Baro.
L'Innocent Exilé, tragi-comedy, by Chevreau.
Les Deux Alcandres, tragi-comedy, by Boisrobert.
Le Mariage d'Orphée et d'Eurydice, ou la Grande Journée des Machines,
    tragedy, by Chappoton.
La Troade, tragedy, by Sallebrai.
Iphigénie, tragedy, by Rotrou.
Palène, tragi-comedy, by Boisrobert.
Méléagre, tragedy, by Benserade.
Marguérite de France, tragi-comedy, by Gilbert.
Reconciliation of Richelieu and Corneille ; marriage of the latter.
Polyeucte, tragedy, by Corneille.

1641.

Declaration of Louis XIII. in reference to players, who are held to be
    " worthy of respect."
Parthenie, tragi-comedy, by Baro.
Le Grand Timoléon de Corinthe, tragi-comedy, by St. Germain.
L'Injustice Punie, tragedy, by Duteil.
Le Gouvernement de Sanche Pansa, comedy, by Bouscal.
Andromire, tragi-comedy, by Scudéri.
Clarice, comedy, by Rotrou.
Phalante, tragedy, by Calprenède.
Belisaire, tragi-comedy, by Desfontaines.
Le Fils Désavoué, ou le Jugement de Théodoric Roi d'Italie, anonymous.
Thomas Morus, ou le Triomphe de la Foi et de la Constance, tragedy in
    prose, by Laserre.
Les Véritables Frères Rivaux, tragi-comedy, by Chevreau.
L'Esprit Follet, comedy, by Douville.
Blanche de Bourbon, Reine d'Espagne, tragi-comedy, by Regnault.

La Couronnement de Darie, tragi-comedy, by Boisrobert.
La Mort de Pompée, tragedy, by Corneille.

1642.

Le Triomphe des Cinq Passions, tragi-comedy, by Tessonnerie.
Alcidiane, ou les Quatre Rivaux, tragi-comedy, by Desfontaines.
Le Martyre de Saint Eustache, tragedy, by Desfontaines.
Francion, comedy, by Tessonnerie.
Aristotime, tragedy, by Levert.
Alinde, tragedy, by Mesnardière.
Ibrahim, ou l'Illustre Bassa, tragi-comedy, by Scudéri.
Cyminde, ou les Deux Victimes, tragi-comedy, by Colletet.
La Belle Egyptienne, tragi-comedy, by Sallebrai.
La Vraie Didon, ou Didon la Chaste, tragedy, by Boisrobert.
L'Amante Ennemie, comedy, by Sallebrai.
Les Galantes Vertueuses, tragi-comedy, by Desfontaines.
La Mort d'Agis, tragedy, by Bouscal.
Le Sac de Carthage, tragedy in prose, by Laserre.
Les Fausses Vérités, ou Croire ce qu'on ne voit pas, et ne pas croire ce qu'on voit, comedy, by Douville.
Philoclée et Téléphonte, tragi-comedy, by Gilbert.
Arminius, ou les Frères Ennemis, tragi-comedy, by Scudéri.
Le Menteur, comedy, by Corneille.
Europe, comedy, by Richelieu and Desmarets.
Death of Richelieu ; the players of the Hôtel de Bourgogne receive a pension of 12,000 livres from the State.
Death of Mondori.
Retirement of Bellerose.

1643.

Floridor, Michel Baron, and Mdlle. Baron appear at the Hôtel de Bourgogne.
Herménigilde, tragedy in prose, by Calprenède.
La Climène, ou la Triomphe de la Vertu, tragi-comedy in prose, by Laserre.
Esther, tragedy, by Duryer.
La Martyre de Ste. Catherine, tragedy in prose, by Laserre.
Roxelane, tragi-comedy, by Desmarets.
La Belle Esclave, tragi-comedy, by L'Etoile.
L'Absent chez soi, comedy, by Douville.
Le Bélisaire, tragedy, by Rotrou.
Axiane, tragi-comedy in prose, by Scudéri.
La Suite du Menteur, comedy, by Corneille.

1644.

La Folie du Sage, tragi-comedy, by Tristan.
Le Jugement Équitable de Charles le Hardi, dernier Duc de Bourgogne, tragedy, by Maréchal.
Thesée, ou le Prince Reconnu, tragi-comedy in prose, by Laserre.
La Stratonice, ou le Malade d'Amour, tragi-comedy, by Debrosse.
Perside, ou la Suite d'Ibrahim Bassa, and *L'Illustre Olympie, ou le Saint Alexis*, tragedies, by Desfontaines.
Rodogune, tragedy, by Gilbert.
Sainte Catherine, tragedy, by St. Germain.

La Mort de Sénèque, tragedy, by Tristan.
Rodogune Princesse des Parthes, tragedy, by Corneille.

1645.

Oroondate, ou les Amants Discrets, tragi-comedy, by Bouscal.
La Virginie Romaine, tragedy, by Leclerc.
Les Innocents Coupables, comedy, by Debrosses.
Célie, ou le Viceroi de Naples, comedy, by Rotrou.
First Italian opera in Paris.
Jodelet, ou le Maître Valet, by Paul Scarron.
L'Art de Regner, ou le Sage Gouverneur, tragi-comedy, by Tessonnerie.
L'Illustre Comédien, ou le Martyre de St. Genest, tragedy, by Desfontaines.
Artaxerxe, tragedy, by Magnon.
La Dame Suivante, comedy, by Douville.
La Mort de Crispe, ou les Malheurs Domestiques du Grand Constantin, tragedy, by Tristan.
Bérénice, tragi-comedy in prose, by Duryer.
Papyre, ou le Dictateur Romain, tragedy, by Maréchal.
Zénobie, Reine des Palmyréniens, tragedy in prose, by the Abbé d'Aubignac.
La Sœur, comedy, by Rotrou.
Théodore, Vierge et Martyre, tragedy, by Corneille.
Le Curieux Impertinent, ou le Jaloux, posthumous comedy, by another Debrosse.
Aimer sans Savoir Qui, and *Les Morts Vivants,* comedies, by Douville.
Retirement of Guillot-Gorju.

1646.

Sigismond Duc de Varsau, tragi-comedy, by Tessonnerie.
Death of Adrien de Montluc.
Jodelet Astrologue, comedy, by Douville.
Perselide, ou la Constance d'Amour, tragi-comedy, anonymous.
La Sœur Généreuse, tragi-comedy, by the Abbé Boyer.
Les Songes des Hommes Eveillés, comedy, by Brosse.
La Porcie Romaine, tragedy, by Boyer.
Josaphat, tragi-comedy, by Magnon.
Le Véritable St. Genest, tragedy, by Rotrou.
Les Boutades du Capitan Matamore, one-act comedy in eight-syllable verse, by Scarron.
Scévole, tragedy, by Duryer.
Aricidie, ou le Mariage de Tite, tragi-comedy, by Levert.
Séjanus, tragedy, by Magnon.
La Coiffeuse à la Mode, comedy, by Douville.
Les Trois Dorothées, ou le Jodelet Soufpleté, comedy, by Scarron.
Le Turne de Virgile, tragedy, by Debrosse.
Hippolyte, ou le Garçon Insensible, tragedy, by Gilbert.
L'Inconnue, comedy, by Boisrobert.
Les Danaïdes, tragedy, by Gombaud.

1647.

Héraclius, Empereur d'Orient, tragedy, by Corneille.
Thémistocle, tragedy, by Duryer.
La Déniaisé, comedy, by Tessonnerie.
La Mort d'Asdrubal, tragedy, by the actor Montfleuri.
Belissante, ou la Fidelité Reconnue, tragi-comedy, by Desfontaines.

La Mort de Roxane, tragedy, anonymous.
Sémiramis, tragedy, by Gilbert.
La Véritable Sémiramis, tragedy, by Desfontaines.
Orfeo, Italian opera.
Don Bernard de Cabrère, tragi-comedy, by Rotrou.
L'Intrigue des Filoux, comedy, by L'Etoile.
Porus, ou la Générosité d'Alexandre, tragedy, by Boyer.
Le Prince Rétabli, tragi-comedy, by Bouscal.
Le Grand Tamerlan, ou la Mort de Bajazet, tragedy, by Magnon.
La Mort des Enfants de Brute, tragedy, anonymous.
Aristodème, tragedy, by Boyer.
Venceslas, tragedy, by Rotrou.
Les Engagements du Hazard, comedy, by Thomas Corneille.

1648.

Le Mariage d'Oroondate et de Statira, ou la Conclusion de Cassandre, tragi-
    comedy, by Magnon.
Tiridate, tragedy, by Boyer.
Le Prince Fugitif, "poëme dramatique," by Baro.
La Mort de Valentinian et d'Isidore, tragedy, by Tessonnerie.
Ulysse dans l'Isle de Circé, ou Euryloche Foudroyé, tragi-comedy, by Boyer.
Le Feint Astrologue, comedy, by T. Corneille.
Cosroès, tragedy, by Rotrou.

1649.

Cariste, ou les Charmes de la Beauté, dramatic poem, and *Rosemonde,*
    tragedy, by Baro.
L'Aveugle Clairvoyant, comedy, by Debrosse.
L'Héritier Ridicule, ou la Dame Intéressée, comedy, by Scarron.
La Florimonde, comedy, by Rotrou.
La Jalouse d'Elle-même, comedy, by Boisrobert.
Nitocris, Reine de Babylone, tragi-comedy, by Duryer.
L'Amante Vindicative, dramatic poem, by Baro.

1650.

Zénobie, Reine d'Arménie, tragedy, by Montauban.
Amours d'Apollon et de Daphné, three-act tragi-comedy, by Dassoucy.
Adolphe, ou le Bigame Généreux, tragi-comedy, by Lebigre.
Les Soupçons sur les Apparences, "heroïco-comédie," by Douville.
Dynamis, Reine de Carie, tragi-comedy, by Duryer.
Don Lope de Cardonne, tragi-comedy, by Rotrou.
Death of Rotrou.
Raimond Poisson and Jean Devilliers appear at the Hôtel de Bourgogne.
Amarillis, pastoral, by Duryer.
Don Bertrand de Cigarral, comedy, by T. Corneille.
Torelli comes to Paris.
Andromède, tragedy, by Corneille.

1651.

Les Charmes de Félicie, pastoral, by Montauban.
Don Sanche d'Arayon, heroic-comedy, by Corneille.
L'Amour à la Mode, comedy, by T. Corneille.
La Folle Gageure, ou les Divertissements de la Comtesse de Pembroc, comedy,
    by Boisrobert.

1652.

Seleuchus, tragi-comédie-héroïque, by Montauban.
Amarillis, pastoral, by Rotrou.
Lubin, ou le Sot Vengé, one-act comedy in eight-syllable verse, by Raimond
     Poisson.
Soliman, ou l'Esclave Généreuse, tragedy, by Jacquelin.
Death of L'Etoile.
Les Illustres Foux, comedy, by Beys.
Les Trois Orontes, comedy, by Boisrobert.
Nicomède, tragedy, by Corneille.
Don Japhet d'Arménie, comedy, by Scarron.

1653.

La Mort d'Agrippine, Veuve de Germanicus, tragedy, by Cirano de Bergerac.
Le Berger Extravagant, comedy, by T. Corneille.
Le Comte de Hollande, tragi-comedy, and *Indégonde,* tragedy, by Montauban.
Le Charme de la Voix, comedy, by T. Corneille.
Cassandre Comtesse de Barcelone, tragi-comedy, by Boisrobert.
Pertharite, Roi des Lombards, tragedy, by Corneille.
Corneille resolves to write no more for the stage.
Les Rivales, comedy, by Quinault.
Establishment of the *part d'auteur.*

1654.

Le Pédant Joué, comedy in prose, by Cirano de Bergerac.
La Généreuse Ingratitude, tragi-comedy-pastoral, by Quinault.
L'Eunuque, comedy, by Lafontaine (it is doubtful whether this piece was
     represented).
La Belle Plaideuse, comedy, by Boisrobert.
Le Parasite, comedy, by Tristan.
Les Illustres Ennemis, comedy, by T. Corneille.
Les Généreux Ennemis, comedy, by Boisrobert.
L'Ecolier de Salamanque, ou les Généreux Ennemis, tragi-comedy, by
     Scarron.
Introduction of Crispin.
L'Amant Indiscret, ou le Maître Etourdi, comedy, by Quinault.
Jeanne de Naples, tragedy, by Magnon.

1655.

Les Apparences Trompeuses, comedy, by Boisrobert.
Anaxandre, tragi-comedy, by Duryer.
L'Amant Ridicule, comedy in one act, by Boisrobert.
Le Gardien de Soi-Même, comedy, by Scarron.
Le Géolier de Soi-Même, by T. Corneille.
La Comédie sans Comédie, by Quinault.
Laroque and Hauteroche appear at the Théâtre du Marais.
Deaths of Tristan, Cirano de Bergerac, Michel Baron, and Vion d'Alibrai.

1656.

Damon et Pythias, tragedy, by Chappuzeau.
Les Coups d'Amour et de Fortune, comedy, by Boisrobert.
Les Coups de l'Amour et de Fortune, comedy, by Quinault.
Osman, tragedy, by Tristan.

La Belle Invisible, ou la Constance Eprouvée, comedy, by Boisrobert.
La Mort de Cyrus, tragedy, by Quinault.
Le Marquis Ridicule, ou la Comtesse fait à la Hâte, comedy, by Scarron.
Timocrate, tragedy, by T. Corneille.

1657.

Le Campagnard, comedy, by Tessonnerie.
Théodore, Reine d'Hongrie, tragi-comedy, by Boisrobert.
Le Mariage de Cambyse, tragi-comedy, by Quinault.
Bérénice, tragedy, by T. Corneille.
Cresphonte, ou le Retour des Héraclides dans le Peloponnèse, tragi-comedy,
    and *Les Amours de Diane et d'Endymion,* tragedy, by Gilbert.
Amalasonte, tragedy, by Quinault.
Le Jugement de Paris et le Ravissement d'Helène, tragi-comedy, by Salle-
    brai.

1658.

Italian players, including Scaramouche and Dominique, appear at the Hôtel
    du Petit Bourbon, receiving a pension of 12,000 livres from the State.
Astianax, tragedy, anonymous.
Le Feint Alcibiade, tragi-comedy, by Quinault.
Les Sœurs Jalouses, ou l'Echarpe et le Brasselet, comedy, by Lambert.
Performance given by MOLIÈRE and his troupe before the King in the guard-
    hall of the old Louvre, October 24.
The Hôtel du Petit Bourbon assigned to the new-comers, who are made
    " Comédiens de Monsieur."
They appear alternately with the Italian players.
Molière's company at the outset consists of himself, Madeleine Béjart,
    Ducroisy, Mdlle. Duparc, Wilquin Debrie, Duparc (Gros-René),
    Geneviève Béjart, Lagrange, the two brothers Béjart, and Mdlle.
    Debrie.
Representation of Molière's *L'Etourdi,* originally produced at Lyons in
    1653.
Duryer died, Nov. 6.
Molière joined by L'Épi and Brécourt.
Le Dépit Amoureux, comedy, by Molière, first played in the provinces.
La Mort de l'Empereur Commode, tragedy, by T. Corneille.

1659.

Pierre Corneille returns to the theatre. His *Œdipe,* tragedy.
Le Festin de Pierre, ou le Fils Criminel, tragi-comedy, by Devilliers.
Death of Colletet.
Clotilde, tragedy, by Boyer.
Death of Béjart the elder, May 21.
Le Fantôme Amoureux, tragi-comedy, by Quinault.
Second Italian opera in France.
Arie et Pétus, ou les Amours de Néron, tragedy, by Gilbert.
Death of Charles Beys.
Ostorius, tragedy, by the Abbé de Pure.
Fédéric, tragedy, by Boyer.
Les Précieuses Ridicules, one-act comedy in prose, by Molière.
Zénobie, Reine de Palmyre, tragedy, by Magnon.
Darius, tragedy, by T. Corneille.
Les Précieuses, comedy, by the Abbé de Pure.

1660.

Stratonice, tragi-comedy, by Quinault.
La Mort de Démétrius, ou le Rétablissement d'Alexandre, Roi d'Epire, tragedy, by Boyer.
Le Mariage de Rien, one-act comedy in eight-syllable verse, by Montfleuri fils.
L'Apothiquaire Dévalisé, comedy, by Devilliers.
Sganarelle, ou le Cocu Imaginaire, one-act comedy, by Molière.
La Toison d'Or, tragedy, by Corneille.
Le Galant Doublé, comedy, by T. Corneille.
La Magie sans Magie, comedy, by Lambert.
Spanish comedians established in Paris.
Death of Jodelet.
La Feinte Mort de Jodelet, comedy, by Brécourt.
Le Cartel de Guillot, ou le Combat Ridicule, one-act comedy, in eight-syllable verse, by Chevalier.
Death of Scarron.
Les Amours de Lysis et d'Hespérie, allegorical-pastoral, by Quinault.
Tigrane, tragedy, by Boyer.

1661.

Troupe de Mademoiselle, headed by Dorimon, established in the Rue des Quatre Vents, Faubourg St. Germain.
Le Festin de Pierre, tragi-comedy, and *L'Amant de sa Femme* and *L'Inconstance Punie*, one-act comedies, by Dorimon.
Camma, tragedy, by T. Corneille.
Erixène, tragedy, anonymous.
Don Garcie de Navarre, ou le Prince Jaloux, heroic comedy, by Molière.
Les Bêtes Raisonnables, one-act comedy, by Montfleuri.
Agrippa Roi d'Albe, ou le Faux Tibérinus, tragi-comedy, by Quinault.
La Femme Industrieuse, La Comédie de la Comédie, and *Les Amours de Trapolin*, one-act comedies, by Dorimon.
L'Ecole des Maris, three-act comedy in verse, by Molière, June 4.
First appearance of Armande Béjart.
La Roselie, ou Don Guillot, comedy, and *L'Ecole des Cocus, ou la Précaution Inutile*, one-act comedy in verse, by Dorimon.
Les Fâcheux, three-act comedy-ballet in verse, by Molière, Nov. 4.
L'Académie des Femmes, three-act comedy in verse, by Chappuzeau.
La Désolation des Filoux sur la défense de porter les armes, ou le Malade qui se portent bien, one-act comedy in eight-syllable verse, by Chevalier.
Le Médecin Volant, one-act comedy in verse, by Boursault.
Pyrrhus, Roi d'Epire, tragedy, by T. Corneille.

1662.

Policrite, tragi-comedy, by Boyer, Jan.
Le Riche Mécontent, ou le Noble Imaginaire, comedy, by Chappuzeau.
Maximian, tragedy, by T. Corneille, Feb.
Sertorius, tragedy, by Corneille, Feb. 25.
Death of Boisrobert, March 30.
Les Ramoneurs, one-act comedy, by Devilliers.
Le Mort Vivant, three-act comedy, by Boursault.
Death of Magnon, April 12.
Les Galantes Ridicules, ou les Amours de Guillot et de Ragotin, one-act

comedy in eight-syllable verse, and *Les Barbons Amoureux et Rivaux de leurs Fils*, three-act comedy, by Chevalier.
Manlius Torquatus, tragedy, by Catherine Desjardins.
Colin-Maillard, one-act comedy in eight-syllable verse, by Chappuzeau.
Le Baron de la Crasse, one-act comedy, including another comedy in eight-syllable verse, *Le Zigzag*, by Poisson.
Théagène, tragedy, by Gilbert.
La Disgrace des Domestiques, one-act comedy in eight-syllable verse, by Chevalier.
Champagne le Coiffeur, one-act comedy in eight-syllable verse, by Boucher.
Oropaste, ou le Faux Tonaxare, tragedy, by Boyer.
Death of Mdlle. Baron.
L'Intrigue des Carrosses à Cinq Sols, three-act comedy in verse, by Chevalier.
Mdlle. Descœillets appears at the Hôtel de Bourgogne.
L'Ecole des Femmes, comedy, by Molière, Dec. 26.
Persée et Démétrius, tragedy, by T. Corneille.

1663.

Sophonisbe, tragedy, by Corneille, Jan. 18.
Nitétis, tragedy, by Mdlle. Desjardins, April 2.
Le Mari sans Femme, comedy, by Montfleuri.
Les Amours d'Ovide, heroic-pastoral, by Gilbert.
Mesnardière died, June 4.
La Critique de l'Ecole des Femmes, one-act comedy in prose, by Molière, June 1.
Zelinde, ou la Véritable Critique de l'Ecole des Femmes, one-act comedy in prose, by Devisé.
Le Portrait du Peintre, ou la Contre Critique de l'Ecole des Femmes, one-act comedy in verse, by Boursault.
Death of Calprenède, October.
Lathorillière and Mdlle. Ducroisy join Molière's company.
L'Impromptu de Versailles, one-act comedy in prose, by Molière.
L'Impromptu de l'Hôtel de Condé, one-act comedy in verse, by Montfleuri fils.
Réponse à l'Impromptu de Versailles, ou la Vengeance des Marquis, one-act comedy in prose, by Devilliers.
La Dame d'Intrigue, ou le Riche Vilain, three-act comedy, by Chappuzeau.
Trasibule, tragi-comedy, by Montfleuri fils.
Les Cadenas, ou le Jaloux Endormi, one-act comedy, by Boursault.

1664.

La Bradamanthe Ridicule, comedy, anonymous.
Les Amours de Calotin, three-act comedy, by Chevalier.
Les Amours d'Angélique et de Médor, tragi-comedy, by Gilbert.
Les Amours Déguisés, ballet danced in by Louis XIV., Feb. 13.
Le Mariage Forcé, three-act comedy-ballet, by Molière, Feb. 15.
Hubert joins Molière's company.
La Princesse d'Elide, comedy-ballet, by Molière.
Representation of the first three acts of *Tartuffe* at Versailles.
Troupe du Dauphin appear at the Palais Royal.
Le Fou Raisonnable, one-act comedy in verse, by Poisson.
La Thébaïde, ou les Frères Ennemis, tragedy, by RACINE, June 20.
L'Ecole des Jaloux, ou le Cocu Volontaire, three-act comedy in verse, by Montfleuri.

La Joueuse Dupée, ou l'Intrigue des Académies, one-act comedy in verse, by
 J. D. L. F.
Les Frères Gémeaux, ou la Menteurs qui ne mentent point, comedy, by
 Boursault.
Othon, tragedy, by Corneille, Nov. 5.
Astrate, Roi de Tyr, tragedy, by Quinault, Dec. 15.
Death of Duparc.

1665.

Les Coteux, ou les Marquis Friants, one-act comedy in verse, by Devilliers,
 January.
Brécourt migrates from the Palais Royal to the Hôtel de Bourgogne.
Don Juan, ou le Festin de Pierre, comedy in prose, by Molière, February.
Molière's company made "Comédiens du Roi" and pensioned.
Riot at the Palais Royal.
Le Favori, tragi-comedy, by Mdlle. Desjardins, June.
L'Après-Soupé des Auberges, one-act comedy in verse, by Poisson.
Laserre died, July.
Le Pédagogue Amoureux, comedy, by Chevalier.
L'Amour Médecin, three-act comedy-ballet, by Molière, Sept. 22.
La Mère Coquette, ou les Amants Brouillés, comedy, by Quinault, Oct. 18.
La Mère Coquette, ou les Amants Brouillés, three-act comedy, by Devisé,
 Oct. 24.
Les Yeux de Philis Changés en Astres, pastoral, by Boursault.
Alexandre le Grand, tragedy, by Racine.

1666.

Les Amours de Jupiter et de Sémélé, tragedy, by Boyer, January.
Arsace Roi des Parthes, tragedy, by De Prade.
Agésilas, tragedy, by Corneille, April.
Antiochus, tragi-comedy, by T. Corneille.
Le Misanthrope, comedy, by Molière, June 4.
Les Intrigues Amoureuses, comedy, by Gilbert.
Mdlle. Duparc goes to the Hôtel de Bourgogne.
La Noce de Village, one-act comedy, by Brécourt.
Les Avantures de Nuit, three-act comedy, by Chevalier.
Le Médecin Malgré Lui, three-act comedy in prose, by Molière, Aug. 6.
L'Ecole des Filles, comedy, by Montfleuri *fils*.
Gombaud died.
Le Jaloux Invisible, three-act comedy, by Brécourt, Aug. 20.
Myrtil et Melicerte, heroic pastoral in two acts, by Molière, Dec. 2.
Michel Baron *fils* made a Comédien du Roi.
Les Poëtes, one-act comedy, anonymous.

1667.

Le Sicilien, ou l'Amour Peintre, one-act comedy-ballet, by Molière, January.
Attila, Roi des Huns, tragedy, by Corneille, February.
La Veuve à la Mode, one-act comedy, by Devisé, May 9.
Scudéri died, May 14.
Production of *Tartuffe* at the Palais Royal under the title of *L'Imposteur*,
 Aug. 5.
The performance stopped, Aug. 6.
Léandre et Ero, tragedy, by Gilbert, Aug. 15.
L'Infante Salicoque, ou le Héros des Romans, comedy, by Brécourt.

Délie, pastoral, October, and *L'Embarras de Godard, ou l'Accouchée,* one-act comedy, November, by Devisé.
Andromaque, tragedy, by Racine, Nov. 26.
Cléopatre, tragedy, by Lathorillière.

1668.

Declaration by Louis XIV. that the calling of a player is not incompatible with the quality of gentleman.
Amphitryon, three-act comedy in irregular verse, by Molière, January.
Beauval and Mdlle. Beauval added to Molière's company.
Death of Montfleuri.
Appearance of Juvenon de Lafleur and of Mdlle. d'Ennebaut.
Laodice, Reine de Cappadoce, tragedy, by T. Corneille, February.
La Folle Querelle, ou la Critique d'Andromaque, three-act comedy, by Subligny, May 18.
La Poëte Basque, one-act comedy, by Poisson, June.
L'Amant qui ne flatte point, comedy, by Hauteroche, July.
George Dandin, ou le Mari Confondu, three-act comedy in prose, by Molière, July.
L'Avare, comedy in prose, by Molière, Sept. 9.
Les Faux Moscovites, one-act comedy, by Poisson, October.
Le Duel Fantasque, ou les Valets Rivaux, one-act comedy in eight-syllable verse, by Rosimont, actor at the Marais.
Le Courtisan Parfait, tragi-comedy, by Gilbert.
Le Soldat Poltron, tragi-comedy in eight-syllable verse, anonymous.
Pausanias, tragedy, by Quinault, Nov. 16.
Les Plaideurs, three-act comedy in verse, by Racine, November.
Death of Mdlle. Duparc.
Le Baron d'Albikrac, comedy, by T. Corneille, December.

1669.

Les Maux sans Remèdes, comedy, anonymous, Jan. 11.
Le Jeune Marius, tragedy, by Boyer, January.
Representation of *Tartuffe* formally sanctioned by Louis XIV. ; reproduction of the play, Feb. 15.
La Fête de Vénus, heroic comedy-pastoral, by Boyer, Feb. 15.
La Femme Juge et Partie, comedy, by Montfleuri, March 2.
Le Souper Mal Aprêté, one-act comedy, by Hauteroche, July.
Le Procès de la Femme Juge et Partie, one-act comedy, by Montfleuri.
La Critique du Tartuffe, one-act comedy, anonymous.
Monsieur de Pourceaugnac, three-act comedy in prose, by Molière, Nov. 15.
Le Nouveau Festin de Pierre, ou l'Athée Foudroyé, tragi-comedy, by Rosimont, November.
La Mort d'Annibal, tragedy, by T. Corneille, November.
Britannicus, tragedy, by Racine, Dec. 15.

1670.

Policrate, heroic comedy, by Boyer, January.
Racan died.
Les Amours de Vénus et Adonis, tragedy in irregular verse, by Devisé, March.
Mdlle. Champmêlé and her husband appear at the Marais.
L'Avocat sans Etude, one-act comedy in verse, by Rosimont.
Le Gentilhomme de Beauce, comedy, by Montfleuri, August.
Le Désespoir Extravagant, comedy, anonymous.

Mdlle. Béjart died.
Le Gentilhomme Guespin, one-act comedy, by Devisé.
Retirement of Béjart and of Devilliers and his wife.
Les Trompeurs Trompés, ou les Femmes Vertueuses, one-act comedy, by
    Rosimont.
Les Intrigues de la Loterie, three-act comedy, by Devisé.
La Dupe Amoureuse, one-act comedy, by Rosimont.
Les Amants Magnifiques, comedy-ballet in prose, by Molière.
Les Femmes Coquettes, comedy, by Poisson.
La Comtesse d'Orgueil, comedy, by T. Corneille.
Mdlle. Marotte Beaupré engaged for the Palais Royal.
Bellerophon, tragedy, by Quinault.
Mdlle. Champmêlé and her husband pass over to the Hôtel de Bourgogne ;
    great success of the former.
Le Bourgeois Gentilhomme, comedy-ballet in prose, by Molière, Oct. 14.
Death of Mdlle. Descœillets, Oct. 25.
Bérénice, tragedy, by Racine, Nov. 21.
Tite et Bérénice, by Corneille, Nov. 28.
Death of Mdlle. Devilliers, actress at the Hôtel de Bourgogne.

1671.

Psyché, tragi-comedy-ballet in irregular verse, by Molière, Corneille, and
    Quinault, July 24.
Retirement of Floridor.
Les Amours du Soleil, tragedy with music, by Devisé, January.
Les Fourberies de Scapin, three-act comedy in prose, by Molière, May 24.
Les Grisettes, three-act comedy, and *Les Grisettes,* one-act comedy, by
    Champmêlé.
Les Qui-Pro-Quo, ou le Valet Etourdi, three-act comedy, by Rosimont.
Le Mariage sans Mariage, comedy, by Marcel.
La Comtesse d'Escarbagnas, one-act comedy in prose, by Molière, December.
Perrin and Cambert establish the opera at a theatre built by the Marquis
    de Sourdéac in the Rue Mazarine.
Lulli causes their privilege to be transferred to himself.
Retirement of Floridor.

1672.

Bajazet, tragedy, by Racine, Jan. 5.
Le Mariage de Bacchus et d'Ariane, heroic comedy in three acts, in irregular
    verse, and with various spectacular effects, by Devisé, Jan. 7.
Ariane, tragedy, by T. Corneille, March 4.
Les Femmes Savantes, comedy, by Molière, March 11.
The Spanish players dismissed.
Lisimène, ou la Jeune Bergère, pastoral, in irregular verse, by Boyer.
L'Heure du Berger, pastoral, by Champmêlé.
La Fille Capitaine, comedy, by Montfleuri.
Marotte Beaupré retired.
Le Fils Supposé, tragedy, by Boyer.
La Hollande Malade, one-act comedy, by Poisson.
Les Apparences Trompeuses, ou les Maris Infidèles, three-act comedy, by
    Hauteroche.
Pulchérie, heroic comedy, by Corneille, November.
Théodat, tragedy, by T. Corneille, November.
Death of Floridor.
Le Deuil, one-act comedy, by Hauteroche.

1673.

Mithridate, tragedy, by Racine, January.

L'Ami de tout le Monde, comedy, anonymous.

L'Ambigu Comique, ou les Amours de Didon et d'Enée, three-act comedy, with comic interludes, by Montfleuri.

Le Malade Imaginaire, three-act comedy-ballet in prose, by Molière, Feb. 10.

Death of Molière, Feb. 17.

The Théâtre du Palais Royal assigned to Lulli.

Secession of Baron, Lathorillière, and the Beauvals from the Troupe de Molière to the Hôtel de Bourgogne.

Occupation by Mdlle. Molière and the rest of her troupe of the theatre in the Rue Mazarine.

Closing of the Théâtre du Marais ; the players there—Laroque, Verneuil, Mdlle. Auzillon, Dupin, Dauvilliers, Madame Dupin, Guérin d'Etriché, Madame Dauvilliers, and Mdlle. Guiot—ordered to join Mdlle. Molière.

Mdlle. Ducroisy retired.

Deaths of the Abbé d'Aubignac, Claveret, and Chevalier.

Demarate, tragedy, by Boyer.

Le Comédien Poëte, by T. Corneille, Nov. 10.

Argelie Reine de Thessalie, tragedy, by Abeille.

La Mort d'Achille, tragedy, by T. Corneille, Dec. 29.

1674.

Pirame et Thisbé, tragedy, by Pradon.

Trigaudin, ou Martin Braillard, comedy, by Montfleuri, Jan. 26.

Iphigénie, tragedy, by Racine, February.

Crispin Musicien, comedy, by Hauteroche, July.

L'Ombre de Molière, one-act comedy in prose, by Brécourt.

Panurge, comedy, by Montauban, Aug. 3.

Crispin Médecin, three-act comedy in prose, by Hauteroche.

Suréna, Général des Parthes, tragedy, by Corneille (his last work).

Don César d'Avalos, comedy, by T. Corneille.

1675.

Gilbert died.

Circé, tragedy, with music and spectacular effects, by T. Corneille and Devisé, March 1.

Iphigénie, tragedy, by Leclerc and Coras, May. 24.

Deaths of Geneviève Béjart and Béjart, June.

L'Inconnu, comedy, with music and spectacular effects, by T. Corneille, Nov. 17.

Tamerlan, ou la Mort de Bajazet, tragedy, by Pradon.

Death of Wilquin Debrie.

1676.

Coriolan, tragedy, by Abeille, Feb. 14.

Deaths of Desmarets and Laroque.

Le Volontaire, one-act comedy in verse, by Rosimont, March 6.

Le Triomphe des Dames, five-act comedy in prose, with divertissements, by T. Corneille, Aug. 7.

1677.

Phèdre et Hippolyte, tragedy, by Racine, Jan. 1.
Phèdre et Hippolyte, tragedy, by Pradon, Jan. 3.
Molière's *Don Juan*, rewritten in verse by T. Corneille, revived Feb. 22.
Crispin Gentilhomme, comedy, by Montfleuri.
Electre, tragedy, by Pradon, Dec. 17.
Hissing first resorted to.

1678.

Le Comte d'Essex, tragedy, by Corneille, January.
Le Comte d'Essex, tragedy, by Boyer.
La Dame Médecin, comedy, by Montfleuri, Jan. 14.
Les Nobles de Province, comedy, by Hauteroche, January.
Lyncée, tragedy, by Abeille, Feb. 25.
Les Nouvellistes, three-act comedy, by Hauteroche.
Le Feint Lourdaut, comedy in one act, anonymous.
Anne de Bretagne, tragedy, by Ferrier, November.
Le Cavalier par Amour, comedy, anonymous, Dec. 2.
La Princesse de Clèves, tragedy, by Boursault, Dec. 20.

1679.

La Troade, tragedy, by Pradon, Jan. 17.
Mdlle. Champmêlé and her husband go over to the theatre in the Rue
    Mazarine.
Jean Baptiste Raisin, Mdlle. Bélonde, and Latuillerie appear at the Hôtel
    de Bourgogne.
Mdlle. Auzillon dismissed.
Le Gentilhomme Meunier, one-act comedy, anonymous, May 9.
Crispin Precepteur, one-act comedy in verse, by Latuillerie.
Death of Lathorillière.
Germanicus, tragedy, by Boursault.
La Devineresse, ou Madame Jobin, by T. Corneille and Devisé.
Statira, tragedy, by Pradon.
It becomes certain that Racine will write no more for the stage.

1680.

Genséric, tragedy, by Madame Deshoulières, January.
Adraste, tragedy, by Ferrier, February.
Agamemnon, tragedy, by D'Assezan, March 12.
La Bassette, one-act comedy, by Hauteroche.
Death of the Abbé de Pure.
La Bassette, comedy, by two anonymous authors.
Death of Lafleur.
Les Carrosses d'Orléans, one-act comedy in prose, by Lachapelle.
Union of the companies of the Hôtel de Bourgogne and the theatre in the
    Rue Mazarine at the latter house.

FORMATION OF THE COMÉDIE FRANÇAISE.

Members of the company at the outset: Baron, Mdlle. Champmêlé and
    her husband, Poisson, Mdlle. Beauval, Dauvilliers, Mdlle. Guérin
    (Molière), Lagrange, Mdlle. Bélonde, Hubert, Mdlle. Debrie, Latuil-
    lerie, Mdlle. d'Ennebaut, Rosimont, Mdlle. Dupin, Hauteroche,
    Mdlle. Guiot, Guérin, Ducroisy, Mdlle. Raisin, Raisin, Mdlle.

Ducroisy, Devilliers, Verneuil, Mdlle. Lagrange, Beauval, and Mdlle. Baron

Retirement of Dupin and Madame Dauvilliers

The Hôtel de Bourgogne asssigned to the Italian players.

Soliman, tragedy, by Abeille (in the name of Latuillerie).

Les Foux Divertissants, three-act comedy in verse, by Poisson, Nov. 14.

Aspar, tragedy, by Fontenelle, Dec. 27.

1681.

Zaïde, tragedy, by Lachapelle, Jan. 26.

La Comète, one-act comedy in prose, by Fontenelle, in the name of Devisé, Jan. 29.

La Pierre Philosophale, five-act comedy in prose, with spectacular effects, by T. Corneille and Devisé, Feb. 23.

Le Laquais Fille, comedy, anonymous, April 30.

Crispin Bel-Esprit, one-act comedy, by Latuillerie, July 11.

Endymion, tragedy, anonymous, July 22.

Oreste, tragedy, by Leclerc and Boyer, Oct. 10.

Hercule, tragedy, by Abeille, in the name of Latuillerie, Nov. 7.

Cléopatre, tragedy, by Lachapelle, Dec. 12.

1682.

Death of Mdlle. Beauchâteau.

Tarquin, tragedy, by Pradon.

Zélonide Princesse de Sparte, tragedy, by Genest, Feb. 4.

Retirement of Hauteroche.

Le Parisien, comedy, by Champmêlé.

Les Bouts Rimés, one-act comedy in prose, by Saint Ussans, May 25.

La Rue St. Denis, one-act comedy in prose, by Champmêlé, June 17.

Subvention first paid to the Comédie Française, Aug. 24.

Artaxerce, tragedy, by Boyer, Nov. 22.

La Rapinière, ou l'Intéressé, comedy, by Robbé, Dec. 4.

Téléphonte, tragedy, by Lachapelle, Dec. 26.

1683.

Les Joueurs, comedy, anonymous, Feb. 5.

Virginie, tragedy, by Campistron, Feb. 12.

Le Mercure Galant, ou la Comédie sans Titre, comedy, by Boursault.

Nitocris, tragedy, anonymous, March 10.

Le Rendezvous, one-act comedy, anonymous, May 7.

La Cassette, comedy, anonymous, June 19.

Le Divorce, comedy, anonymous, Sept. 6.

Death of Mdlle. Desjardins (Marquise de Chatté).

Marie Stuart, tragedy, by Boursault.

1684.

Le Docteur Extravagant, comedy, by Beauregard, Jan. 14.

Pénelope, tragedy, by Genest, Jan. 22.

Arminius, tragedy, by Campistron, Feb. 19.

La Dame Invisible, ou l'Esprit Follet, comedy, by Hauteroche, Feb. 22.

Retirements of Mdlle. Guiot and Verneuil.

Débuts of Jacques Raisin, Lathorillière, Madame Bertrand, and Madame Desbrosses.

Ragotin, comedy, by Lafontaine, April 21.

Les Fragments de Molière, two-act comedy in prose, by Champmêlé, May 4.

La Mère Ridicule, one-act comedy, anonymous, May 8.
La Mort d'Alexandre, tragedy, anonymous, May 26.
Le Cocher Supposé, one-act comedy, by Hauteroche, June 9.
L'Amante Amant, comedy in prose, by Campistron, August 2.
Timon, one-act comedy in prose, by Brécourt, Aug. 13.
Death of Corneille, Sept. 30.
Ajax, tragedy, by Lachapelle, Dec. 2.

1685.

Andronic, tragedy, by Campistron, Feb. 8.
L'Usurier, comedy, anonymous, Feb. 13.
Deaths of Brécourt and Montauban.
Le Rendezvous des Tuileries, ou le Coquet Trompé, three-act comedy in prose, by Baron, March 3.
Management of the Comédie assigned to the Dauphiness ; new regulations issued.
Retirement of Raimond Poisson, Mdlle. Debrie, Hubert, Mdlle. d'Ennebaut, and Mdlle. Dupin.
Débuts of Nicolas Desmares, Durieu and Madame Durieu, Dancourt and Madame Dancourt.
Le Notaire Obligeant, three-act comedy in prose, by Dancourt, June 8.
Les Enlèvements, one-act comedy in prose, by Baron, July 6.
Le Florentin, one-act comedy in verse, by Lafontaine, July 23.
Angelique et Médor, one-act comedy in prose, by Dancourt, Aug. 1.
L'Héroïne, one-act comedy, anonymous, Sept. 10.
L'Opérateur, one-act comedy, anonymous, Oct. 24.
Aristobule, tragedy, anonymous, Nov. 30.
More regulations as to the Comédie Française issued.
Les Façons du Temps, comedy in prose, by Saintyon, Dec. 13.
Alcibiade, tragedy, by Campistron, Dec. 28.
Death of Montfleuri *fils*.

1686.

Death of Devilliers.
Le Baron de Fondrières, comedy, by T. Corneille, Jan. 14.
L'Homme à Bonne Fortune, comedy in prose, by Baron, Jan. 30.
First appearance of Etienne Baron and of Paul Poisson.
Death of Mairet, Jan. 30, and of Rosimont.
Burial of the latter without Christian rites.
Antigone, tragedy, by D'Assezan, March 14.
Merlin Dragon, one-act comedy in prose, by Desmares, April 26.
Le Brutal de Sangfroid, one-act comedy, anonymous, May 3.
Le Niais de Sologne, one-act comedy, by Raisin the elder, June 3.
Renaud et Armide, one-act comedy in prose, by Dancourt, July 31.
Les Nouvellistes, one-act comedy, anonymous.
L'Homme de Guerre, comedy, anonymous.
Phraate, tragedy, by Campistron, Dec. 26.
La Coquette et la Fausse Prude, comedy in prose, by Baron, Dec. 28.

1687.

Géta, tragedy, by Péchantré, Jan. 29.
Le Rival de son Maître, comedy, anonymous, April 28.
Le Badaut, comedy in one act, anonymous, May 10.
Le Petit Homme de la Foire, one-act comedy, by the elder Raisin, May 20.
Merlin Peintre, one-act comedy, by La Tuillerie, July 20.

La Désolation des Joueuses, one-act comedy, in prose, by Dancourt, August 23.

Le Chevalier à la Mode, comedy in prose, by Saintyon and Dancourt, Oct. 24.

Le Voleur, ou Titapapouf, comedy in prose, by Mdlle. Longchamps, Nov. 4.

Varron, tragedy, by Dupuy, Nov. 14.

Le Jaloux, comedy, by Baron, Dec. 17.

1688.

Régulus, tragedy, by Pradon, Jan. 4.

Latuillerie died, Feb. 13.

His place taken by Gourlin de Roselis.

Reception of Sévigny at the theatre.

Le Faux Gascon, one-act comedy, by Raisin the elder, May 28.

La Coupe Enchantée, one-act comedy in prose, by Lafontaine, July 16.

L'Epreuve Dangereuse, comedy, anonymous, Aug. 4.

La Maison de Campagne, one-act comedy in prose, by Dancourt, Aug. 17.

Les Amants Magnifiques, by Molière, originally produced at Court, performed for the first time in Paris, Oct. 15.

Annibal, tragedy, by Riuperous, Nov. 5.

Coriolan, tragedy, anonymous, Nov. 26.

Death of Quinault, Nov. 26.

Phocion, tragedy, by Campistron, Dec. 16.

First début of Fonpré.

1689.

La Dame à la Mode, ou la Coquette, comedy, by Dancourt, Jan. 3.

Laodamie, tragedy, by Mdlle. Bernard, Feb. 11.

Esther, tragedy, by Racine, played at St. Cyr.

Migration of the Comédiens du Roi to a theatre they had built in the Rue des Fosses St. Germain des Prés, April 18.

Retirement of Ducroisy.

Dauvilliers sent away.

Les Fontanges Maltraitées, ou les Vapeurs, one-act comedy, by Baron, May 11.

Démétrius, tragedy, by Daubry, June 10.

La Répétition, one-act comedy in prose, by Baron, July 10.

Le Veau Perdu, one-act comedy in prose, by Lafontaine, Aug. 22.

Le Concert Ridicule, one-act comedy in prose, by Brueys and Palaprat, Sept. 14.

Le Debauché, comedy, by Baron, Dec. 8.

1690.

Adrien, tragedy, by Campistron, Jan. 11.

Les Fables d'Esope, comedy, by Boursault, Jan. 18.

Agathocle, tragedy, by Daubry.

La Folle Enchère, one-act comedy in prose, by Dancourt, May 30.

Le Ballet Extravagant, one-act comedy in prose, by Palaprat, June 21.

L'Eté des Coquettes, one-act comedy in prose, by Dancourt, July 12.

Les Bourgeois de Qualité, comedy, by Hauteroche, July 26.

Merlin Deserteur, one-act comedy, by Dancourt, August 8.

Le Cadet de Gascogne, comedy, anonymous, Aug. 21.

First appearance of Mdlle. Desmares.

Le Secret Révélé, one-act comedy in prose, by Brueys and Palaprat, Sept. 13.
Merlin Gascon, one-act comedy, by Raisin the elder, Oct. 7.
Valérien, tragedy, by Riuperous, Nov. 22.
Brutus, tragedy, by Mdlle. Bernard.
Le Carnaval de Venise, heroic comedy, by Dancourt, Dec. 29.
Raimond Poisson dead.

1691.

Le Grondeur, three-act comedy, in prose, by Brueys and Palaprat, Feb. 3.
Tiridate, tragedy, by Campistron, Feb. 12.
La Parisienne, one-act comedy in prose, by Dancourt, June 13.
Le Muet, comedy in prose, by Brueys and Palaprat, June 22.
La Chasse Ridicule, one-act comedy, anonymous, July 25.
Le Bon Soldat, one-act comedy in verse, by Poisson and Dancourt, Oct. 10.
Benserade died, Oct. 15.
Retirement of Baron, Oct. 21.
Débuts of Durocher, Rosidor, Beaubourg, and Biet.
Leclerc died, Dec. 8.
Début of Mdlle. Devilliers.
Phaëton, comedy in irregular verse, by Boursault.

1692.

La Femme d'Intrigues, comedy in prose, by Dancourt, Jan. 30.
Le Négligent, three-act comedy in prose, by Dufresny, Feb. 27.
Beaubourg received.
Athalie, tragedy, by Racine, played at Versailles.
Death of Lagrange.
Retirement of his wife.
La Gazette de Hollande, one-act comedy in prose, by Dancourt, May 14.
L'Opéra de Village, one-act comedy in prose, by Dancourt, June 20.
L'Impromptu de Garnison, one-act comedy in prose, anonymous, but edited by Dancourt, July 26.
Les Bourgeoises à la Mode, comedy in prose, by Saintyon and Dancourt, Nov. 15.
Jugurtha, tragedy, by Péchantré, Dec. 17. .

1693.

Les Saturnales, ou la Prude du Temps, comedy, by Palaprat, Jan. 7.
Aëtius, tragedy, by Campistron, Jan. 18.
Le Fourbe Parachevé, three-act comedy in prose, anonymous, Feb. 14.
La Baguette, one-act comedy in prose, by Dancourt, April 4.
Je vous prends sans Verd, one-act comedy in verse, by Champmêlé, May 1.
Le Sot Toujours Sot, ou le Marquis Paysan, one-act comedy in prose, by Brueys, July 3.
Death of Mdlle. Auzillon, July 8.
Death of Jean Baptiste Raisin, Sept. 5.
Débuts of Devilliers *fils*, Poisson de Grandville, Lebrun, Quinault, Provost, Lavoy, and Dufey.
Reception of Quinault and Madame Godefroi.
Début of Mdlle. Duclos, Oct. 28.
Zénobie, tragedy, anonymous, Nov. 18.
L'Important, comedy in prose, by Brueys, Dec. 16.
Reception of Mdlle. Duclos.

1694.

Adherbal, tragedy, by Lagrange-Chancel, Jan. 8.
Sancho Pansa, three-act comedy in prose, by Dufresny, Jan. 17.
Médée, tragedy, by Longepierre, Feb. 13.
Death of Madame Deshoulières, Feb. 17.
Le Dédit, comedy, anonymous.
Hercule et Omphale, comedy, by Palaprat, May 7.
Attendez-moi sous l'Orme, one-act comedy in prose, attributed to Regnard,
    but written by him in conjunction with Dufresny, May 19.
L'Entêté, one-act comedy, anonymous, June 3.
La Sérénade, one-act comedy in prose, by Regnard, July 3.
Le Café, one-act comedy in prose, by Jean Baptiste Rousseau, Aug. 2.
Les Mots à la Mode, one-act comedy in verse, by Boursault, Aug. 19.
Les Vendanges, one-act comedy in prose, by Dancourt, Sept. 30.
Retirement of Armande Béjart and Madame Poisson.
Le Jeune Homme, one-act comedy, anonymous, Oct. 14.
Retirement of Jacques Raisin, Oct. 31.
Les Mœurs du Temps, comedy, anonymous, Nov. 29.
Le Triomphe de l'Hiver, comedy, anonymous, Nov. 29.
Germanicus, tragedy, by Pradon, Dec. 22.

1695.

Les Héraclides, tragedy, by Debrie, Feb. 9.
Les Dames Vengées, comedy in prose, by Devisé, Feb. 21.
Judith, tragedy, by Boyer, March 4.
Flight of Sévigny from Paris.
Death of Ducroisy.
Death of Lafontaine, March 31.
Le Jaloux Masqué, three-act comedy, anonymous, April 16.
Reception of Etienne Baron, Lavoy, Quinault, Mdlle. Clavel, Dufey, and
    Madame Champvallon.
Le Genois, one-act comedy, anonymous, June 6.
Le Tuteur, July 13, *La Foire de Bézons*, Aug. 13, and *Les Vendanges de
    Surêne*, Oct. 15, one-act comedies in prose, by Dancourt.
First appearance of Marie and Mimi Dancourt.
Bradamanthe, tragedy, by T. Corneille, Nov. 18.
Sésostris, tragedy, by Longepierre, Dec. 28.

1696.

L'Avanturier, comedy in prose, by Devisé, Jan. 2.
La Foire Saint Germain, one-act comedy in prose, by Dancourt, Jan. 18.
Polixène, tragedy, by Lafosse, Feb. 3.
Agrippa, ou la Mort d'Auguste, tragedy, by Riuperous, March 19.
Le Vieillard Couru, ou les Différends Caractères des Femmes, comedy in
    prose, by Devisé, March 24.
Mdlle. Bélonde and Mdlle. Devilliers retired.
Le Maréchal Médecin, ou les Houssarts, one-act comedy in prose, anonymous,
    May 12.
Le Bal, one-act comedy in verse, by Regnard, June 14.
Le Moulin de Javelle, one-act comedy in prose, with divertissement, by
    Michault, edited by Dancourt, July 7.
Deaths of Dupin and Assezan.
Les Sœurs Rivales, one-act comedy, anonymous.

Les Eaux de Bourbon, one-act comedy : prose, with divertissement, by
  Dancourt, Oct. 4.
Les Vacances, one-act comedy in prose, with divertissement, by Dancourt,
  Oct. 31.
Le Flatteur, comedy in prose, by Rousseau, Nov. 24.
Polymnestor, tragedy, by Genest, Dec. 12.
Le Joueur, comedy, by Regnard, Dec. 19.

1697.

Scipion l'Afriquain, tragedy, by Pradon, Feb. 22.
Le Chevalier Joueur, comedy in prose, by Dufresny, Feb. 27.
La Fille Médecin, one-act comedy in prose, anonymous, March 9.
Le Lourdat, one-act comedy, by Debrie.
Dismissal of the Italian players.
Le Bourget, one-act comedy in prose, with divertissement, anonymous,
  May 23.
Les Empiriques, three-act comedy in prose, by Brueys, June 4.
La Loterie, one-act comedy in prose, by Dancourt, July 10.
L'Enfant Gâté, one-act comedy, anonymous, Aug. 23.
Le Charivari, one-act comedy in prose, with divertissement, by Dancourt,
  Sept. 19.
Le Retour des Officiers, one-act comedy in prose, with divertissement, by
  Dancourt, Oct. 19.
Le Distrait, comedy, by Regnard, Dec. 2.
Oreste et Pylade, tragedy, by Lagrange-Chancel, Dec. 11.

1698.

Disgrace of Racine at Court.
Manlius Capitolinus, tragedy, by Lafosse, Jan. 18.
Le Marquis de l'Industrie, comedy, anonymous, Jan. 25.
Deaths of Mdlle. Champmêlé, May 15, and of Boyer, July 22.
First début of Sallé.
Les Curieux de Compiègne, Oct. 4, and *Le Mari Retrouvé,* Oct. 29, one-act
  comedies in prose, with divertissements, by Dancourt.
Pradon dead.

1699.

La Mort d'Othon, tragedy, by Belin, Jan. 5.
Myrtil et Melicerte, heroic pastoral in three acts, with interludes, by Guérin
  fils, Jan. 10.
Méléagre, tragedy, by Lagrange-Chancel, Jan. 28.
Début of Mdlle. Desmares.
Gabinie, tragedy, by Brueys, March 14.
Death of Racine, April 21.

LOUIS XIV.

INDEX.